Women and the City

Women and the City

Visibility and Voice in Urban Space

Edited by

Jane Darke
Senior Lecturer
School of Planning
Oxford Brookes University

Sue Ledwith
Research Fellow
Business School
Oxford Brookes University

Roberta Woods
Professor of Social, Economic and Political Sciences
University of Nothumbria

Preface by Helena Kennedy

Consultant Editor: Jo Campling

First published 2000 by
PALGRAVE
Houndmills, Basingstoke, Hampshire RG21 6XS and
175 Fifth Avenue, New York, N.Y. 10010
Companies and representatives throughout the world

PALGRAVE is the new global academic imprint of
St. Martin's Press LLC Scholarly and Reference Division and
Palgrave Publishers Ltd (formerly Macmillan Press Ltd).

ISBN 0–333–77485–X

This book is printed on paper suitable for recycling and
made from fully managed and sustained forest sources.

A catalogue record for this book is available
from the British Library.

Library of Congress Cataloging-in-Publication Data
Women and the city : visibility and voice in urban space / edited by Jane
Darke, Sue Ledwith, Roberta Woods ; preface by Helena Kennedy.
        p. cm.
Includes bibliographical references and index.
ISBN 0–333–77485–X
   1. Urban women—Social conditions—Case studies. 2. Urban women–
–Economic conditions—Case studies. 3. Urban women—Employment–
–Case studies. 4. Women in city planning—Case studies. I. Darke, Jane,
1943– II. Ledwith, Sue. III. Woods, Roberta, 1957–
HQ1154 .W823 2000
305.42'09173'2—dc21
                                                    00–031115

10   9   8   7   6   5   4   3   2   1
09   08 07 06 05 04 03 02 01 00

Printed and bound in Great Britain by
Antony Rowe Ltd, Chippenham, Wiltshire

Contents

List of Tables

Foreword

Baroness Helena Kennedy QC

I am a woman of the city. My urban childhood in working-class Glasgow and my professional life in the criminal courts of London and other cities has given me a particular skew on city life. I love it. It is what I know. I like the sprawl and the noise and the seething life. But I am also clear that there should be no romancing of the wretchedness that exists within that urban vitality: the poverty, the homelessness, the paucity of local authority housing and the squalor of what is available, the crisis of public transport, the inequalities in employment, the lack of affordable childcare, the crime. Many of the problems of city life are not dissimilar to those experienced by people in rural communities but the surprise is that those who are closest to seats of power should have such little access to it. Women in cities often feel as distant from decision making as any country dweller.

I had the great pleasure of opening the 1997 conference on Women and the City in Oxford, where, indeed, this book was conceived. Labour had only recently been elected and a question hung in the air as to whether women's voices would now be heard in the corridors of power. Would the significant increase of women in Parliament change the dynamics of the government and introduce another perspective? The initial appointment of a Minister for Women, who unlike every other minister would receive no salary, did not inspire confidence. The attack upon the level of welfare benefits paid to single mothers sent a shock-wave through traditional Labour circles.

Yet, despite these anxieties, the Oxford conference hummed with confidence and the belief that change was possible. After so many years of hostile government the participants seemed to feel that a great weight had been lifted. Although we revisited familiar debates about the undervaluing of women's contribution, the ways that women are inevitably blamed for male transgression, the continuing hostility of the workplace and inequality in pay, the flavour of the discussions was new and the context changed because a different government presented a different hope. Speakers addressed the absence of women's views in urban planning, the diverse nature of women's needs, depending on age, ethnicity and class, and the experience of women in other parts of the world. The globalised economy had changed the nature of work and the possibilities for women. Yet with it had come the growth of social exclusion and even greater divisions between rich and poor.

Since the conference there have been highs and lows for women. Many of us were alarmed at the government's vision of employment as the answer to all the problems of lone parents. Compensating for the reduction in single parents' benefits, the 1998 Budget brought a rise in child benefit and we are now seeing the introduction of tax credits for families on low incomes, which will redistribute wealth in ways that will benefit many women. Single parents are now able to receive advice on ways back into employment, sometimes through education and training, but the element of compulsion is happily missing.

In the 1998 summer reshuffle a women's unit was created in the Cabinet Office with Margaret Jay, Leader of the House of Lords, becoming the cabinet minister responsible for keeping the interests of women on the agenda. There were fears that this might simply be another gesture towards women rather than a meaningful portfolio. However, the unit has conducted a consultation process, asking 30000 women around the country their views, and produced an interesting document called 'Voices'. It makes clear that women want more government support in balancing work and family life, equal pay, help in setting up small businesses, better career and life skills advice for girls and a greater effort to ensure that women's perspectives are acknowledged in policy making. They want their caring roles, looking after children and ageing relatives, acknowledged.

The results tell most of us what we already knew but provide the kind of popular confirmation so persuasive to politicians. These divine revelations now mean there is recognition that the gender pay gap is a major factor in child poverty. Because women lamented the lack of support if they wanted to set up small businesses, the Chancellor of the Exchequer is examining a scheme which would convert state benefits into capital loans for would-be entrepreneurs. There will also be incentives for small and medium-sized firms to offer women job flexibility. It is yet to be decided how the government will take on the issue of the 'female forfeit', namely the disparity in income which starts as soon as boys and girls leave education. Moves are already underway to speed up sluggish equal pay tribunals, but it is recognised that more dramatic steps will be required.

One of my own special areas of concern, though not a special subject at the conference, is the issue of violence towards women. It is slowly being acknowledged internationally as an issue of human rights. Domestic violence is a scourge faced by huge numbers of women here in Britain and around the world. For too long it has been seen as different from other crime, yet the violent home is the seedbed of so many social problems, including mental ill health, behavioural problems in children and other forms of crime. If government is intent on being tough on crime here is an area where it could really make a difference.

Women's organisations have done an amazing job in creating support structures, such as the refuge movement, and in campaigning for public awareness, as in the Zero Tolerance Campaign, but still insufficient resources are being placed at their disposal. Some positive initiatives are taking place such as a pilot project in Fulham, West London, bringing together police, courts and Women's Aid to address some of the failures of the criminal justice system by creating a collaborative response. There is also a special domestic violence court, with trained magistrates, being tried out in Leeds. The Judicial Studies Board is introducing training for judges.

In sexual cases such as rape, new legislation withdraws the right of a man personally to cross-examine the complainant when he is representing himself: the judge will act as intermediary or appoint someone to act on behalf of an accused for that purpose. The change was introduced because of cases where women were victimised by invasive questioning from the very person who had violated them. Cross-examination of a woman about her sexual history with or without a lawyer will not be allowed, save in a very few specified situations. These changes are ones which women have sought for years and only gained support when an administration was sufficiently committed to the issues.

Having seen the processes up close, I am all too aware of the difficulties in delivering on everyone's expectations. I do not expect that this government will satisfy all of the women all of the time. However, we have to keep up the pressure, especially on behalf of the women who have least voice within the system. So far, for women, this is as good as it has got. But that must not stop us still wanting more. This book not only makes the arguments but also makes proposals for change. It is thought provoking in its analysis and exciting in its conclusions. What was clear at the conference and remains so is that postfeminism is a myth. Thinking has evolved, the discourse is more nuanced, new generations of women are bringing different aspirations and perspectives, but women are on the move. We may have come a long way but we still have a long way to go.

Acknowledgements

The editors would like to thank the Oxford Women's Studies Network, which includes women from the University of Oxford, Ruskin College and Oxford Brookes University as well as associates from elsewhere, for their support for the Women and the City conference at which earlier versions of these papers were presented. Oxford Brookes University and the Open University assisted in the preparation of this volume. It has been a pleasure to work with Jo Campling as consultant editor and Karen Brazier at Macmillan. Finally we thank all those who attended the Women and the City conference and made it such a stimulating event.

Notes on Contributors

Mavis Bayton is a sociology tutor at Ruskin College. Her main research interests lie in the area of women and rock music. She has recently published a book on this topic *Frock Rock* with Oxford University Press. Formerly a member of the Oxford band The Mistakes, Mavis is now a solo blues and folk performer.

Sue Brownill teaches at the School of Planning, Oxford Brookes University. Previously she worked at the Docklands Forum, a community planning organisation on London docklands, working especially with women on planning issues. Her research has also analysed race and regeneration.

Beatrix Campbell is a feminist writer and journalist. She is widely known for her analysis of women's involvement in community politics. Previous books have also commented on the nature of contemporary masculinity, women in Conservative politics and the impact of the death of Princess Diana. She holds an Honorary Doctorate at Oxford Brookes University, and is currently Visiting Professor of Women's Studies at Newcastle University.

Charlotte Coleman is a qualified transport planner with a consultancy background. She is now a Senior Lecturer and Research Associate in Transport Planning at Oxford Brookes University. Her research and teaching interests include green commuter plans, rural transport and women's transport issues.

Jane Darke has been researching and teaching on housing issues and on women and the urban environment for several years, and has also worked as a housing manager. She teaches at Oxford Brookes University. She has written extensively on housing, often collaboratively, including editing *Changing Places: Women's Lives in the City*, with Chris Booth and Sue Yeandle (Paul Chapman, 1996).

Liz Doherty, Simonetta Manfredi and Hilary Rollin have worked together as part of a larger research team since 1993; they have given papers, and published independently and jointly on issues relating to women's employment in Britain, Italy, Spain and France. They all work at Oxford Brookes University; Simonetta and Hilary in the School of Languages (Italian and Spanish departments respectively), and Liz in the School of Hotel and Restaurant Management. Liz and Simonetta have in turn been seconded as Head of Equal Opportunities for the University.

Susanna Graham-Jones is a practising general practitioner and lecturer at the University of Oxford, where she is exploring the management of anxiety and depression is primary care. She previously worked in Nepal and Liverpool.

Sarah Harper is a senior research fellow and Director of the Oxford Centre on population and ageing. She has written widely on the health needs of elderly women in an international context. During the research for her chapter is this book Sarah was Visiting Associate Professor at the Irving B. Harris School of Public Policy Studies, Chicago.

Satya Kartara has worked in the field of equal opportunities for over ten years, first in community education then for a women's college. She is currently Equal Opportunities Officer for Oxford City Council, advising all council departments and other organisations on equal opportunities.

Helena Kennedy grew up in Glasgow, is a practising barrister and was created a Labour life peer in 1997. She is Chancellor of Oxford Brookes University.

Karen Kuehne has worked in the field of housing in America and Britain since 1987. The research described in her chapter was part of an MSc in Housing at Oxford Brookes University. She has published poetry on the issues of women and homelessness, most recently in *Feminist Review*.

Sue Ledwith is a founder member of Oxford Women's Studies Network and is both a writer and practitioner around women's issues. She is a Research Fellow and lectures on employment and equality issues at Oxford Brookes University and at Ruskin College, where she teaches women's studies. With Fiona Colgan she edited '*Women in Organisations*: challenging gender politics' (Macmillan, 1996). Her main research interest is women and trade unions.

Cecilia Nathansen Milwertz is a research fellow at the Nordic Institute of Asian Studies in Copenhagen, and was European Science Foundation research fellow at Oxford University, the Institute of Chinese Studies. She has published research on women's perspectives on the Chinese population policy and her current research is on the newly emerging grass-roots women's organisations in Beijing.

Caroline Morrell completed her PhD in 1999 on 'Housing and the Women's Movement 1860–1940'. She has worked in homelessness projects and been a lecturer in housing studies and history at Ruskin College and Oxford Brookes University.

Siobhan Reilly has seven years experience working as a health service researcher in primary healthcare and community mental health. She is currently working as a research associate in the School of Psychiatry and Behavioural Sciences, University of Manchester, where she completed her doctoral thesis on the effectiveness of health and social care for homeless people.

Verna Rowland has been a front-line housing practitioner for over ten years, working in both local authority and registered social landlord sectors. For the past three years she has concentrated on part-time housing research, specialising in tenant participation and tenant empowerment. She is currently bringing up a family, studying and doing voluntary work in housing.

Helen Russell, formerly at Nuffield College, Oxford University, is a research officer at the Economic and Social Research Institute, Dublin. Her main research interests include gender and the labour market, social disadvantage and unemployment. Much of her research involves cross-national comparisons and she has published work on unemployment among young people in the EU and gender wage differentials in Ireland.

Hilary Simpson is the Human Resources Manager at Oxfordshire County Council. She has a particular interest in women's employment patterns. She has also undertaken research on the equal opportunities aspects of university employment in Oxford.

Elizabeth Wilson is a feminist and socialist who was active in a number of the campaigns in the 1970s and since. She is the author of numerous books, including *Adorned in Dreams: Fashion and Modernity* and *The Sphinx in the City*, and of many articles including 'The unbearable lightness of Diana' in *After Diana*, edited by Mandy Merck. She is Professor of Cultural Studies at the University of North London and lives in North London with her partner and daughter.

Roberta Woods has worked formerly at Ruskin College, Oxford and the Open University. She is currently Professor and Head of Social, Economic and Political Sciences at the University of Northumbria at Newcastle. Her background includes academic research, teaching and local government. She is a founder member of the Oxford Women's Studies Network. She edited *Housing Women* with Rose Gilroy (Routledge, 1994) and is a co-editor of *Social Policy Review*. Her main research interests are gender issues and housing, local government and social exclusion.

1
Women and the City

Sue Ledwith, Roberta Woods and Jane Darke

Introduction

> I propose we hand the city's business over
> To women. After all, inside our homes
> They hold the purse strings tight and run our affairs.
> ... Quite wonderful. Let's hear some more.

> (Aristophanes 393BC)

This is a book about women and our lived experiences in cities. It was conceived by women in a city – Oxford – and was born from a conference organised there. Women academics from the three main higher education institutions in Oxford, Oxford University, Oxford Brookes University and Ruskin College, came together in 1996 to form the Oxford Women's Studies Network, aiming to offer a multidisciplinary, cross-institutional network of mutual support, to share our research, develop joint initiatives and enjoy ourselves. Most of us work primarily in subject areas other than gender or women's studies but also carry out research and teaching on gender in relation to our own disciplines.

Our launch event was a one-day conference, Women and the City, held in September 1997. A hundred women came, from all over the country as well as, predominantly, from Oxford itself. Academics and practitioners, including trade unionists, voluntary workers, students and city councillors, met together to debate, discuss and respond to research papers, many of which make up this book. There were films about homeless women and about the women supporting the striking Liverpool dockers. There were women's walks around Oxford, one following the suffragette trail, and the other around women's spaces in the contemporary city. As Elizabeth Wilson commented, it was an inspirational day. She couldn't recall being at a *women's* conference for a long time. As at the conference, Elizabeth's paper rounds off this book.

So, from this flavour of excitement and a one-day stirring of the women's movement, to the shape of this book. Reflecting the academic and personal concerns of the contributors, it concentrates on women's many and varied roles, positions and activities in relation to modern urban life. We are aware that there are aspects of city life which are not addressed here and that this is both an eclectic and a particular collection. The emphasis here is on challenging the discrimination women still face in everyday life in cities rather than glamour and romance and dreaming spires. For example, as Helena Kennedy reminds us in the Foreword, although a major issue for women is domestic violence, a detailed discussion is absent from this collection. Nevertheless it is the 'urgent' issues of women's urban lives which are mainly addressed here, reflecting, as Elizabeth Wilson comments, the unequal chances of women in terms of public services, income, health, childcare and employment. We hope that in these scholarly and research-based contributions readers will be interested to find and make connections with their own lives. After all it was the women's movement which first dismantled the divide between public and private life, and we still feel, despite postmodernism, that feminist analysis provides an overarching 'grand narrative'.

The book has also been shaped by another set of influences. Our conference was held after 18 years of Conservative government in Britain, accompanied by increasingly rampant globalisation. Women had borne the brunt of policies of government spending cuts in public services, health, education and welfare; of privatisation ideology and practices which had devastated public housing, decimated manufacturing industry and shattered communities. Women coping, alone, or holding together families and neighbourhoods, is a recurring theme. But men's lives too have been altered, and thus relationships between men and women, between masculinity and men, have been fractured and reformed, with women often picking up the pieces. Some of this is mapped in Beatrix Campbell's opening essay, which traces the recent history and transformation of women's and men's lives on suburban council estates. She charts how the loss of jobs in the manufacturing sector has led to pauperisation and how the consequent 'bad behaviour' of boys has been laid at the feet of the morals of mothers.

Dispossession and the hardships endured by women is a motif of several chapters. Yet there is often an upside: women are resourceful and resilient. For example, as Sarah Harper describes, the African-American grandmothers of Chicago, marginalised by poverty and racism, lacking support, old and ill themselves, make creative use of the hospital emergency rooms for their own and their families' survival. Survival in the face of homelessness is another strand of the book. Caroline Morrell and Karen Kuehne show how the position of single homeless women in late nineteenth-century Oxford had a particular form and character, with charity provision centering on the need to protect young single women from the sexual dangers of the city. When they researched the contemporary situation in Oxford they found that, despite huge changes, women's homelessness remained a feature of city life, with some of the same causes. Yet despite the problems of keeping up with such a transient population, it is possible to provide effective support systems, as Susanna Graham-Jones and Siobhan Reilly report. They describe how an experimental system of health advocacy for the homeless in one health centre's catchment area in Liverpool was able to improve significantly the quality of life of their homeless patients, eighty per cent of whom were women. This programme of primary healthcare was an example of the kind of practical, hands on, local neighbourhood initiative which women are so used to delivering. Its success also led to it being extended by the health authority to other neighbourhoods and target groups.

Significantly, in all of the papers in this collection, in different ways, women's interests were absent at national-level government policy making about those very issues which are critical to women's lives: housing planning, health, transport, social benefits and systems. While the new Labour Government has started to address some of these, such exclusion nevertheless gives rise to a positive paradox whereby marginalisation stimulates consciousness and action. Outsidership has always been a catalyst for creativity and challenge, as the women writing here show by providing research-based evidence. The borderlands which women inhabit can be fertile ground in which to sow the seeds of insubordination, and where women can both build their own organisation and develop and shape agendas to take into mainstream urban life. Some of this is demonstrated through the voices of women music makers, which Mavis Bayton presents, in their attempts to storm the male redoubts in the clubs of Oxford and other cities. Mavis, herself a rock musician, shows from her research that a strategy of separatism for encouraging and increasing the number of young women musicians can be effective. However, when competing in the 'malestream', survival tactics of rock and 'Indie' music women are often to return the male abuse in kind, risking reinforcing the culture of sexist denigration.

It should be clear by now that the city women who appear in these chapters are diverse, their voices various, and their agendas and demands different. This diversity means that the arguments in this book, made by different women about different issues, are detailed and divergent, and sometimes in opposition to one another; the picture is complex. Some women may place a high value on environmentalism but, for others, private transport is central to their ability to run their lives, careers and families. For women marooned in run down suburbs with poor transport, priorities are quite different. Women are divided by class, culture and ethnicity, by sexuality and family, but are bound together by being women. This book is about women's absence and presence, their invisibility and visibility; their 'braided lives' (Piercy, 1983) in urban spaces, in cities.

Women: space, policy and activism

In addition to the paradoxes discussed so far, there are other important themes running through the chapters. These are, first, women's relationship to space, or lack of it, both literally and metaphorically. From women's homelessness to access for women to local authority housing, from their absence from urban policy and planning, contributors show how women, on the one hand, remain objectified and invisible in the gendered processes of policy determination and, on the other, are excluded from practical decision making. Sue Brownill provides ample evidence of the absence of women from the arena of urban planning and what can happen as a result; how the consequent configuration of the built environment shapes, breaks and reshapes families and communities. Similarly, local authorities continue to ignore the needs of certain ethnic and religious communities. As Sue concludes, moving gender and diversity from the margins to the centre can transform theory and practice. There are many examples of the impact that gender-aware thinking can have. For some European examples see several case studies in Otties et al. (1995). The chapter by Roberta Woods also suggests some positive trends. She reports empirical evidence about access to public housing for women. The findings showed that most allocations went to families or lone mothers, but scotched the myth that women become pregnant in order to get housed. She also found that many local authorities do not hold data in a form which would help them analyse the diversity of needs among their tenants. Some only kept manual records; in others the data lacked consistency and uniformity.

This second, overlapping theme of women's relationship with policy making pervades another whole area – roads and transport. As Charlotte Coleman points out, at a time when governments are pursuing environmental policies of public transport, the growth in Britain in women's car ownership and use has outstripped that among men, precisely because this is often the only way for women to be able to pursue their multiple roles such as home maker, mother, worker, carer. Elsewhere, as Jane Darke and Verna Rowland demonstrate, in the London Borough of Kensington and Chelsea's Tenant Management Organisation, women are becoming active in managing their own housing because of their common interest in having a say, and also because of support from some men.

Third, as already discussed, women's agency in both responding to and challenging their exclusion, takes many forms in many places. A link between some of these chapters is the localised nature of women's grass-roots activism. The nearer to home and the workplace, the higher the level of women's activity, whether in formal representative situations in trade unions or political groups, or informally in the community, as Beatrix Campbell's chapter especially shows. Cecilia Milwertz's chapter also illustrates this through the particularism of the situation of rural migrants in China. In her case study, women's collective organising is vested in well-educated women 'imposing' their feminist ideology on the development of rural women as autonomous citizens when they move into Beijing. While such a 'maternalist' approach might well be seen in the west as inappropriate, both it and the Migrant Women's Club's affiliation to state structures illustrate the diversity of forms of lived feminism across cultures. In the Beijing women's case these forms are clearly important means, at this point in time, of gaining the legitimacy and resources needed to sustain the rural women in their new and precarious existence in the city.

More often, however, women find themselves working individually to claim and hold on to their spaces. For instance, while the mass movement of women moving into the workforce has led to better family-friendly policies and practices, domestic returners – women attempting to re-enter the labour market following a period of full-time housework – are largely excluded from official unemployment counts and most are denied any form of unemployment benefit. Liz Doherty, Simonetta

Manfredi and Hilary Rollin's findings of how some employers in Oxford have responded to the challenge and recognised the need for reconciling home and work, contrast sharply with Helen Russell's assessment of the persistent invisibility of unemployed women and women returners and how this squares with the new (1997–) British government's initiatives. Hilary Simpson and Satya Kartara take up the theme with their evidence of women being materially critical to the running of the city, but seemingly being invisible. What a shock it would be if, as Hilary and Satya suggest, no women turned up for work one day and the city came to a halt.

Context

The work presented in this book builds on a generation of feminist analysis. Thirty years ago the Women's Liberation Movement and second-wave feminism were developing in Britain. They were exhilarating times, providing the genesis for so many new ideas, for turning gender-blind assumptions on their head. By the late 1970s many subject-specific groups were forming, including geographers, historians and those analysing the built environment. Women practitioners and academics uncovered the gendered assumptions built into the man-made environment, (Matrix, 1984; Boys, 1989; Ravetz, 1989; Roberts, 1991; Darke, 1996), but argued that women (and men) were active agents who could creatively transcend these contraints. Historians were influenced by the research of Davidoff and her co-authors (Davidoff, 1974; Davidoff et al., 1976). Davidoff and Hall (1987) demonstrated that polarised gender roles were formed at particular historical conjunctures and that these social constructions of gender had their counterparts in the physical arrangements of spaces, for example the suburban home predicated on the traditional family structure of a breadwinner husband whose wife ran the home and used local facilities.

A further influence came from North American research (Hayden, 1981; Wekerle et al., 1980; Wright, 1980), showing how women's participation in public life has been contingent on their role in the home and how some women had attempted to liberate themselves by reorganising domestic labour. Women planners started to analyse their profession's assumptions on gender (Greed, 1994; Booth et al., 1996; GLC, 1986). In these studies it has been axiomatic that the role of women as practitioners and as users of the environment are seen as equally important, true also of studies of women and housing (Brion, 1995; Gilroy and Woods, 1994; Mama, 1989).

The flux and change in cities and the way in which this can provide opportunities for women as well as presenting risks and danger is reflected in the new global/urban geography literature (Massey et al., 1999). McDowell (1999) highlights the contradictions that cities pose for women, showing that fluidity and change can open up new possibilities for women organising around and getting involved in new political structures or forging new social relations where space is not clearly defined in terms of gender. She also points out that spatial and social circumstances can entrap women. This literature is relevant to much of the discussion in this book because it highlights issues of diversity and unequal power relationships, both of which have a particular resonance for women. Elizabeth Wilson's essay ranges over these and other issues raised by contributors to the book; ways in which masculinity has difⁿferiated spheres and locations for men and women in both private and public realms, and that cities spell danger, disempowerment and deprivation for women but pleasure and excitement for men. She reminds us that urban life, like women's lives, is inherently contradictory, and through invocation of Marxism, postmodernism and, of course, feminism begins to draw us a map to take us into this new, twenty-first century.

Activism

Above all, this book sees women as active agents, engaged in building our own spaces or challenging traditions. The next question for women then becomes that of the political interests of gender. To achieve substantive change, is it necessary that women's individual and group projects become 'joined up'? Is there a place for a new women's movement, not only to maintain and increase women's voices and places, but to transform social and political structures and cultures and recreate women's roles and places in the city?

Some members of the Oxford Women's Studies Network are active in urban politics. As we write this, we are arguing to retain our women's space within a 'modernisation' agenda of streamlining local authority structures which sees spaces for self-organisation, such as a women's committee, as unnecessary when women are increasingly being elected to office. In our view this argument misses the point and is used as a disingenuous or seductive attempt to head off women's challenges. In most political arenas women are not elected solely to represent women and their interests. They are there to represent women, men and children from all sections of the community and whose interests often

collide and conflict. In spite of increasing numbers of women in politics in many countries, there seems to be no direct relationshipship with
sex equality policy, although change in the political culture can sometimes be discerned once women are no longer just 'tokens' (Marinez-
Hernandez and Elizondo, 1997; Hedlund, 1988:100). As Jones and
Jonasdottir (1988; p. 5) point out, to expect that the '*mere* integration
of more women will be sufficient to realize the full transformative
potential of the feminist challenge is niaive'. For women adequately to
represent women's interests, what is needed are women with a political
gender consciousness and a mandate from women. Where else should
this come from but a movement of women, albeit recognising the fragmentation and diversity of women's interests and the tensions around
notions of women's difference?

Without women's collective consciousness *and* activism it seems,
both locally and nationally, that gender policy, practice and traditions
will not substantially change (see Colgan and Ledwith, 2000). We
opened this chapter with a quote from the Greek comic playwright
Aristophanes who over two millennia ago observed that putting women
in charge of the city was to transform it. In his play *Assembly-Women*
(Ecclesiazousai) women took over the Athenian assembly, establishing
a 'revolutionary gynaecocracy'. The new regime moved to establish
economic communism, abolished private property (including slavery),
and created public dining halls. The family unit was to be replaced by
a new sense of general kinship (Halliwell, 1998; pp. 147–8). For Plato,
thought to be the source of some of Aristophanes's ideas, the position
assigned to women in Greek society was a gross waste of the talents of
'one half of the human race' (Lee, 1987:xxi) and some means had to
be found to free women to a greater or lesser extent from the ties of
family life.

When such vision is set alongside the minimalist family-friendly
policies and practice of the late twentieth and early twenty-first
century, it fills us with dismay that so little has been achieved for and
by women, and that so much is still resisted. Only when life comes to
be structured around family, in all its modern forms, and is based
in humanity, perhaps women can be said to have truly taken over
the city.

References

Aristophanes, *Birds. Lysistrata. Assembly-Women. Wealth.* (1998) Translated by
S. Halliwell, Oxford: Oxford University Press.

Booth, C., Darke, J. and Yeandle, S. (eds) (1996) *Changing Places: women's lives in the city.* London: Paul Chapman.

Boys, J. (1989) 'From Alcatraz to the OK Corral: Images of class and gender'. In Attfield and Kirkham (eds), op. cit., ch. 4.

Brion, M. (1995) *Women in the housing service.* London: Routledge.

Colgan, F. and Ledwith, S. (2000) 'Diversity, Identities and Strategies of Women Trade Union Activists'. In *Gender, Work and Organization.* vol. 7. No 4 October, Oxford: Blackwell.

Darke, J. (1996) 'The man-shaped city'. In Booth, Darke and Yeandle, op. cit., ch. 7.

Davidoff, L. (1974) 'Mastered for life: servant and wife in Victorian and Edwardian England'. In *Journal of Social History,* 7(4).

Davidoff, L., L'Esperance, J. and Newby, H. (1976) 'Landscape with figures: home and community in English society.' In J. Mitchell, and A. Oakley, *The Rights and Wrongs of Women,* Harmondsworh: Penguin.

Davidoff, L. and Hall, C. (1987) *Family Fortunes: men and women of the English middle class 1780–1850.* London: Hutchinson.

Gilroy, R. and Woods, R. (eds) (1994) *Housing Women.* London: Routledge.

GLC (Greater London Council) (1986) *Changing places: positive action on women and planning.* London: GLC.

Greed, C. (1994) *Women and planning: creating gendered realities.* London: Routledge.

Halliwell, S. (1998) *Translated, Introduction and Notes in Aristophanes; Birds and other plays.* Oxford: Oxford University Press.

Hayden, D. (1981) *The Grand Domestic Revolution: a history of feminist design for American houses, neighbourhoods and cities.* Cambridge, MA: MIT Press.

Hedlund, G. (1988) 'Women's Interests in Local Politics'. In K. B. Jones and A. G. Jonasdottir (eds), op. cit., ch. 5.

Jones, K. B. and Jonasdottir, A. G. (eds) (1988) The Political Interests of Gender. London: Sage.

Lee, D. (1987) Translated and Introduction in *Plato, The Republic.* Harmondsworth, Penguin Books.

Mama, A. (1989) *The Hidden Struggle.* London: Race and Housing Research Unit.

Marinez-Hernandez, E. and Elizondo, A. (1997) 'Women in Politics: are they really concerned about equality?', *The European Journal of Women's Studies,* 4, 451–72, London: Sage.

Massey, D., Allen, J. and Pile, S. (1999) *City Worlds.* London: Routledge in association with the Open University.

Matrix (1984*) Making space: women and the man-made environment.* London: Pluto.

McDowell, L. (1999) 'City life and difference: negotiating diversity'. In J. Allen, D. Massey and M. Pryke (eds), *Unsettling Cities,* London: Routledge in association with the Open University.

Ottes, L., Poventud, E., van Schendelen, M. and von Banchet, G. S. (eds) (1995) *Gender and the Built Environment: Emancipation in planning, housing and mobility in Europe.* Assen, The Netherlands: Van Gorcum.

Piercy, M. (1983) *Braided Lives.* Harmondsworth: Penguin Books.

Plato, *The Republic,* translated by D. Lee, 2nd edn, (revised), 1987, Harmondsworth: Penguin Books.

Ravetz, A. (1989) 'A view from the interior.' In Attfield and Kirkham (eds), op. cit., ch. 13.

Roberts, M. (1991) *Living in a man-made world: gender assumptions in modern housing design*. London: Routledge.

Wekerle, G., Petersen, R. and Morley, D. (1980) (eds), *New Space for Women*. Boulder, CO: Westview Press.

Wright, G. (1980) *Moralism and the Model Home: Domestic Architecture and Cultural Conflict in Chicago 1873–1913*. Chicago: University of Chicago Press.

2
Gender, Crime and Community

Beatrix Campbell

While Elizabeth Wilson's work has explored the city as a place of both pleasure and danger, a place in which women discover the pleasurable and promiscuous company of strangers, as a place of performance and display (Wilson, 1992), these notes are concerned with contemporary concerns about a perceived crisis of community and suburbanity in the locale of peripheral neighbourhoods. This perceived crisis, which in political discourse is rarely contextualised in the protracted exit of public and private capital, by the 1990s began to be aired as a crisis of gender and generation, of morals and motherhood. To be specific, it became almost hegemonic in the 1990s to read the difficulties of dispossessed neighbourhoods through the filter of community crime and a kind of chaos generated, it was claimed, by the morals of mothers and the fading legitimacy of the patriarchal order. I want to suggest, on the contrary, that the problem of crime and chaos in pauperised places is an effect neither of mothers' morals nor the collapse of patriarchal order, but a phenomena common to many countries and classes in a late twentieth-century world characterised by both class polarisations and by an exponential growth in high value added, and mobile, commodities; that community crime is a context in which masculinity is made and reasserted as difference and dominance. The poignancy of this, as a political problem, is that what is often asserted as a crisis of identity among young men, is rather the reassertion of traditional templates of masculine power at precisely that point in history where, globally, patriarchy is losing its hegemony and locally its manifestation as sexual separatism, both spatial and temporal, is undermined by the impact of feminism on the labour market, and by the emergence of enduring employment crises in specific locales within most British cities, particularly those municipal suburbias built to house the respectable, male working class. The argument here is that the survival strategies of pauperised peripheral neighbourhoods are intensely gendered, no less than the anxious and alienated political commentaries which have dominated debates about community and crime in the 1990s. But while political rhetoric draws attention to gender it also swerves away from the cultural and political history of masculinity and redirects its accusing anxieties towards women. The effect is to spread a kind of panic about masculinity's loss of power across debates about community, and simultaneously to dissemble potential political alliances with women. Indeed, one of the remarkable features of politics in Britain in the 1990s has been the retreat of labourism from its brief and precarious dalliance with pro-feminism or egalitarianism in the 1970s and l980s. Furthermore, New Labour's community and crime discourse reveals a crisis of empathy between 'the people's party' and the poorest people, particularly the women and children of the poorest communities.

While in the 1970s the crisis of the city was rhetorically located in the inner city, a newly derelict, but deliciously dangerous, magnet for illicit urban pleasures, in the 1990s settled with equivalent anxiety on peripheral municipal suburbias, a monument to the successes and failures of British welfarism and municipalism. Built to warehouse the respectable, waged working class, these homesteads, by the end of the century, became the locales of working-class households pauperised by the collapse of manufacturing. These communities starved of both public and private investment and effective public stewardship, also became the site of political panic and intra-community conflict.

These neighbourhoods were designed to pacify the raucous, rude and clamourous working class, clear them from the inner city to the clean and empty edges of the cities where the people would breathe fresh air and be improved. By the end of the century these communities were deemed peripheral estates populated by peripheral people. Or as the doyen of the New Right put it in a radio debate with the author, by 'sub-populations.'

It was not always so. Millions of people, like my mother, regarded rehousing in our 1950s council house as the threshold to paradise. We had a washhouse, front and back garden, and built-in cupboards. Happiness was built-in cupboards.

The stereoscope belonged to children. There were no cars, no trees, no shops. Eventually we got a church and a chip shop. The street was our social space. Only uppity and snobbish parents sequestered their children in the sanctuary of the house, uncontaminated by the society of their own generation.

These same places, by the 1990s, were deemed dangerous: stripped of ready access to a legal living, permanent pauperisation seemed to be their fate. The exponential growth in crime across all classes in Britain came to be assigned, in political rhetoric, to the poor. For the Right, crime merely confirmed the congenital criminogenic characteristics of the great unwashed. For the Left, crime was blithely cited as an unsurprising effect of poverty. For both ends of the political firmament, crime was both a pathology and a subpolitical response to dispossession.

The great unsaid, however, was that crime was almost exclusively associated with one gender. Indeed the history of crime cannot be understood without reference to gender. More importantly, if we are to avoid the risk of essentialism and an easy equation between testosterone and criminality, then we must make sense of crime as a culture and context – like many others – which manifests a functional, rational, performance of masculinity. My own work in neighbourhoods overwhelmed by community crime revealed that crime was a means by which masculinity addressed the world and expressed itself as spatial and sexual dominion. Far from being pathological the values and cultures associated with criminalised coteries cascaded from the ancient lore of masculine assemblies, whether the police or the House of Commons.

The Australian academic Bob Connell also adopts this approach in his argument that masculinity 'is something that has to be made, and criminal behaviour is one of the ways of its making'. Crime, therefore, can be seen as a resource for the making of gender; and in most cases that means it is a strategy for masculinity.

Community and crime came to be coupled in political discourse in the 1990s, particularly in 1993 when Tony Blair made a germinal speech in response to the murder of Jamie Bulger. Communities, he said, needed to wake up, take responsibility, teach children the difference between right and wrong. This founding speech of New Labourism was followed by a determined moral crusade by a caucus of men within the Labour Cabinet which (wrongly) correlated crime with single parenthood, permissiveness, the Sixties, standards . . . In turn it pinpointed a purported problem of incivility in hard-pressed communities by promoting morals and marriage. By implication the criminality of children in impoverished communities was a failure of mothering and marriage.

The crisis of community crime in the 1980s and 1990s, which exasperated neighbourhoods in cities all over Britain already exhausted by the withdrawal of waged work and the decline of public services and stewardship, sustained the new law-and-order agenda of New Labour. But it also provided a clear case for challenging the traditional attempts to simultaneously erase the gendering of crime and yet explain crime as an effect of gender.

Two tendencies became evident, indeed achieved an almost hegemonic status: the bad behaviour of boys came to be associated with the morals of the mothers, rather than with the cultural history of masculinity bequeathed by men to boys; the correlation between masculinity, incivility and crime, found explanations in common sense which assumed that the attraction of crime for boys was self-evident, a fact of biology, an essentialist and pessimistic reading of masculinity as intrinsically dangerous unless properly policed, either by other men or by the discipline of domestication, marriage and breadwinning. As Dench (1994) has argued, in his candid case for patriarchy, making men the privileged breadwinner is the price women have to pay for peace.

My own work, as a journalist, in communities living in conditions of economic extremity at the end of the 1980s and early 1990s, explored the stark evidence that crime provided a context – much like the military, the police, traditional trade unionism, sport or the House of Commons – in which young men enunciated their masculinity as both difference and dominion. As Connell has said, crime is a context in which masculinity is made. By contrast, the vigorous networks of community activism and self-help systems – which constituted virtually the only political resource in neighbourhoods bereft of representation or resources – were almost exclusively sustained by mothers. In some respects this gendered polarisation could be seen as a reiteration of the gender polarisation which shaped the local landscape before the impact of global economic restructuring transformed working-class conditions of existence.

In the era of industrialisation the way that men and women inhabited social space in general, and the neighbourhood in particular, revealed a spatialised struggle for power between the genders. The men's movement – the trade union movement – in a historic compromise with capital, successfully created the breadwinner as a masculine identity. Men moved in and out of the community they shared with women and children and, *en masse*, congregated in workplaces characterised by sexual separatism. Women and children, largely excluded from the world of waged work, were expected to occupy a domestic domain that was to be visited, rather than inhabited, by men. Masculinity, it was believed, could only be constructed in the crucible of the waged work-place or social spaces from which women and children were excluded. Sexual separatism, and supremacy, split social spaces. This episodic and estranged relationship to the home and the locality has been reinter-preted recently, by communitarians and ethical socialists on the one hand and right-wing political commentators on the other, as a more permanent presence. Lack of it, so the argument goes, from Charles Murray (Murray, 1990) to Amitai Etzioni (1995), from the maverick think-tank Demos to the Institute for Community Studies, from Bill Clinton to Tony Blair, has left communities unfathered, in a state of nature, in chaos and without culture.

But as Collier (1996) has argued, the position of the male breadwinner is characterised by 'a random polarisation between absence and author-ity'. Far from being a halcyon pasture peacefully occupied by kith and kin who shared the same interests, language, and priorities – the iconic landscape invoked as a lost land to be reclaimed – the 'local commu-nity' was always fissured by conflict between gender and generation. Local community was, as de Certeau puts it, 'a space of enunciation' (de Certeau, 1984) which organised conflict and solidarity. In the late twen-tieth century, pauperised community space became a locale in which young men made their mark as men, in which they made their mas-culinity, not by taking political power, but rather by seizing spatial power. Women's traditional relationship to social space – coming and going between shops, schools, homes, neighbours, hospitals, the solici-tors', the courts (observe any school foyer or courthouse waiting room, populated by mothers escorting and explaining, and supporting their children) – was by now amplified by their access to waged work on the one hand and, crucially, the political imperatives produced by the extreme conditions of existence of their own, often unrepresented, neighbourhoods.

Political confidence and political necessity together launched these women into a domain best described as the boundary between public and private. In this context it was the work of mothering that posi-tioned these women on that boundary. Indeed, predictably, women's work as active citizens often blurred the rhetorical distinction between public and private. It is the women who navigate neighbourhoods, weaving not only in and out but also across (while research on men's traffic across community space suggests coming and going, leaving and returning) and who also negotiate with public institutions, with the schools, the clinics, the courts, on behalf of their men and their children. In impoverished places, men's traditional dominance of class institutions – primarily associated with the world of waged work – did not translate into a presence within the community organisations and networks which became the crucial agents in community relations with the State and other public institutions. Indeed, many municipal, criminal justice and urban regeneration professionals fully expected working men to offer their services as skilled negotiators in the world of waged work to the ever-more elaborate task of community representation, only to be disappointed. Community politics, it seemed, was women's work.

This has happened in the context of global simultaneous economic restructuring and the reform of relations between men and women. This does not mean that the world has been feminised; far from it. Rather, it means that the construction of masculinities and femininities in cities and communities in the late twentieth century occurs in new political conditions: patriarchy is not dead but, as Connell (1993) has argued, it is losing its legitimacy. Women, including poor women, have acquired agency in the world of waged work, the locality, and in their relationships to men. Poor men with little or no access to the exclusive assemblies associated with production (work) and power (pleasure and politics) have found themselves sharing space and time with women and therefore find themselves making their masculinity in new political conditions.

Ideologically, the proliferation of identities emerging in late twentieth-century cities simultaneously sponsor a traditional struggle for supremacy and sexual separatism and yet invite a new culture of co-operation between the genders. It is among poor and working-class men, above all, that we witness the most potent evidence of change as well as muscular expressions of masculine fundamentalism, while among middle-class and professional men, gender is still organised in their relationship to waged work and social power, their relative absence from the domestic domain, and their ability to buy solutions to the struggle for a more democratic distribution of domestic labour.

Community crime

It is among poor and working-class men, confined to the locality, that the impact of the power struggle between genders is most manifest in the streets. Traditionally crime has been represented as a pathology. This argument takes a different position, that crime is a rational, functional context in which masculinity is made, and in which young men assert spatial control over the rest of their community, in which control is expressed through chaos.

Criminalised coteries, like the great assemblies of archetypal and respectable masculinity, are structured by militaristic, exclusive, hierarchical and sexually separatist codes. They do not express dysfunctional masculinity, a gender in search of an identity, as is often claimed, but a purposive context in which young men assert their dominion over both public and private space.

Criminalised coteries reiterate the structures and priorities associated with respectable masculinities: militaristic, hierarchical, exclusive, secretive. All of these characteristics are hallmarks of congregations which have shaped the culture of modernity: from the trade unions to the Orange Order, from the House of Commons to the working man's club, from the police to the professions.

But it is not merely misogynist politicians who recycle common-sense laments about the loss of patriarchal power and a resistance to a project that puts the cultures of masculinity under scrutiny, it is also a tendency manifest in traditional socialism, which cannot countenance any disruption of its representation of class as the dominant contradiction, and in a form of feminism which will not tolerate the constitution of masculinity as a political subject: feminism was, it seems, merely an arena in which women could organise their noble ambitions, not a politics which produced a critique of both femininities and masculinities constructed in patriarchal conditions. In England Rosalind Coward exemplified the resistance to the constitution of masculinity as a political subject, and a tendency to either represent masculinity as victimised by the shift in the balance and power between men and women, or femininity as somehow omnipotent and, therefore, culpable in the construction of gender identities. This drove Coward to traduce feminist history and politics (Coward, 1997). In a bizarre but malevolent muddling of political imperatives Coward accused feminists interested in problematising masculinities as somehow offering succour to the malice of New Right ideologues such as Charles Murray, whose notions of the underclass, intensely infused with racial and class contempt, sponsored in Britain by the right-wing think-tank, the Institute of Economic Affairs, were extraordinarily influential in Britain in the 1990s.

Additionally, the assertion that the traditional work of mothering, in the changing conditions of the 1990s, emerged as not only private, unremunerated, domestic toil but also as public, community work, and sometimes as the practice of political representation in poor, unstewarded, unchampioned neighbourhoods, seems to have affronted critics (including some socialist-feminists) for whom class is always structurally defined and, therefore, scarcely mediated by gender. Masculinity, by their account, therefore has no history.

References

Collier, R. (1996) 'Coming together? Post heterosexuality, masculine crisis and the new men's movement'. *Feminist Legal Studies*, 4(1), 3–48.

Connell, R. W. (1993) *Masculinities and Crime*. Boston: Rowman and Littlefield.

Coward, R. (1997) *Symbols of our Sex*. London: HarperCollins.

de Certeau, M. (1984) *The Practice of Everyday Life*. Berkeley: University of California Press.

Dench, G. (1994) *The Frog, the Prince and the Problem of Men*. London: Neanderthal Books.

Etzioni, A. (1995) *The Spirit of Community: Rights, Responsibilities and Communication Agenda*. London: Fontana Press.

Murray, C. (1990) *The Emerging British Underclass*. IEA Choice in Welfare Series No. 20, London: Institute of Economic Affairs.

Wilson, E. (1992) *The sphinx in the city*. London: Virago.

3

Five Voices from Southside Chicago: Healthcare Experiences of Elderly African-American Women[1]

Sarah Harper

My granddaughter had got all messed up, and she had these five kids, really six, but I had already raised the one that's 20 now. But then she left all these five and they were gonna take them into a home, and they was gonna be split up. So then I went and got a place big enough for us and her too. And then I just had a nervous breakdown, because she was a baby . . . she was a baby and she had been drugged, drugs and hollerin' all night. And I would just sit down and cry . . . then I sent her down South to my cousin's 'cause they're in school too, trying to keep her from the bad folks.

So you took the kids in 1990?
Five of them. The oldest one made 13 and he's a boy. The oldest, a girl, is 11, and [the youngest] is five . . . she was a baby then [8 months old].

And they were your great-grandchildren?
Yeah, they're my great-grandchildren.

(Hattie, Great-grandmother, Chicago)

Introduction

Hattie lives in one of the USA's most racially segregated cities – Chicago[2]. With an African-American population of 1.1 million, comprising 39 per cent, the city has the second largest African-American population in the country. These segregated communities are clustered mainly to the south and west of the downtown metropolitan area, and experience some of the highest crime and disease rates in the US. Rates of homicide, infant mortality, teen birth, sexually transmitted disease and most forms of cancer are far higher in these black communities than in the surrounding white suburban areas. Thus, with a population death rate of 50 per 10 000 in the US, and 70 per 10 000 in Chicago, the African-American population of the city experiences a rate of 99 per 10 000, and those living in the southside communities 133 per 10 000 – two-and-a-half times that of the nation as a whole. This is exacerbated by high poverty rates, with male unemployment reaching 80 per cent in some communities. It is has long been recognised that women play a key role in the support and continuation of African-American families in America. Less understood are the stresses placed upon older women as they continue to head households, typically all-female, well into later life. These women may have responsibility for the care and upbringing of two or even three generations of children in an urban society where gun- and drug-associated violence affects even children of primary school age. In addition they may find themselves caring for elderly dependant mothers. The chapter discusses the stress this places on older women's own health and welfare, drawing on oral and life history material collected in Chicago's emergency rooms.

Research context

This paper reports on a study funded by the Chicago Community Trust and the National Institute on Aging, into the healthcare experiences of black and Chinese older adults. The under use of primary care and over use of emergency care by the African-American population is well documented (Ruiz and Herbert, 1984). This can lead to the duplication of services, unnecessary testing, lack of co-ordinated treatment and follow-up, and neglect of a holistic approach to healthcare. Our starting point was that emergency rooms are not necessarily appropriate entry points for older persons into hospital medical care, but instead may be a manifestation of a failure in primary, community and home healthcare (Harper et al., 1998; Kaplan and Harper, 1996). We thus wished to use these 'events' in an elderly person's life to explore possible breakdown in both formal primary and preventative healthcare, and the informal care-giving structure provided by family, neighbours and friends. The wider study aims to identify preventable failure in primary and preventative healthcare, social support and community care which may lead to unnecessary use of emergency care and to suggest policy interventions which may increase their use compared to emergency provision.

Southside Chicago

Chicago's population of 2.8 million is divided into 77 formally designated community areas. The African-American ethnic group is the
largest with 38.6 per cent of the population, Whites comprise 37.9 per
cent and Hispanics 19.6 per cent. This population is strongly residen-
tially segregated, with the black population comprising 95 per cent of
the population in the south and west sides. The ethnographic research
occurred in southside Chicago comprising the community areas of Near
South Side, Armour Square, Douglas, Oakland, Fuller Park, Grand
Boulevard, Washington Park, Woodlawn and South Shore. In terms of
socioeconomic and health status indicators these communities consistently fall into the bottom 20 of all communities in the city, and in
most cases comprised 8 of the bottom 10 (Chicago Department of Public
Health, 1994). These community areas are among those with the lowest
median income (less than $10 000), with on average over half this
population below twice poverty level and over half receiving public
aid. These areas have the highest mortality rates of the Chicago area at
over 1 per cent, three times that of some of the northern white community areas. Death from heart disease, stroke, lung cancer, pneumo-
nia, influenza, chronic liver disease and diabetes is twice as prevalent as
in the Chicago area as a whole. Infant, child and young adult mortality ranks at twice the average for the city as a whole, and five times that
of the affluent white suburbs. These communities have a very high
homicide rate, three to four times that of Chicago, and ten times that
of the national average. In one southside community, the homicide rate
for 1996 was 27 times that of the US as a whole, with two murders per
1000 people. The impact on the families within these communities is
highlighted by the fact that 11 per cent of all murder victims in this
year were of juveniles (under 17), and more strikingly 33 per cent of
those arrested for homicide were juveniles. Several of these community
areas immediately adjacent to the hospital have a higher than average
(13 per cent for Chicago) population aged over 65.[3] In addition nearly
50 per cent of this elderly community live alone, the highest percentage in the Chicago area. These communities thus include a high percentage of vulnerable elderly people.

Life histories and ethnographies

In her overview of feminism and qualitative research, Olesen (1998)
concludes that qualitative feminist research is not homogenous but

highly differentiated and complex, with differing potentials for influence on the disciplines. Despite this we can identify three broad feminist models of research which have been used by qualitative researchers. Starting from the work of Smith (1974), who highlighted the importance of women's perspectives, and Harstock (1983), who started with the privileging of women's experiences, 'standpoint research' raised women's view as particular and privileged. Dorothy Smith, aware of women's exclusions and silencings, conceptualised the everyday world as being continually shaped and known by the women within. Thus to understand this world, women researchers must not create it as an object for study, but instead participate as subjects in the orders of ruling. While this approach has inevitably fallen under the postmodern gaze, attracting such concern as the understanding of fragmented identities, its essentialist tone and the possibility of encapsulating experience, the work was clearly a necessary move to instate women's lives and experiences at the centre and not the margins of the research question.

Feminist empiricism, a commitment to traditional research methods, proceeds on the assumption of intersubjectivity, commonly created meanings and realities between researcher and participant. As Olesen (1998) points out, in spite of concern and respect for women's lived experiences, such research may well replicate current disciplinary boundaries and women's status. Similarly, Hawkesworth (1989) argues that it cannot be possible to achieve the neutrality/objectivity demanded by traditional qualitative approaches while stressing the subjectivity of one's work.

Both these traditions have clearly been overshadowed in recent years by postmodernism and its many and varied demands on the collection of truth and reality. Qualitative research on women's health, in particular, is being heavily influenced by this, the dismembering of Western rational thought as scientific discourse is deconstructed to reveal its practises, discourses and implications for the control of women's lives (Haraway, 1991; Jacobus et al., 1990; Harper, 1997a). It is this literature which forms the theoretical framework for this chapter.

There is a small but growing British tradition (Finch, 1986; McIntyre, 1985; Stacey, 1992) of qualitative feminist research, mirrored by a smaller North-American group (Romalis, 1988), which aims to make women's own perceptions of their needs central to the policy debate. The voices from this study typify the experiences of women in the African-American community, and this material can thus help to inform those policies aimed at reducing the high mortality and morbidity figures for this elderly population.

The current account, while acknowledging that these voices are but few among millions, attempts to allow five women to tell their story, and in the telling to reveal their positioning in relation to the needs of their communities as seen by the policy makers, providers and deliverers. The complex methodological questions that surround such work have been fully explored elsewhere (Harper, 1997b). Collection, analysis and reporting are as problematic as the use of such words to describe the methodology. Sixty-three life histories and/or ethnographic stories were collected from older women visiting the emergency rooms of three Chicago hospitals, with further conversations taking place in some cases following admittance in one of the hospitals. Although each story is clearly unique, each reveals pertinent issues concerning the health of older African-American women in Chicago. The five stories have been chosen to illustrate aspects of the caring relationship and the way this impacts upon health in later life. The women all lived in the surrounding communities, which had the highest rates of social deprivation, disease and mortality in the city. The two issues we shall discuss focus on the stress of multigenerational care, and problems of access to care for older black women living in these communities.

The voices and stories

One aim of ethnographic and life history research is to allow voices to speak that normally go unheard. I have tried to present the complete voice that tells its story intact, and to interpret these stories. Clearly, there are ethical questions to be considered, especially when dealing with women at such vulnerable times. In particular the promise of complete confidentiality and anonymity requires that some details are changed, with due sensitivity to the story being told.

The matriarchal family and household

Of the 63 women taking part in the study, just under half (29) lived alone. Race, gender and age all contribute to this, with elderly, black women likely to live alone. Thus in the predominantly African-American study area 47 per cent of older men and women (over 65) live alone, compared with 32 per cent for Chicago as a whole (Chicago Department of Health, 1994). National figures for the African-American population indicate that 80 per cent of black women over 65 are without a spouse (Chatters and Taylor, 1990), and in the study communities between 60 per cent and 85 per cent of the households were headed by women, compared with 39 per cent for Chicago as a whole

(Chicago Department of Health, 1994). Most strikingly, however, the majority of those living with a family member lived in an extended family. Furthermore, in addition to those living with a variety of family members in the household, many more had family living in the same building – the majority of the women living in high-rise apartment blocks. This is in sharp contrast to the men interviewed as part of the same study (Harper, 1998; Harper, Walter and Kaplan, 1998) where most of the men living with a family member were with a spouse or female partner. And it appears not only to be due to necessity.

Mildred

Mildred, 80, is middle class, well educated and can afford a private housekeeper to attend to her each afternoon. She lives in a private house converted into three apartments. Barbara, her daughter, lives upstairs and owns the building, Julie, Barbara's daughter, lives in the basement with her four-year-old daughter. Julie visits each morning and brings her grandmother breakfast before taking her young child to the babysitter. Barbara brings her lunch, and the housekeeper provides supper.

Such predisposition for families to be female headed has been well documented (Chatters and Taylor, 1990) and in particular the hesitancy of women to remarry or set up a cohabiting relationship following divorce or separation is seen as an important contributing factor to this trend, though it is still unclear whether Cazenave's (1979) telling point that black men as husbands and fathers qualify as 'phantoms of American family studies' reflects substance or neglect. In addition, there is well-established evidence of the extendedness of the black family: both at the household level, through the inclusion of those beyond the nuclear family, and through the extension of the family network and family life itself across several households (Jackson, 1991; Chatters and Taylor, 1993). What is less well researched is the stress experienced by older members of these families, and in particular the pressure on health. I have explored the impact of this family structure for healthcare and older African-American men elsewhere (Harper, 1998). Here I turn to address some of the issues arising for older women due to the experience of heading a multigenerational extended family well in to late age, and problems of access to care for these older women.

Hattie

Hattie is in her late seventies and providing full-time sole care for her five great-grandchildren. She is a frequent visitor to the emergency room. She is a single parent to a daughter and son, now in their fifties. Her son was conspicuously and deliberately absent from her story. Her daughter, also a single parent, was described by Hattie as unable to care for her own daughter, Hattie's grand-daughter, now in her mid thirties. This woman had borne her first child whilst in her early teens, and Hattie had then solely raised her from birth. In 1990, whilst the grand-daughter was under surveillance for drug abuse, Hattie took in her other five children, then aged between eight months and seven years, and had been their sole carer since then. Hattie's own health was frail, she was a heavy smoker, had cataracts, asthma, and had recently suffered an acute wrist fracture following a fall. She was very heavily stressed, had undergone a severe psychological trauma episode some ten years earlier, and was a habitual user of valium.

Hattie's account of her household was quoted at the start of the chapter. She continued:

I went up to the school to see about one of them, and I kept feeling that something was gonna happen to me. I was trying to prevent it, you know. I didn't wanna have no heart attack or a stroke. And I would just take it easy, you know, sometimes. I was doing a lot of work around the house and doing a lot of washing and stuff, and running to the clinic with them, and running to court with them. And so, I didn't know what it was. So I went up to the school, and I missed a step, and I kept saying that I got to do something 'cause they gettin' worse.

Have you had something done about them? (Her cataracts)
I ain't had nothin' done, that's why half the time I can't hardly see, you know. That's why I missed that bottom step.

So that's why you're here today?
I fell, I missed the bottom step and step on that street.

So, and then what did you do last night?
Yeah, the boy, they worried, come to do something. They said 'Grandma what can we do, what can we do, do you want some pills?' They told me if I needed them, call 'em. So I had gotten some kosher hot dogs and they love those, and some hot dog rolls and some pickle, and they eat that. I can't cook no dinner for them . . . all of them is on punishment anyway until I get their report cards, 'cause that's what I been runnin' up to the school for . . . AFDC just keep you so busy, with running to the clinic and running to the house and check on you . . . I got two workers – an Asian, she come in twice a month to check. And then a nice African come and check the clothes for spring and summer

and their shoes. . . . I'm happy when they are doing good in school. I try to make them my best.

Are they doing better?
Yeah, one of them is very, very slow, very slow. I don't know maybe the stuff had got to her brains or somethin . . . that's the one I'm having trouble with. Every time I look round the teacher sending me a letter, sayin' she gone fail.

Hattie's story needs little accompaniment. The family story is complex, and embedded in the social problems of the city. Yet her daily responsibilities are made more difficult as the broad spectrum of health and social care is provided by diverse agencies, occupying multisites across the community areas and wider city. Thus maternal and child welfare clinics, adult male health clinics, primary and preventative health clinics, social services, public aid, substance abuse services, mental health services, are provided by different agencies in different locations. She, and many other women, would be greatly assisted by a single-site community health and social care centre, with safe access and extended opening hours. She knows that this will not happen in her lifetime. Hattie thus lives day to day, hoping to prevent her great-grandchildren from falling into the substance abuse cycle that has dictated the passage of their mother's and grandmother's lives.

Ada and Cleo

Ada, in her mid seventies, is under the stress of the responsibility of caring for two adult children, in particular her disturbed daughter. She is an insulin-dependent diabetic with high blood pressure, the reason for her latest emergency room visit, and cataracts. She lives with three of her 13 children (five died in infancy). The others live in various parts of the US, several in Chicago, and she has 11 grandchildren. She also helps care for an elderly aunt (88) who is primarily cared for by her sisters. Ada's daughter Darlene and son Winston, in their fifties, are also insulin-dependent diabetics and both heavily dependent on their mother. Darlene is disabled and mentally impaired, having been shot as a child whilst playing at home. Ada's youngest son, Earl, also lives with them, works full time in the post office, and relies on his mother to cook, clean and wash, but in return drives his mother. Ada's main concern is that if she should die, Darlene would have to go into a home.

In a way you helped take care of them more than they helped take care of you.
Yeah.

Do you worry about them if you're not able to take care of them?
Yeah, I worry about them. My daughter, I worry more about her because . . . if something happens to me, she will have to go in a home.

Does she know what that means?
No, I don't think she does. That's what they would have to do.

That's a real worry for you.
Yeah, it's a worry for me.
[Several minutes later following a conversation about Ada's seventy-fifth birthday party]
Well, my daughter.

That's a big worry.
I don't like it if something happens to me . . .

Does she have a social worker or somebody that kind of keeps track of her, and what's going on with her?
No. I tried to get her up at M— home . . . she was smoking since she's 14 years old, and this lady at the home, I was gonna try and get her there, she said they don't take people who smoke . . .
[Conversation on smoking]
That's my one worry, if something happened to me, and my daughter.

While Darlene is too young to qualify for help under Medicare (free healthcare for those 65 and over), she is eligible for help thorough Medicaid (means-tested health care payment). Yet Medicaid beneficiaries in Illinois are very restricted, with home health expenditures being well under 50 per cent of the national average. Only around half all home healthcare provision is covered by public aid, and there is concern in the city that despite a growth in these services, they are not well targeted and may not reach those in need. Adult day care centres, which provide needed respite for care givers, rely on private payments and local fund-raising to match the limited public funds available. It is difficult for them to provide adequate comprehensive services to the poorer communities of the city. Southside Chicago is served by four such centres, all of which must limit their intake for financial reasons.

However, it is not only the stress of responsibility for her family, it is Ada's own health that is of concern. Yet Ada, Darlene and Earl, three insulin-dependent diabetics, live in one of Chicago's primary healthcare professional shortage areas (HPSAs). Health planning in the city is by its very nature multidimensional. The Chicago Department of Health planning process thus includes representations from the Chicago and Cook County Ambulatory Care Council[4], and city, county, state and federal health-related public agency representatives, residents and service providers on the seven community-based facility health boards, task forces and planning councils for HIV, TB, women's health, alcohol and drug abuse, lead elimination and the Chicago Medical Society. While the above suggests an attempt to develop a broad and all-inclusive health plan, it also highlights the diverse array of healthcare providers, and the potential tensions of operating with such a variety of interest groups and agendas. Thus, while the private sector has ensured a broad spectrum of hospital-based services, public health and primary care is less complete. Analysis of sentinel events indicating lack of access to primary care, such as late-diagnosed cancer, TB, and uncontrolled hypertension among adults, and dehydration, asthma and vaccine-preventable diseases for children, indicates that certain groups and community areas in Chicago suffer from a low level of access to preventative and primary care (Chicago Department of Health, 1994). While 27 per cent of Chicago's population live in a HPSA, (US Department of Health and Human Services, 1994), 53 per cent of African-Americans do so, and within the 19 community areas which comprise Chicago's HPSAs, 75 per cent of the residents are African-American. Indeed, the Chicago and Cook County Health Care Summit Action Plan estimated that shortage of primary care in this area was so acute that the volume of ambulatory care *required* for the medical needy exceeded existing capacity by more than 2 million visits (Chicago Department of Health, 1990). Among this population, the rate of adult-onset diabetes is nearly twice that of the State.

Cleo's experience illustrates this lack of primary and preventative care vividly. She came to the emergency room with a very sore throat. A scrape diagnosed advanced throat cancer. Cleo missed a hospital appointment four days later, and came the following day with acute nausea, stomach pain, lack of appetite. She appeared to be in shock, and was depressed, and sad about her family. Of her four sons, one had eight grandchildren, and one great-grandchild lived in California. Cleo was admitted to hospital. One of our research team helped her settle into hospital room and promised to return. She found her in bed the next morning with a sheet pulled over her face. Cleo had died a few minutes earlier. Cleo died alone and neglected in her sixties from undiagnosed throat cancer. Not only are the mortality rates from cancer significantly higher than for other population groups in the city, but those cancers which can be treated if caught early also kill a far higher percentage. For example, while the cervical cancer rate is virtually the same for both white and African-American women, the death rate for African-American women is 150 per cent that of White. It is striking that in their designation of provider categories, the Department of Health recognises maternal and child welfare and adult male provision (Chicago Department of Health, 1994). Women beyond reproductive age are thus not specifically highlighted as a needy category.

Mavis and Elizabeth

Mavis, a women in her eighties with advanced Alzheimer's Disease, is being cared for full time by her extended family. She has minimal education, and worked 30 years as a presser in a laundry. Mavis's daughter is partially blind and frail and so Mavis helped raise her five children. The family provide all support but no one wishes her to go into a home. As Mavis's daughter is partially blind and frail, her granddaughter is her legal guardian, and cares for both mother and grandmother. She brought Mavis to the emergency room because of a cold.

There's a nurse that comes . . . for my mother [*who is blind*]. Nobody comes for my grandmother. When she has to go to her clinic appointments, either myself or my other sister, Doreen, bring her. Basically she's a real healthy old lady. No one knew she had Alzheimer's until somebody just happened to bring her, you know.

How long has she had Alzheimer's?
For the last two years, that I know about.

Oh really? Before that, she was pretty much OK?
Before that, she was pretty much OK, 'til she started wandering off.

So somebody's got to watch her all the time, or she'll just go, huh?
'Cause she had her own apartment . . . [We] just went over and checked. . . . I cleaned up for her, me and my sisters. But she basically was taking care of herself, then she got so she couldn't remember too much anything, so we just sent for her to come with us.

Eugenie is a woman in her eighties with Alzheimer's Disease, being cared for by her siblings with apparently no help forthcoming from her daughters. Eugenie's elder sister Elizabeth has just moved in to look after her. Her brother Eugene pays her bills and gives her money, and her son

Terry calls most days. Her daughters have nothing to do with her, which clearly causes friction. Elizabeth, a former medical worker, 'knows a bit about medicine' and brought Eugenie to the emergency room because of a bad headache.

Eugenie

She started complaining of headaches. And I gave her Extra-Strength Tylenol. It didn't seem to help. She kept complaining. And I fed her and she dozed off to sleep, and I thought she was all right. Then she said she was going to bed. I went in and checked on her and she looked all right. But this morning when I woke her, she work me up telling me her head was hurting. So I said what is it? She said I don't know and she started staggering around the room. So I said, I'd better get her down here. Because not being familiar with Alzheimer's I have the brochures and I've read up on it, but I didn't know if the pain and ache could have caused pressure, or fluid on the brain, or irritated some of the brain cells, or not.

Does she take any medicine?
The medicine they gave her was too strong, so I don't give them to her . . . it just made her so sick, I didn't give it to her. And then they gave her another pain medication, I can't remember what it was, but when I give that to her, she's hyper. When we got the diagnosis that she had Alzheimer's I read up on the brochures. I talked to Dr T— at the first meeting and he felt that she shouldn't be alone. So I say, 'Are you saying to me that she needs someone 24 hours a day?' and he says 'Yes'.

How did you and your sister decided who that was going to be?
Well, my sister's not going to stay from her home at night . . . *it was a matter of who was able to* . . . Who was willing to really sleep there all night, and be there 24 hours a day.

So was it a tough decision to make?
No, I just buried my mom on the fourth of November after five years. Its just . . . there's usually only one person left going to do it.

That's tough. That tough on you, I imagine.
Well, if its something that's got to be done you just ask God for the strength to do it. [*Eugenie's daughters give no support*] They have their own place. And then, their lifestyle is not conducive to our lifestyle. Leave it like that.

So the people she gets the most help from, then, are her sisters and brothers,
and not so much from her own kids.
That's true.

Both these families could have benefited from home healthcare. Yet
home health agencies are particularly constrained in their provision of
care to elderly people. Both Medicaid and Medicare will only provide
these services on the recommendation of a physician, and following
strict eligibility criteria. The US General Accounting Office 1987
national survey suggested that Medicare rules and regulations were the
key barrier to home healthcare for the elderly population. This med-
ically based model of home healthcare severely restricts access for the
elderly population as a whole, and reflects a severe lack of fit between
the need for social support services and the historic emphasis on
medical services.

The Illinois Community Care Program is run by the Departments on
Aging and of Rehabilitation Services, to enable older people to remain
in their own homes. This is an entitlement program designed to provide
both home services and adult day care for those with assets under
$10 000 at risk for a nursing home placement. Around three-quarters
of those served under this programme are widowed women over 70, of
whom around half are black. Alongside this runs a variety of home
healthcare services which provide nursing, therapy and medical social
services. These include private and for-profit agencies. In addition,
because Medicare home health services have been increasingly restricted
over the past decade, the chronically ill may not be receiving
needed services. Data from the US Senate, for example, reveals a significant decline in Medicare beneficiaries receiving home care, a decline in the number of visits per beneficiary, and decreased outlays
for home care.

Women's voices and the policy debate

Little attention appears to be given to the tremendous stress experienced
by older women who still head multigenerational households, particularly those sited in extreme environmental conditions: abandoned
and deteriorating housing, overcrowding, high crime rates. These daily
stresses of dwelling in substandard conditions compound the severe
psychological and emotional strains of managing children (including
adult children) damaged by crime, drug and alcohol abuse. The stories
also underline the need for a greater recognition in healthcare planning,

of the diverse health needs of this group, and increased sensitivity towards various healthcare perceptions. Through the stories run the lack of autonomy, fatalism and dependency felt by many of these women.

As is also clear, access to high-quality primary care is denied to many of these women. Three broad barriers can be identified – fragmentation of provision, fear and social isolation, and perceived patient resources. The diversity and scatter of agencies creates confusion and requires time-consuming travel around the city, but also frequently leads to duplication of administration and services. Both the extended family and the individual are treated for specific social and health problems, rather than holistically.

This fragmentation is compounded by fear and social isolation which prevents access to parts of the community. Overuse of ambulances, for example, can in part be accounted for by those who view this as a safe means of transport in and out of a residential area dominated by gangs and drug dealers. While elderly African-American women generally qualify for Medicare and/or public aid, many were unaware of their rights to this form of insurance. In addition, as earlier discussed, neither of these public insurances covers the full spectrum of care required in later life. Transport costs and the perceived barriers to receiving free transport tokens militates against taking up the broad range of care scattered across the community, while lack of access to telephones in the home raises difficulty in finding out clinic hours, scheduling and follow-up care.

Lack of dissemination of information concerning primary and preventative healthcare is a final barrier to achieving a comprehensive service. Older women find the complexities of gaining knowledge about possible healthcare and associated services particularly daunting.

These are the described experiences of a small group of African-American women living in Chicago. Our study wished to allow the voices of these women themselves to inform those policy debates which will have a direct impact on their lives.

Notes

1 The research discussed in this chapter was undertaken while the author was Visiting Associate Professor at the Irving B. Harris School of Public Policy Studies. The study was jointly funded by the National Institute on Aging and The Chicago Community Trust.
2 By the index the least number of blacks to see a white person in their daily lives.

3 Fuller Park 19 per cent, Armour Square 18 per cent, Woodlawn 16 per cent,
   Kenwood 16 per cent, Grand Boulevard 14 per cent over 65 years of age.
4 A conglomerate of public, private and voluntary sector healthcare providers
   and social service professionals.

References

Cazenave, N. (1979) 'Middle-income black fathers'. *Family Co-ordinator*, 28, 583,
   quoted in C. Kart 1990, 'Diversity among aged black males'. In Z. Harel et al.,
   Black Aged, Newbury Park: Sage.
Chatters, L. and Taylor, R. (1990) 'Social integration'. In Z. Harel et al., *Black Aged*,
   Newbury Park: Sage.
Chatters, L. and Taylor, R. (1993) 'Intergenerational Support'. In Jackson et al.,
   1993, *Aging in Black America*, Newbury Park: Sage.
Chicago Department of Health (1990) *Chicago and Cook County Health Care
   Summit Action Plan*, Chicago: Department of Health and Illinois Department
   of Public Health.
Chicago Department of Health (1994) *Chicago IPLAN Community Health Needs
   Assessment and Public Health Plan*, Phase One, Chicago, Illinois.
Finch, J. (1986) *Research and Policy*. London: Falmer.
Haraway, D. (1991) *Simians, Cyborgs and Women*. London: Routledge.
Harper, S. (1997a) 'Constructing the body/constructing later life'. In A. Jamieson,
   S. Harper and C. Victor (eds), *Critical Approaches to Ageing and Later Life*, Milton
   Keynes: Open University Press.
Harper, S. (1997b) *Health Care Experiences for Elderly African-American Women –
   the collection of life histories in Chicago's emergency rooms*. Paper presented to the
   Women in the City Conference, Oxford, September 1997.
Harper, S. (1998) *The health and social welfare of an African-American elderly
   population: research in Chicago's Emergency Room*. WP298 Oxford: Centre on
   Population Ageing.
Harper, S. Walter and Kaplan (1998) *Under use of primary care overuse of emergency
   care: Chicago's African-American population*. WP498 Oxford: Centre on Popula-
   tion Ageing.
Harstock, N. (1983) 'The feminist standpoint'. In S. Harding and M. Hintikka
   (eds), *Discovering reality*, Amsterdam: D. Reidel, 283–310.
Hawkesworth, M. (1989) 'Knowers, knowing, known'. *Signs*, 14, 533–57.
Jackson, J. (ed.) (1991) *Life in Black America*. Newbury Park: Sage.
Jacobus, M., Keller, E. and Shuttleworth, S. (1990) *Body/politics*. New York:
   Routledge.
Kaplan, L. and Harper, S. (1996) *Emergency Room Use by Chicago's African
   American Population*. Washington: Gerontological Society of America,
   November.
McIntyre, S. (1985) 'Gynaecologist/women interaction'. In C. Ungerson (ed),
   Women and Social Policy, London: Macmillan, 175–84.
Olesen, V. (1998) 'Feminisms and models of qualitative research'. In N. Denzin
   and Y. Lincoln, *The Landscape of Qualitative Research*, California: Sage.
Romalis, S. (1988) 'Struggle between providers and recipients'. In E. Lewin and
   V. Olesen (eds), *Women, Health and Healing*, London: Tavistock.

Ruiz, D. and Herbert, T. (1984) 'The economics of health care for elderly blacks'. *Journal of the National Medical Association*, 76(9), 849–53.

Smith, D. (1974) 'Women's perspective as a radical critique of sociology'. *Sociological Inquiry*, 4, 1–13.

Stacey, M. (1992) *Regulating British Medicine*. New York: Wiley.

Stack, C. (1974) *All our Kin*. New York: Harper and Row.

US Department of Health and Human Services (1994). Washington DC.

4
Homeless Women and Health Advocacy in Inner-city Liverpool

Susanna Graham-Jones and Siobhan Reilly

Introduction

It is a shocking fact that the divide between rich and poor is widening, not narrowing, despite fifty years of relative peace and prosperity in Britain. The 'inverse care law' invoked thirty years ago to describe patterns of health and social service provision rings stark and true today: the more you need, the less you get (Hart, 1971). One hundred and fifty years after Dickens's descriptions of the urban underclass in London, vulnerable city dwellers are still being traumatised by multiple deprivation.

People in poor housing have a range of social problems which increase the risk of ill health, such as relationship breakdown, unemployment and poverty (Acheson, 1998). The association between poverty, homelessness and ill health is well documented (Conway, 1988; Standing Conference on Public Health, 1994). But the homeless are not well served by mainstream health services. This chapter is an account of an attempt to improve the care of homeless families in Liverpool.

The cornerstone of British 'cradle-to-grave' general practice has been the provision of continuing, personal medical care to individuals registered with a given practitioner with whom they can develop a personal and trusting relationship. 'Short-stay' residents can be catered for, as temporary patients, but without continuity of care and often in a perfunctory manner. General practitioners are often reluctant to register homeless people; because of their multiple needs, they are perceived as difficult patients (Wood et al., 1997). Many homeless people will therefore turn to accident and emergency departments which are open 24 hours a day, only to be told they should register with a general practitioner instead. Acute medical care is grudgingly delivered to this most needy sector of the population. As for health promotion, now regarded as integral to mainstream primary care, there is no incentive for practices to offer even a basic health check to a temporarily registered patient.

The cycle of deprivation also affects providers of care. Homeless people tend to congregate in urban areas; such shelters, handouts and charitable services as there are tend to be centred on the inner city. Health and social service professionals are under-resourced, overburdened and stressed by the needs of multiply deprived patients. New services, set up by idealistic and dedicated workers, rapidly attract new users, and the inner-city grapevine ensures that news of sympathetic treatment of substance abusers, homeless clients or hostel dwellers is passed on rapidly throughout the 'underclass'. One of the dangers of such success, however, is burn-out among service providers (Hagen and Hutchison, 1988); many such projects are unable to sustain the initial momentum.

What do we know about the effective ways of tackling the problems of homeless people? Lessons from a systematic review of the literature

A recent estimate of the size of the statutorily recognised homeless population in Britain was 400 000 individuals, making up 166 000 households (Shelter, 1997). The 10 per cent who are roofless single males have been highlighted as a source of inner-city nuisance because of a high prevalence of alcoholism, substance abuse and severe mental illness. There is high morbidity in this group – a survey in Sheffield suggested that one-third had been admitted to a psychiatric hospital at some time (George et al., 1991). But it is homeless women – often as heads of one-parent families – who predominate in the temporarily housed population (in bed-and-breakfast accommodation, hostels and cheap hotels), often as a result of distressing events such as eviction from rented housing, relationship difficulties within families, domestic violence and unwanted pregnancy. A recent survey of temporarily homeless people in northwest Thames showed a 'mental morbidity' prevalence of 45 per cent compared with 18 per cent for the local permanently housed residents. Another survey of women in a London hostel reported that one-third of the residents had severe mental illness and another quarter had minor mental health problems (Marriott et al., 1997; Winkleby and Boyce, 1994). Women's particular experiences of homelessness and its consequences, such as loss of control of the home environment and worrying about safety, have been thoughtfully explored by Bunston and Breton, 1992; Hatton, 1997; Buckner et al., 1993 and Watson, 1986.

As for addressing the problems faced by homeless people, much has been attempted by dedicated inner-city workers. Different models of service provision for the homeless include specialised teams and premises, mobile multidisciplinary teams, soup kitchens with add-on medical services, and attempts at integration with mainstream health and social services, including primary care (Lowry, 1990; Balasz, 1994). Most projects described served roofless men, but some have targeted homeless families and women (Hatton, 1997; Marriot et al., 1997; Hayden, 1992; Mercier and Racine, 1993; Cohen et al., 1997).

In relation to documented effectiveness of service provision, one recurring debate centres on the benefits of 'mainstream' versus 'dedicated' healthcare for the homeless (Victor, 1996). Another question is the extent to which 'social support plays a role in mitigating the adverse effects of housing stress' (Smith et al., 1993). But the disappointing conclusion from a systematic review of health and social care intervention studies (Reilly, 2000) is that there is very little reliable evidence about effective practice for ameliorating the health and well-being of homeless women or men. Projects in deprived areas are beset by distinct pitfalls for researchers, one of which is the difficulty of following up short-stay residents (Victor, 1996; Power et al., 1999). Another derives from the fact that funding decisions are driven by political need. The most sophisticated attempts at evaluation in American homeless populations relate to problems of mental illness, substance abuse, or both. Outcome indicators specific to such problems (time out of hospital, abstinence from substance abuse, etc.) are therefore the main currency in the reports of these studies. Severe mental illness and substance abuse are indeed problems highly associated with the roofless population of the inner cities, but they are not necessarily the main stumbling blocks for homeless or temporarily housed women, who need the whole range of primary care services for themselves and their children. Indicators of outcome which are specific to diagnosis are less useful, in terms of health policy formulation, than more general – or multidimensional – measures of quality of life suitable for use in heterogeneous populations. To date, unfortunately, there are very few studies using quality of life measures in the homelessness literature.

The other major problem uncovered by the review is that of inadequate design and methods. Very few housing project reports are able to address questions about the efficacy of the interventions they describe. The vast majority of so-called evaluations comprise 'before and after' surveys of clients of a given project, and are inevitably subject to multiple sources of bias (selection bias, response bias, and so on). Mant (1993) refers to these studies as 'almost useless'. The vital question – which of a number of interventions is most effective – can only be satisfactorily addressed in the context of randomised controlled studies, in which selection bias is minimised. When unselected clients from a given population are randomly allocated to different interventions and studied prospectively, then statistically significant differences in outcomes measured in these groups can reasonably be attributed to the interventions. The promotion of 'evidence-based' health and social care means that attempts to address social inequalities in society are now expected to provide measurable evidence of success.

Despite the lack of unambiguous evidence to guide initiatives intended to improve life for homeless women and families, Winkleby and Boyce (1994) concluded that 'homeless women living with children may be simultaneously the most vulnerable . . . but also most likely to benefit from case management and educational and occupational interventions, given their less frequent past experiences with alcohol abuse and psychiatric hospitalization'. Reilly's (2000) systematic review reaches a similar conclusion, sifting the most reliable evidence to identify three characteristics of successful projects. She suggests that the most worthwhile initiatives are likely to be those which bring together expertise from several different perspectives for the benefit of the client; which use a case-management model for individual care packages; and which empower women to access mainstream health and social services rather than directing them to specific services for homeless people.

Homeless temporary residents and general practice: a case study

Princes Park Health Centre was founded in the early 1970s to respond to the social and psychological needs of an inner-city, multiracial neighbourhood (Taylor, 1987). As in all such caring institutions, morale tends to fluctuate (Grieve, 1997; Mercier and Racine, 1993; Hagen and Hutchinson, 1988). In 1989, when Liverpool Family Health Services Authority circulated a mission statement for its new policy on addressing deprivation in the city, the practice team was showing signs of overwork and burnout. The request for comments from general practitioners was met with unaccustomed cynicism. The verdict – at a late-night practice meeting – was 'words, nothing but words and management-speak'. The partners put the strategy paper on one side and went on to discuss the out-of-hours rota, always a bone of contention in times of stress. Because of a nationwide change in housing policy which led to a peak in the numbers of homeless applications being accepted by local councils (Victor, 1996) local hostels and bed-and-breakfast hotels were filling up with homeless families in the area. This meant an increase in temporary registrations and also in night and emergency calls, often for minor illnesses in the children of refugee families or for one-parent families in which the mothers were victims of domestic violence. Having treated the presenting complaint (a child's ear infection, perhaps) it was often impossible for the doctor to ignore the parent's distress and its other causes. Notwithstanding the extra payment for the late-night home visit, the abyss beckoned for the weary doctor. That night or the following day, a long consultation would reveal a mass of problems, leaving both doctor and patient exhausted and frustrated. This scenario eventually prompted us to reopen the discussion on the 'deprivation strategy'. A letter was written to the health authority saying that although we recognised the needs of short-stay patients with complex psychosocial problems, it was wasteful for the doctors to use the same approach for short-stay and permanent residents. We pointed out that the existing undifferentiated system of care led to unrealistic expectations of the doctor–patient relationship on both sides. For our permanently registered patients, we were proud to offer the 'cradle-to-grave' service guaranteed by the NHS. For short-stay temporary residents, some other resource needed to be found.

Alternative models of care

We sketched out some alternatives for discussion. The existing undifferentiated system of accepting all-comers at Princes Park Health Centre now seemed untenable for the practice. An alternative would be to share out applications for temporary registrations among neighbouring practices, or for the practice to close the list and refuse all new registrations. These measures would relieve the burden on the practice in the short term but would not ensure that the needs of homeless patients were met elsewhere. A case could be made for a specialist team to serve incoming homeless temporary residents, a model implemented in several London-based projects (El-Kabir, 1996). This option was expensive and not feasible in the short term.

It became clear that our preferred option was additional in-house provision at our own health centre. We proposed to make a positive response by taking on a dedicated worker to respond to the needs of homeless people registering temporarily with the practice. We wanted someone to interview temporary residents, to help with access to health and social services in the area and to deal with all non-medical concerns. We envisaged that this new member of the team might be a health visitor, with experience in both community development and health work; the majority of our new temporary residents were single mothers and young couples with children.

The aims of the project are outlined in Table 4.1. The proactive approach to newly registered patients with complex needs would, we hoped, ensure that subsequent consultations with general practitioners would focus on medical rather than social problems and would hence be less time consuming, reducing stress for receptionists, doctors and nurses as well as patients.

We felt it would be important to pilot the new scheme and to let it evolve; once established, however, we wanted to measure its impact on patients and on the practice team, using the format of a prospective controlled trial. A full-time research support worker was needed to administer questionnaires, to oversee the data collection and undertake the analysis needed to assess the impact of the health advocacy input. The assistance of the chief executive of the FHSA was vital to the enterprise, as she submitted a bid to the Department of Health for ring-fenced monies for 'General Medical Services for homeless people' (a total allocation of £3 million under Section 56 of the 1977 NHS Act). The project ran for three and a half years from January 1992.

The health advocacy approach

The health advocacy intervention at the practice level (see Table 4.2) was the addition of a designated family health worker, an experienced registered general and mental nurse with excellent counselling skills. Her role was to advise eligible temporary residents, helping them to prioritise their needs and work through their problems. The aim was to empower patients to access services for themselves rather than creating

Table 4.1   Aims of the Family Health Project

---

1   To improve care for homeless people temporarily living in the practice area, offering health needs assessment, accessible health care, health promotion and empowerment through advocacy work
2   To reduce the workload and stress of general practitioners and receptionists which is associated with the care of homeless people and hostel residents
3   To evaluate the efficacy of health advocacy work using patient-centred assessment of quality of life as well as workload statistics from the practice

---

Table 4.2   Health advocacy: the family health worker's role

- Informing people living in local hostels, refuges and bed and breakfast hotels about health care facilities in the area and how to access services effectively.
- Registering individuals or family groups with a health centre, making appointments, and helping patients to list and prioritise their health needs.
- Providing health checks, recording blood pressure, weight, family history, smear & immunisation status.
- Allowing people time to talk and 'off load'. Counselling, focusing on 'here and now' issues.
- Practical help – organising clothes, toys, baby equipment, pot and pans and furniture.
- Liaison and referral to other agencies – social services, health visitors, drug dependency agencies, education welfare.
- Advocacy work with other agencies (housing departments, hospitals, social security offices); writing letters and making telephone calls on behalf of clients.
- Giving information and advice about health promotion, family planning and immunisation to individuals or groups.
- Advising hostel and refuge staff on health related issues and local health services.
- Visiting ex-clients, once re-housed, to terminate relationship and to assist them to access local primary health care services.

---

dependency. Preventive health measures were also offered, since homeless people may not otherwise take up screening tests such as blood pressure measurement and immunisations (Victor, 1996). Besides liaison with health visitors, the family health worker also provided information about housing, childcare, schools, drug dependency units and psychiatric care; and she worked with staff at hostels and hotels, as well as link-workers and interpreters, providing information and support (Gaulton-Berks, 1994).

The evaluation: a controlled trial

As specified above, the Princes Park Family Health Project dealt primarily with a temporarily homeless, transient population. In total there were 1000 patients eligible for the project over three and a half years, including 438 children. A large majority (80 per cent) of the adults were women and a majority of the households (69 per cent) consisted of families with children. About half (55 per cent) of these families were headed by lone parents and half had no current support from health or welfare agencies when they arrived in the area. A third of the individual patients reported having no supportive current partner or confidant; 70 per cent were unemployed or had chronic illness (Reilly, et al., 1996).

In order to evaluate the impact of the health advocacy approach, we designed a system whereby up to half the eligible patients were offered the health advocacy intervention while the others accessed the primary health care team in the usual way. This was done by allocating newly registered patients either to 'health advocacy' or to 'usual care', depending on the month of registration. Although this did not constitute random allocation, it could be described as quasi-randomisation, the basis of group allocation being sequential and otherwise unbiased (Cook and Campbell, 1979; Mant 1993). During 'usual care' months, temporary residents registered at the health centre in the normal way. During 'health advocacy' months, they were referred on to the family health worker. These formed the 'reactive advocacy' group. In addition, the family health worker visited hostels and bed-and-breakfast hotels to initiate contact and register new arrivals ('proactive advocacy' group). Table 4.3 shows that the women in these three groups were statistically comparable in demographic terms.

Baseline information gathering was undertaken in both 'intervention' and 'usual care' periods. Contact with the health advocate varied from a short interview and registration of the patient to visits which might take place up to three times a week. Needs and outcomes for women in contact with the health advocacy worker were compared, over a three-month interval, with those of women given 'usual care'.

Evaluation tools and outcome measures

We used three different quality of life measures to evaluate the health advocacy intervention. These were: the Nottingham Health Profile (Hunt, et al., 1986), a validated measure of 'health-related distress' previously used in a homeless population; the Life Fulfilment Scale (adapted from Baker, et al., 1994), previously used in a large-scale primary care study (Buck, et al., 1996); and the Faces Scale (Andrews and Withey, 1976). All these measures are self-report questionnaires. They are used in this context to assess and quantify levels of distress and dissatisfaction rather than to record the presence or absence of a particular disease.

The workload generated for the practice by each of the three groups of temporarily registered patients was also measured, to give a rough estimate of cost-effectiveness of the project in the light of the original 'burden of work' rationale (see Table 4.1).

Table 4.3 Homeless women: composition of the three study groups

	Control (*n* = 26)	Groups Reactive advocacy (*n* = 18)	Proactive advocacy (*n* = 40)
Age (mean) in years	26.4	27.9	24.5
	%	%	%
Marital status			
Single	46	72	60
Divorced	46	17	23
Married	8	11	17
Temporary accommodation			
Women's refuges	50	39	40
Family hostels	14	28	28
Alcohol rehab. hostel	9	6	——
Hotels and B&Bs	9	22	22
Young persons' hostel	18	6	10
Ethnic group			
White British	82	83	95
Living situation			
With family (children & partner, parents)	14	22	21
With children	55	56	56
With partner	4	11	10
Alone*	27	11	13
Long-term illness reported	27	33	46
Length of time homeless before registration (median) in months	3	3	1.5

Note: no significant differences were found between groups on any demographic variable.
*People are described as living alone if they do not live with any other family member or partner/spouse (but they may live in the young persons' hostel with other residents).

Strenuous efforts were made to follow up both 'usual care' and 'health advocacy' patients three months after registration. Others have pointed out the difficulties of tracking change in a transient population (Williams and Allen, 1989); form filling was unlikely to be a high priority for women whose basic needs remained unmet during this period of their lives. We did not therefore expect to be able to follow up all the women registered for the project, but tried to ensure that comparisons were made on a valid basis by documenting between-group differences at all stages.

Our main hypothesis was that the health advocacy input would lead to an improvement in quality of life and alleviation of distress over the three-month period following temporary registration at the health centre, relative to any changes found in 'usual care' patients. We also hoped to reduce the workload for the health centre team by providing a streamlined service for the homeless temporary residents.

Did the health advocate make a difference?

Baseline questionnaires were completed by 226 homeless people over the three years of the project. Approximately 50 per cent of these (117 people, of whom 84 were women) were successfully followed up for three months each. There were 18 women in the reactive advocacy group, 40 in the proactive advocacy group, and 26 in the 'usual care' control group. The design of the evaluation was such that as far as possible we were comparing 'like with like', with the major difference between groups being the offer of help from the health advocate.

The principal means of measuring the effect of this assistance were the quality of life scales. The Life Fulfilment Scale (LFS) is intended to measure the difference between people's expectations in life and their actual feelings of fulfilment or satisfaction. The relative importance of each of a number of aspects of everyday life is rated in the first part of the questionnaire, and then the reader is asked to rate (on a 4-point scale) his or her current degree of satisfaction, or fulfilment, in relation to each of the same ten items. These are as follows: family life, close friendships, happy marriage (or similar relationship), being able to do enjoyable leisure activities, being in good health, being happy as a person, having a secure job, being happy with the area, adequacy of housing, and having enough money to do desirable things. A high score on this instrument represents a wide gap between what is desired and what is experienced at the time of filling in the questionnaire. The higher the importance rating of each item and the lower the level of satisfaction, the higher the 'gap' score will be.

There were no significant overall baseline differences between control and intervention groups on the LFS scores (women and men). Table 4.4 shows the results for the three groups of women who were followed up three months after registration at the health centre in terms of change scores on all three quantitative measures. A positive change score denotes improvement. LFS change scores show significant variation between groups in personal fulfilment (fulfilment with oneself, family,

Table 4.4 Change in quality of life for homeless women in temporary accommodation over the three-month follow-up period

	Control (*n* = 26)	Groups Reactive advocacy (*n* = 18)	Proactive advocacy (*n* = 40)	Analysis of variance significance level **p** <
LFS mean change scores				
Personal fulfilment subscale	1.42	7.22	10.50	0.03
Material fulfilment subscale	0.65	5.47	6.60	——
Overall life fulfilment	2.38	11.94	17.17	0.02
NHP mean change scores				
Emotional reactions	−4.68	10.08	21.60	0.01
Energy	−5.29	6.31	16.35	0.05
Social isolation	−11.30	16.59	5.56	0.02
Sleep	4.09	16.35	15.95	——
Pain	−0.80	1.34	8.76	——
Physical mobility	0.69	0.57	4.31	——
Faces scale mean change scores				
	0.54	0.88	1.25	——

Note: Negative score (–) denotes deterioration; positive score denotes improvement.

friends, spare time, partner and health) and overall fulfilment. Group-to-group comparisons were limited by the small number of women involved, but the improvement was significantly greater for the proactive advocacy group than for the 'usual care' patients, whose quality of life on the LFS did not improve and in some cases declined. Changes in the material fulfilment subscale were not statistically significant, although many women had been rehoused within the three-month follow-up interval.

The Nottingham Health Profile (NHP) results also highlighted the emotional impact of homelessness. Significantly more improvement was reported by the proactive advocacy group than the 'usual care' group on two of the six dimensions, namely emotional distress and social isolation. Other dimensions of the NHP showed no significant changes associated with the advocacy intervention (Hunt and McKenna, 1991).

The Faces scale measures 'global' quality of life, or emotional state. The patient is asked which of seven diagrammatic faces most closely represents their current feelings. The faces range from 'delighted' (happy smile, score = 1) to 'terrible' (downturned mouth, score = 7). The results in Table 4.4 suggest somewhat more improvement for the patients given

access to health advocacy than the 'usual care' patients, but the difference was not statistically significant on this small sample of women.

Of the other factors which might also have a major influence on perceived quality of life and fulfilment, rehousing was an obvious confounding variable; we were aware that health advocacy support might
have helped women to get rehoused. The proportion rehoused within
the three-month follow up period was 80 per cent for the proactive
advocacy group and 83 per cent for the reactive advocacy group, compared with 68 per cent of the 'usual care' group; but the difference was
not statistically significant and it was noted that almost all the women
were rehoused within a four-month waiting period because of the local
authority strategy.

Although it is not possible to state unambiguously that the health
advocacy input was the sole cause of the improvement in quality of life
for women in this study, the three independent sets of results shown in
Table 4.4 suggest that the quality of life of people supported by a health
advocate during their stay in temporary housing improved more than
that of people given 'usual care' at the health centre. Two of the instruments used were sensitive enough to demonstrate statistically significant differences; we were able to show that proactive health advocacy,
in particular, was associated with positive outcomes for women.

What about the workload at the health centre?

The aim of the project was to achieve health gain for a group of particularly needy patients whilst protecting the regular health centre team
from overload. The numbers of encounters with various members of the
health centre and project teams were logged for both adults and children in the follow-up study. We assumed that patients who registered
themselves at the health centre were, a priori, likely to want to see a
doctor, whereas patients proactively registered at their hostel address
were not necessarily in need of medical attention at that time. The
average number of GP consultations was one per month over the three-
month follow-up period; but differences in consultation rates with
general practitioners or nurses between the women in the three study
groups were not significant (see Table 4.5). The two intervention groups
had similar levels of contact with the family health worker (Tables 4.5
and 4.6).

Clearly, we did not achieve a statistically significant reduction of workload for the health centre as a result of the expenditure on the health
advocacy intervention. Neither, however, did we realise fears that the
project would actually increase the workload of the team. Although the

Table 4.5 Primary healthcare workload associated with homeless patients over a three-month period

	Control (*n* = 26)	Groups Reactive advocacy (*n* = 18)	Proactive advocacy (*n* = 40)
GP contact	2.23	2.89	1.78
FHW contacts			
Initiated by FHW		3.99	3.90
Initiated by patient		4.67	7.94

Note: no significant difference between groups.

Table 4.6 Rating of how much support the family health worker has given the patient over a three-month period

	Intervention groups	
	Reactive advocacy (*n* = 18) %	Proactive advocacy (*n* = 40) %
Registration and health assessment only	5.6	2.5
1 or 2 additional contacts	27.8	25.0
3–6 contacts	27.8	25.0
6 or more contacts	38.9	47.5

Note: no significant difference between groups.

needs assessment process undoubtedly uncovered significant problems for many families and individuals, these were largely addressed within the remit of the health advocate, and other members of the team reported, from early on in the three-year project, that it was less stressful dealing with temporary residents knowing that their complex needs would be addressed by the family health worker in her advocacy role.

Interviews with clients were undertaken to complement the quantitative investigation; these highlighted the women's sensitivity about relationships with professionals.

The most important thing about her [the FHW] was the way she was relaxed, not abrupt at all. When you're homeless you have such low self-esteem. If she's the first person from the health centre that you have contact with she doesn't look down on you or anything. And being a woman, that was quite important.

Action research in the inner city

The Family Health Project was one of 34 projects funded by the Department of Health with the aim of developing more satisfactory healthcare for the homeless. Williams's (1995) report for the DoH on the scheme, however, reveals that none of the other projects was formally evaluated in respect either of value for money or of the efficacy of the various methodologies employed by different projects. This represents a missed opportunity for addressing, and perhaps resolving, some of the unanswered questions about how to deal with the problems of homeless people in the UK which have been repeatedly pointed out in the literature. We have already referred to the ongoing debates about the role of social support and the question 'whether the health needs of (homeless) families are best met by generic or specialist forms of service organisation' . . . 'In the absence of rigorously conducted evaluative studies it is impossible to conclude which model of care most effectively meets the very obvious health care needs of homeless people' (Victor, 1996).

Working from an inner-city health centre meant that we could, in this project, provide both mainstream (generic) and specialist (health advocacy) services for temporarily homeless patients. Of the various models considered at the outset, the health centre 'additional in-house provision' seemed the most appropriate to implement and evaluate, on the ground that if it was successful it could relatively easily be replicated in other inner-city practices across the country. This model also shares the characteristics identified in the systematic review (Reilly, 2000) as being associated with positive outcomes.

Action research of this kind requires a dedicated and skilled team and full co-operation from the host institution and from the client group. We were extremely fortunate in all these respects. Our conclusions are based on a small sample of homeless people, but we have taken account of potential confounding variables in putting forward evidence to support the hypothesis that the family health worker's client-led approach to her work, which we have termed health advocacy, played an important part in generating positive outcomes for homeless women.

The health advocacy intervention was complex, and a job description and protocol were developed in consultation with a steering group which identified key principles (Table 4.7) and oversaw the implementation and evaluation of the project (Reilly, et al., 1996; Gaulton-Berks, 1998). The approach was tailored to clients' and hostel workers' needs by an experienced nurse. The 'case management' protocol involved, in sequence: engagement of the client (building rapport); needs assessment; a proactive response to both social and medical requirements; attempted reintegration into mainstream service provision; and, finally, attention to the proper termination of a therapeutic relationship with each client. All these aspects seemed important at different times for different people. Another quote from a patient: 'She was like everything rolled into one [all the agencies] . . . Any problems we had we could talk to her, and if she could help you she would.'

Anticipatory care: a challenge to the 'inverse care' law

A particularly good case can be made from our results for the anticipatory care of homeless women and families, since the outreach service provided by the family health worker to women on arrival in the area was the most beneficial pattern of care. Given the high morbidity associated with homelessness, proactive and permanent registration of homeless patients with a GP in the locality is promoted by some enthusiasts (Lowry, 1990; Balasz, 1994). We used temporary registration, needs assessment and streamlined care for short-stay patients in our area.

We were unable to show that the project reduced the burden of care on primary and secondary healthcare providers. Nevertheless, as far as the health centre was concerned, the Family Health Project transformed

Table 4.7 Key principles for the health advocacy approach

- The FHW was an additional resource in an established mainstream service.
- Effective intervention necessitated collaboration and inter agency work. The needs of homeless individuals and families were often complex. Health needs were interwoven with social and housing needs.
- Emphasis was placed on outreach work, encouraging needy people in the practice area to access services, and making links with the primary health care team and other agencies.
- A flexible and holistic approach to health care was necessary. All interventions were related to the needs of the individual or family.
- Advocacy was a major part of this service, helping homeless people's voices to be heard and their health needs to be met.
- Giving people adequate information, both written and verbal, is vital. It was important not to assume that people knew how to access services.

a near-burnout situation into an exciting action-research project. Paradoxically, the initial rejection of the Health Authority's 'mission statement management-speak' by idealistic but stressed general practitioners evolved into a collaboration which became highly organised and goal driven. Support from an imaginative health authority, leading to the timely injection of ring-fenced funds from the Department of Health, permitted a disaffected group of health workers to define a workload problem, articulate possible responses, and design and implement a social experiment within the setting of primary healthcare. The formal evaluation framework (quasi-randomised controlled trial) and consistent results allow a positive conclusion to be drawn about the efficacy of health advocacy in an inner-city setting with regard to the quality of life of temporarily housed women.

Liverpool Health Authority has demonstrated its confidence in the practice-based health advocacy/anticipatory care model by funding an expansion of the project. The family health worker has taken on the role of primary care development nurse and now covers a wider area for outreach work. This includes training and supervision of lay advocacy workers based in several practices and helping practice staff to identify people who will benefit from additional support (Gaulton-Berks, 1998). Further evaluation is in progress to demonstrate whether the health advocacy model can be successfully and economically adapted for other groups of disadvantaged people.

References

Acheson, D. (1998) *Independent Inquiry into Health Inequalities*. London: HMSO.

Andrews, F. and Withey, S. (1976) *Social Indicators of Well-Being. Americans' Perception of Quality of Life*. New York: Plenum Press.

Baker, G., Jacoby, A., Smith, D., Dewey, M. and Chadwick, D. W. (1994) 'The development of a novel scale to assess life fulfilment as part of the further refinement of a quality of life model for epilepsy'. *Epilepsia*, 35, 591–6.

Balasz, J. (1994) 'Health care for single homeless people'. In K. Fisher and J. Collims (eds), *Homelessness, Health Care and Welfare Provision*. London: Routledge.

Buck, D., Jacoby, A., Baker, G. A., Graham-Jones, S. and Chadwick, D. W. (1996) Patients' experiences of and satisfaction with care for their epilepsy. *Epilepsia*, 37, 841–9.

Buckner, J. C., Bassuk, E. L. and Zima, B. T. (1993) 'Mental health issues affecting homeless women: implications for intervention'. *American Journal of Orthopsychiatry*: 63(3), 385–99.

Bunston, T. and Breton, M. (1992) 'Homes and homeless women'. *Journal of Environmental Psychology*, 12, 149–62.

Cohen, I. C., Ramirez, M., Teresi, J., Gallagher, M. and Sokolovsky, J. (1997) 'Predictors of becoming redomiciled among older homeless women'. *The Gerontologist*, 37(1), 67–74.

Conway, J. (1988) *Prescription for poor health: The health crisis for homeless families*. London: London Food Commission, Maternity Alliance, Shac and Shelter.

Cook, T. D. and Campbell, D. T. (1979) *Quasi-experimentation: Design and analysis for field settings*. Boston: Houghton Mifflin Company.

El-Kabir, D. (1996) 'On creating a culture of care for the homeless'. *Journal of Interprofessional Care* 10, 3, 267–9.

Gaulton-Berks, L. (1994) Homeless but not helpless. *Nursing Times*, 9(15), 53–5.

Gaulton-Berks, L. (1998) 'Equity in health: lightening the primary care load'. *Primary Health Care*, 8, 26–9.

George, S. L., Shanks, N. J. and Westlake, L. (1991) 'Census of single homeless people in Sheffield'. *British Medical Journal*, 302, 1387–9.

Grieve, S. (1997) 'Measuring morale – does practice area deprivation affect doctors' well-being?' *British Journal of General Practice*, 47, 547–52.

Hagen, J. L. and Hutchison, E. (1988) 'Who's serving the homeless?' *Social Casework: The Journal of Contemporary Social Work*, 69(8), 491–7.

Hart, J. T. (1971) 'The inverse care law', *The Lancet* (i), 405–12.

Hatton, D. C. (1997) 'Managing health problems among homeless women with children in a transitional shelter'. *Journal of Nursing Scholarship*, 29(1), 33–7.

Hayden, C. (1992) 'Bed and breakfast blues'. *Health Service Journal*, 8 October, 22–4.

Hunt, S., McEwan, P. and McKenna, S. (1986) *Measuring health status*. London: Croom Helm.

Hunt, S. and McKenna, S. (1991) *The Nottingham Health Profile User's Manual*. Manchester: Galen Research & Consultancy.

Lowry, S. (1990) 'Housing and health: Health and homelessness'. *British Medical Journal*, 300, 32–4.

Mant, D. (1993) 'Understanding the problems of health and housing research'. In R. Burridge and D. Ormandy (eds), *Unhealthy Housing: research, remedies and reform*, London: E. & F.N. Spon.

Marriott, S., Harvey, R. and Bonner, D. (1997) 'Health in hostels: a survey of hostel dwelling women'. *Psychiatric Bulletin*, 21, 618–21.

Mercier, C. and Racine, G. (1993) 'A follow-up study of homeless women'. *Journal of social distress and the homeless*, 2(3), 207–22.

Power, R., French, R., Connelly, J., George, S., Hawes, D., Hinton, T., Klee, H., Robinson, D., Senior, J., Timms, P. and Warner, D. (1999) 'Health, health promotion and homelessness'. *British Medical Journal*, 318, 590–2.

Reilly, S. (2000) 'Addressing the health problems of the (inner-city) homeless: a systematic review and a controlled trial'. John Moores University, Liverpool (unpublished PHd thesis).

Reilly, S., Gaulton, L., Graham-Jones, S. and Davidson, L. (1996) *Effective primary health care for homeless people: an evaluation of the Family Health Project*. Princes Park Health Centre/Liverpool Health Authority, Liverpool, unpublished report.

Shelter (1997 *et seq*) Updates on homeless population figures. (http//:www.shelter.org.uk/)

Smith, C. A., Smith, C. J., Kearns, R. and Abbot, M. (1993) 'Housing Stressors, Social Support and Psychological Distress', in *Social Science Medicine*, 37(5), 603–12.

Standing Conference on Public Health (1994) *Housing, homelessness and health.* Nuffield Provisional Hospital Trust.

Taylor, C. (1987) 'Primary care in Liverpool'. *Medicine in Society*, 7.

Victor, C. (1996) 'The health of the temporary homeless population'. *Journal of Interprofessional Care*, 10(3), 257–66.

Watson, S. (1986) *Housing and homelessness: A feminist perspective.* London: Routledge and Kegan Paul.

Williams, S. (1995) Review of primary care projects for homeless people. Final Report. Department of Health.

Williams, S. and Allen, I. (1989) *Health Care for Single Homeless People.* London: Policy Studies Institute.

Winkleby, M. and Boyce, T. (1994) 'Health related risk factors of homeless families and single adults'. *Journal of community health*, 19(1), 7–23.

Wood, N., Wilkinson, C. and Kumar, A. (1997) 'Do the homeless get a fair deal from general practitioners?' *Journal of Royal Society of Health*, 117(5), 292–7.

5

Concentration, Marginalisation and Exclusion: Women's Housing Needs and the City

Roberta Woods

Introduction

The concentration of female-headed households in social rented housing is now well documented. This phenomenon reflects a wider-gendered social geography of British cities. Women can find themselves in inner-city housing areas with little access to leisure and other community facilities, or in similarly adverse circumstances on outer estates.

Not all social housing conforms to the stereotype, particularly associated with council housing, of run-down areas where crime and drug taking are rife. Indeed, women have been prime movers in community campaigns to stop or reverse the decline and neglect of many areas (Grayson and Walker, 1996). Nevertheless, many women can end up living in neighbourhoods characterised by social deprivation (Social Exclusion Unit, 1998). The current Labour Government's Social Exclusion Unit has made such areas a priority focus for its work, and part of this chapter will assess whether the strategies put forward by the Social Exclusion Unit and the Urban Task Force are likely to improve women's housing experience of the city. The chapter will also discuss a research project, undertaken between 1992 and 1995, which examined how women access local authority housing – an issue where there is still little empirical evidence but which is important in understanding why female-headed households occupy particular locations in the social geography of cities.

Since 1980 a number of publications have sought to address the issue of gender inequality in the housing market. This seems to have become a particularly crucial issue during the 1980s given the thrust of government policy towards support for owner occupation with a residual social sector to accommodate those not able to purchase on the open market. Literature on this subject has considered issues which disadvantage women in gaining access to owner occupation, but it has also gone further to outline aspects of policy which undermine women's needs or, at a more theoretical level, has sought to examine the role of housing form in reproducing stereotyped gender roles and the dominance of the nuclear family (see Watson, 1986, 1989; for a different perspective see Saunders and Williams, 1988; Saunders, 1989).

In the literature, much attention has been given to the structural disadvantages that women face and which place them in a weak position with regard to the provision of housing. Empirical evidence on women's actual experience of housing and how this relates to housing management practice is rare; the literature focuses on the barriers to owner occupation and difficulties faced in gaining access to council housing (for a review of this see Woods, 1996).

Despite advances in women's employment opportunities and a rise in female participation rates in the labour market, earning differentials between men and women persist (Rubery et al., 1999; ONS, 1999). Lack of earning potential and discriminatory policies pursued by building societies have traditionally been used to account for women having less ability to enter owner occupation than men. Deregulation of building societies and the operation of sex discrimination legislation appear to have changed the lending practices of mortgage lenders and there is currently little evidence that building society policies by themselves restrict women's access to mortgages. Women's differentiated position with regard to owner occupation is now likely to be associated with lower earnings rather than discrimination in terms of mortgage lending.

Data from the General Household Survey (1996) show that female-headed households are more likely to be tenants of social rented housing and less likely to be home owners than their male counterparts (see Table 5.1).

Restricted access to owner occupation is partly the explanation of female-headed households being more reliant on social housing. But there are additional reasons. Bull (1993) has demonstrated the greater reliance that women place on accessing council housing following relationship breakdown. Furthermore, following realtionship breakdown only 6 per cent of female-headed households move from the social rented sector into owner ocupation, compared to 33 per cent of male-headed households (ONS, 1999). The way in which women have been treated by local authority housing departments when seeking rehousing in these circumstances has long been subject to criticism (see Logan,

Table 5.1 Tenure by sex of head of household, 1996

	All male households (%)	All female households (%)
Owner occupied outright and with mortgage	74	47
Social rented housing association and council	18	41
Private rented	8	12

Source: General Household Survey (1996).

1986; Morris and Winn, 1990). Recent guidelines produced by the Department of Environment, Transport and Regions (DETR, 1999) are intended to serve as a good practice guide for local authorities and to discourage policies that are not sufficiently responsive to the needs of people facing problems of this nature. The guidelines promote the importance of dealing sensitively with applicants experiencing relationship breakdown and highlight the need to have supportive policies and practices in place for dealing with those who have been subject to domestic violence. They also stress the importance of preventing homelessness amongst this group.

Much of the literature engages with the debate in urban geography about the relationship between gender roles and the form of the built environment. Of importance here are planning policies, architecture and design (Greed, 1994). These studies reflect upon safety and design and architectural impediments to supportive living, such as nuclear family housing or deck-access high rise. Underground walkways and carparks, poor lighting and excessive shrubbery have also been identified as neglecting women's needs for safety. These aspects lead to more theoretical questions relating to gender divisions of space or the ways in which the home, location and environment curtail or enhance women's choice (McDowell, 1998). However, many writers have sought to counter homogenising the needs of all women with regard to housing by stressing the differing housing needs or different experiences of housing services of young women (Douglas and Gilroy, 1994), elderly women (Sykes, 1994) and Black women (Dhillon-Kashyap, 1994; Woods, 1996).

Social housing is thus particularly important for women. Within this sector, in some areas at least, council housing is still the most important form of social housing. How this housing is allocated to women is, then, a significant issue. The literature, whilst addressing a wide range of issues with regard to women and housing, has focused on economic constraints, weaknesses in the law relating to family breakdown, inadequacies in homeless persons legislation, general problems in allocations systems and, more latterly, the concentration of women in the public sector. There is a lack of empirical information about local authority allocations with specific reference to gender. It is this lack of empirical evidence which the research project described in this chapter sought to address.

To date, little information is available concerning women's experience of council housing. Brailey (1985) went some way towards filling this gap in Scotland. She carried out a study of four local authorities to examine composition of waiting lists, rehousing chances, the reasons for requiring housing and the way homeless persons procedures relate to various categories of women. In England, some surveys have been carried out in local areas (for example, the London Borough of Haringey) to investigate the suitability of public housing for women. But there has been an absence of studies that take a wider, national look at the policies of local authorities as they relate specifically to gender. In addition, there has been a lack of information about how female-headed households fare on the waiting list *vis-à-vis* other groups regarding length of time waiting, quality of housing offered and type of area offered.

Karn (1991) report a large-scale survey of local authority allocations systems and point to the wide variety of such systems. Karn's study was important in enabling the drawing of a sample for the present study, and in framing some of the questions to be addressed.

The research project

The research project described sought to provide much-needed empirical evidence as to the suitability of council housing for women. It had three aspects:

1 An examination of the waiting lists, allocation records, tenant files, rent accounts and repairs information of 18 local authorities in England and Wales.
2 Interviews with relevant housing management staff in each local authority to ascertain detailed information about allocations systems and the operation of homeless persons legislation. Information about

the estates in each local authority area were collected, with the estates being rated on a continuum of good to bad according to a range of housing management indicators.
3 A survey of a sample of tenants from each local authority who were allocated a property in the research period to measure tenant satisfaction.

Local authorities were asked to make accessible information relating to size of waiting list, the composition of the waiting list by household type, the sex and ethnic group of the applicant, reason for being on the waiting list, details of any offers made, state of current accommodation, points and priority grouping if appropriate. For those who had been granted a tenancy within the previous 12 months, information was obtained about family or household structure, sex and ethnic background of the head of household, the reasons for rehousing, number of offers made, the types of offer made, the type of dwelling requested and the type of dwelling accepted, the state of repair of the dwelling, amenities in the dwelling which was accepted and the area in which it was located.

Not all local authorities held this data in a relatively accessible form. There were variations in methods of record keeping. In some authorities data extraction was a very time-consuming business as some local authorities kept only manual records and this was sometimes complicated by a decentralized recording system. In order to add detailed information about the authorities' housing management practices and housing stock, interviews were held with relevant housing managers in each authority.

In order to gauge tenant satisfaction with the allocations system a postal survey was administered to a sample of tenants (2000) across ten of the authorities.

Given the size of the project, only a few of the findings can be outlined here. Table 5.2 shows that for the most part the pattern of letting of properties was broadly similar. The table shows that most allocations went to families or female lone parents. In authority ND the situation was different because local factors (sheltered housing coming onstream) led to a relatively high number of allocations going to elderly people.

What was the route that led to housing/rehousing? Tables 5.3 and 5.4 show the mechanism for housing/rehousing: for example, whether from the waiting list or through homeless priority. The two authorities represented in these tables are very different in character and yet a similar

Table 5.2   Allocation by household type

Local authority	C	FA	LPF	LPM	SF	SM	EF	EM	EC	O
AH	9.0	31.9	18.3	1.3	5.0	4.6	13.2	4.0	9.3	4.6
NA	4.1	28.8	24.4	0.8	3.1	4.1	18.4	3.6	8.5	5.5
ND	2.3	26.4	10.3	——	——	3.4	33.3	3.4	19.5	1.4
NW	8.7	34.1	19.2	1.0	2.9	2.0	20.7	4.4	7.9	——

Key: C = couple; FA = family; LPF = lone parent female; LPM = lone parent male; SF = single female; SM = single male; EF = elderly female; EM = elderly male; EC = elderly couple; O = other.

pattern in the routes to rehousing can be determined. In some ways the findings about the routes to local authority housing were quite surprising. A great deal of concern was expressed by the 1979–97 Conservative Government about people and, in particular, lone parents jumping the housing queue via the homelessness route. Yet it can be seen that, regardless of the type of authority, allocations to the homeless accounted for a relatively small number of total allocations. Most allocations were made via transfers or the waiting list.

Tables 5.5 and 5.6 show for two authorities the pattern of allocations for family type by house type. These tables show results that would be expected. For the most part houses go to families and lone parents. Flats go to single people or couples and bungalows to elderly people. One interesting finding is the reliance of lone parents on maisonettes – a generally unpopular type of accommodation.

The reasons given from the tenant survey for seeking rehousing were many. The main reasons given were health reasons (13.5 per cent); previous accommodation unsuitable (12.9 per cent) and overcrowding (10 per cent). We might like to note that becoming pregnant was listed by only 3.2 per cent of those surveyed and this includes those seeking a larger house for an increase in children in addition to those becoming pregnant for the first time.

The largest area of dissatisfaction centred on accommodation being too small (8.5 per cent), bad neighbours (4.6 per cent); draughty (4.6 per cent); and in need of repair (4.3 per cent). The best things were considered to be large rooms (15.9 per cent); central heating (10.1 per cent); quiet area (7.6 per cent); and easy to manage (6.9 per cent).

Most tenants were satisfied with the service from the housing department, with 15.6 per cent being completely satisfied. Suggestions given for improving the service included more training (7.3 per cent) and more appropriate lettings (4.3 per cent).

Table 5.3 Major reasons for wanting to be rehoused: ED (small rural local authority)

Recorded reason	Couple (%)	Family (%)	Elderly female (%)	Elderly male (%)	Elderly couple (%)	Single female (%)	Single male (%)	Single parent female (%)	Reasons given (%)
Direct exchange	26.7	26.7	6.7	—	6.7	13.3	—	20.0	9.6
Homelessness	—	50.0	—	—	—	—	16.7	33.3	3.8
Transfer	12.8	10.3	17.9	10.3	5.1	20.5	7.7	15.4	25.0
Waiting list	15.8	31.6	13.7	7.4	10.5	7.4	6.3	7.4	60.9

Table 5.4 Major reasons for wanting to be rehoused: NC (large metropolitan local authority)

Recorded reason	Couple (%)	Family (%)	Elderly female (%)	Elderly male (%)	Elderly couple (%)	Single female (%)	Single male (%)	Single parent female (%)	Single parent male (%)	Reasons given (%)
Clearance	5.2	41.7	—	3.8	—	1.4	12.3	21.8	2.4	3.6
Homelessness	0.6	22.7	0.6	0.4	—	16.2	10.6	47.3	1.1	8.0
Transfer	6.0	35.2	11.2	7.0	—	6.2	8.8	21.1	1.4	30.6
Waiting list	7.3	26.6	4.6	1.8	—	11.0	26.7	16.4	1.8	54.0
Other priority	6.9	27.1	8.5	13.3	—	7.4	6.4	27.1	2.1	3.2

Table 5.5 Local authority A: house type by family type

Family type	Bungalow	Bedsit	Flat	House	Maisonnette	Unknown	%
Single male	5.9	17.6	64.7	8.8	—	2.9	99.9
Single female	13.5	5.4	56.8	18.9	5.4	—	100
Couple	13.4	—	47.8	25.4	3.0	10.4	100
Lone parent family, female	—	—	33.1	50.7	13.2	2.9	99.9
Family	0.4	—	11.4	67.9	15.2	5.1	100
Elderly male	33.3	26.7	40.0	—	—	—	100
Elderly female	36.7	15.3	46.9	—	—	1.0	99.9
Elderly couple	65.2	—	30.4	—	2.9	1.4	99.9
Lone parent, male	—	—	50.0	30.0	10.0	10.0	100
Female and NDC	7.7	—	—	69.2	7.7	15.4	100

Table 5.6   Local authority CO: accommodation by household type

Household type	Bungalow	Flat	House	Maisonnette
Single male	11.1	9.8	——	16.7
Single female	11.1	10.5	——	8.3
Couple	11.1	4.6	——	——
Lone parent	——	20.9	52.7	33.3
Family	——	12.4	39.1	25.0
Elderly male	5.6	11.8	——	8.3
Elderly female	16.7	19.6	1.8	8.3
Elderly couple	50.0	8.5	0.9	——
Lone parent, male	——	——	2.7	——
Lone parent, female	——	——	——	——

The context of housing policy

Although only a few research findings have been reported in this chapter, the information shows the effects of the housing policies of the 1979–97 Conservative governments and presents challenges to those policies. These figures indicate that the obsession of those governments with lone parents jumping the housing queue was not based on fact. Many were housed from the waiting list and most housing still goes to families (couples with children). In addition, lone parents do not necessarily get good-quality housing.

The data from the research study showed that women are concerned about their areas becoming residualised (see below) and characterised by a poor environment and bad neighbours. That such residualisation of areas of social housing happened as a result of the market-based nature of Conservative housing legislation is well documented (Malpass and Means, 1993; Cole and Furbey, 1994; Lund, 1996). In a market-based housing system, the social rented sector was to exist, if at all, only for those who were not able to avail themselves of owner occupation or secure housing for themselves through private renting.

The term 'residualisation' has been used to describe the consequences of these policies. This refers to the process whereby social housing has increasingly catered for those on very low incomes rather than 'general needs' (English, 1987; Malpass, 1990). It is a term that has increasingly been linked with social exclusion, whereby people living on estates in the social rented sector are set apart both physically and economically from the rest of the population (Malpass and Murie, 1994). Given the importance of the council sector to female-headed households, residualisation has had a particular impact on women (Maye-Banbury, 1999).

The concentration of low-income families in council housing estates has also produced problems for local authorities in management terms. Housing managers and tenants had to contend with not only a deteriorating physical environment but also rising levels of crime and record levels of unemployment. Crime rates have risen in general in inner-city areas for both household offences and personal offences compared to non inner-city areas (Social Trends, 1997). Rising crime and fear of crime led many local authority housing departments to respond by improving security measures for individual dwellings while diverting spending away from other types of maintenance and improvement. Other initiatives included supporting neighbourhood watch schemes or employing security guards to patrol estates. Such measures can be very physically unattractive and the use of security guards and closed-circuit television, whilst helping residents cope with the actuality and fear of crime, can also stigmatise these areas as unattractive and unsafe places in which to live.

A number of reports sought to address this issue (Coleman, 1985; Page, 1994). Power and Tunstall (1995) suggest that crime prevention policies could be based more soundly on a community reconstruction approach that recognises the need for longer-term investment in social and economic development (see also Passmore and Brown, 1997). This is a clear acknowledgement of the lack of investment in such areas by the 1981–97 Conservative government. Power and Tunstall (1995) also make the point that as far as estate improvement is concerned the answer, in policy terms, was seen in the 1980s to lie with one-off flagship initiatives such as City Challenge, Estate Action or schemes funded by the Single Regeneration Budget. This, however, means that resources were often unavailable for ongoing planned maintenance and incremental improvements. Where additional resources were made available the reponse was often patchy and piecemeal and failed to tackle the underlying causes of degeneration.

In addition to having concentrations of low-income people, local authorities have also had to contend with greater movement in and out of local authority housing. A study commissioned by the Rowntree Foundation found that the annual turnover of properties had risen sharply in the past ten years (Centre for Housing Policy, 1997). A high turnover of stock makes it more difficult to develop community spirit and identity and harder to achieve sustainable and supportive communities. The report also noted that those moving out of the sector were generally couples aged under 45 where one or both people were working. On the other hand, those moving into the sector were in the 16–29 age group and unemployed.

Not all tenants have been equally affected by the problems facing social housing, and many estates represent vibrant and stable communities. Nevertheless, problems of neighbour nuisance and racial harassment have been increasing, leaving ethnic minority communities and individuals at particular risk of attack or abuse (Henderson and Karn, 1987). It has traditionally been the case that local authorities have moved families to a 'safer' environment when they have been subject to racial harassment. This has partly been a response to the difficulty of securing evidence against the perpetrators. More recently, local authorities have sought to take action against perpetrators by obtaining injunctions or seeking eviction. The Housing Act 1996 has strengthened the legislative basis for such action and indeed makes it easier for all social landlords to address the issue of antisocial behaviour among tenants.

It is, however, important to stress that women have actively engaged in campaigns to prevent the deterioration of their communities and to provide community facilities to help support the most vulnerable and counter some of the worst impact of neglect by central government (Grayson and Walker, 1996; Naples, 1998). Local authoriites have in some circumstances supported tenants in this endeavour. The Labour government has sought to tackle this issue by making the improvenment of disadvantaged estates a priority of the Social Exclusion Unit (SEU, 1998). A number of action teams have been put in place to address the mutifaceted nature of the problems facing these areas and to propose solutions, and a new regeneration intiative – the 'New Deal for Communities' – is rolling out in 17 pilot areas.

Homelessness

This study shows in a rather dramatic way that homelessness, whilst being a route to local authority housing, does not in fact dwarf other forms of access. Nevertheless, the Labour government has sought to alter the changes in homelssness legislation that were implemented by the Conservative government in 1996. Under the 1996 Housing Act the right to permanent accommodation for homeless households was removed and replaced with a duty on local authorities to house homeless households in temporary accommodation for two years only. In order to secure permanent accommodation, those presenting as homeless had to be placed on the general waiting list (Cowan, 1997). The Labour government has issued a circular that encourages local authorities to treat homeless applicants as a priority, although legislative change is still awaited. The use of temporary accommodation by women (and in many cases their children also) has been shown to lead to problems of ill health and huge disruption in children's education and development (Conway, 1988; Connolly and Crown, 1994). As such, the move away from the requirement to use temporary accommodation to meet the needs of homeless people, including women and chidren, is a step forward, but the general practice of using temporary accommodation for this group in some areas is not likely to be solved without a substantial investment in afforable housing.

Conclusions

The research reported in this chapter shows the importance of council housing for female-headed households, the need for improvements in the quality of housing obtained, and a safer and better wider environment. The policies put forward by the current government do start to address the issue of reinvestment in housing by the staged release of capital receipts for social housing development, and there may be further changes in capital spending (Armstrong, 1997). However, what is necessary in order to improve housing fitness standards and poor environments is a multifaceted approach to tackle poor housing, unemployment, urban decay and unhealthy environments. The housing minister does seem to be aware of the problems faced by many tenants and the need for such a multifaceted approach to improve some areas of local authority housing (Armstrong, 1999).

It is still too early to say whether the recently announced review of the council housing sector will produce houses and neighbourhoods that are accessible to women and that are pleasant to live in. It also remains to be seen whether the review of housing benefit will lead to properties becoming more affordable for those on low incomes, including women. What is clear is that the current government does have a commitment to revitalising some of the neighbourhoods that have produced circumstances in which women are vulnerable, isolated and impoverished. The 'New Deal for Communities' is not only providing additional resouces to some neighbourhoods, it is also seeking to encourage the active participation of residents in area regeneration. Women are particularly well placed to take on this role, but the problems should not be underestimated. (Naples, 1998 documents the successes and failures of this approach in the United States.)

So whilst this chapter has sought to argue that some improvements may be in the pipeline regarding women's housing experiences, it is perhaps wise to be cautious. Maye-Banbury (1999) gives us a powerful reminder that although the European Parliament supported a housing policy aimed at providing decent housing for all in 1997, no specific policies have been put in place to implement this or evaluate gender aspects of housing inequality. Much, therefore, remains to be done.

References

Armstrong, H. (1997) Text of speech given to the Local Government Association, Manchester, July 25.

Armstrong, H. (1999) 'The puzzle of social exclusion'. *Housing*, April, 20–1.

Brailey, M. (1985) Women's Access to Council Housing. Occasional Paper No. 25, Glasgow, The Planning Exchange.

Bull, J. (1993) *The Housing Consequences of Relationship Breakdown*. London: HMSO.

Centre for Housing Policy (1997) *Contemporary patterns of residential mobility in relation to social housing in England*. York: Centre for Housing Policy.

Cole, I. and Furbey, R. (1994) *The Eclipse of Council Housing*. London: Routledge.

Coleman, A. (1985) *Utopia on Trial*. London: Hilary Shipman.

Connolly, J. and Crown, J. (1994) *Homelessness and Ill Health*. London: Royal College of Physicians of London.

Conway, J. (ed.) (1988) *Prescription for Poor Health: the crisis for homeless families*. London: SHAC.

Cowan, D. (ed.) (1997) *The Housing Act 1996: A Practical Guide*. Bristol: Jordans.

DETR (Deportment of Enviroment, Transport and Regions) (1999) *Relationship Breakdown: A guide for social landlords*. July, London.

Dhillon-Kashyap, P. (1994) 'Black women and housing'. In R. Gilroy and R. Woods (eds), *Housing Women*. London: Routledge, 101–26.

Douglas, A. and Gilroy, R. (1994) 'Young women and homelessness'. In R. Giroy and R. Woods (eds), *Housing women*. London: Routledge, 127–51.

English, J. (1987) 'The Changing Public Sector'. In D. Clapham and J. English (eds), *Public Housing: Current Trends and Future Developments*. London: Croom Helm.

Grayson and Walker (1996) *Opening the Window: Revealing the Hidden History of Tenants Organisations*. Salford: TPAS (Tenant Participation Advisory Service) and Northern College.

Greed, C. (1994) *Women and Planning: Creating gendered realities*. London: Routledge.

Henderson, J. and Karn, V. (1987) *Race, Class and State Housing; inequality and the allocation of public housing in Britain*. Aldershot: Gower.

Karn, V. (1991) *Housing Allocations*. London: Institute of Housing.

Logan, F. (1986) *Homelessness and Relationship Breakdown: How the Law and Housing Policy Affects Women*. London: One Parent Families Association.

Lund, B. (1996) *Housing Problems and Housing Policy*. London: Longman.

Malpass, P. (1990) *Reshaping Housing Policy; subsidies, rents and residualisation*. London: Routledge.

Malpass, P. and Means, R. (1993) 'The politics of implementation'. In P. Malpass and R. Means (eds), *Implementing Housing Policy*. Buckingham: Open University Press, 185–94.

Malpass, P. and Murie, A. (1994) *Housing Policy and Practice* (4th edn). Basingstoke: Macmillan.

Maye-Banbury, A. (1999) 'A woman's lot'. *Inside Housing*, 9 April, 12–13.

McDowell, L. (1998) 'City life and difference: negotiating diversity'. In J. Allen, D. Massey and M. Pryke (eds), *Unsettling Cities*, London: Sage (in association with the Open University).

Morris, J. and Winn, M. (1990) *Housing and Social Inequality*. London: Hilary Shipman.

Naples, N. (ed.) (1998) *Community Activism and Feminist Politics*. London and New York: Routledge.

ONS (Office for National Statistics) (1999) *Social Trends 29*. London: the Stationery Office.

Page, D. (1994) *Developing Communities*. Teddington: Sutton Hastoe Housing Association.

Passmore, J. and Brown, T. (1997) 'Closing the Gap'. *Housing*, July/August, 24–5.

Power, A. (1987) *Property Before People*. London: Allen and Unwin.

Power, A. and Tunstall, R. (1995) *Swimming Against the Tide: Progress or polarisation on twenty unpopular estates*. York, Joseph Rowntree Foundation.

Rubery, J., Smith, M. and Fagan, C. (1999) *Women's Employment in Europe*. London: Routledge.

Saunders, P. (1989) 'The Meaning of Home in Contemporary English Culture'. *Housing Studies*, 4(3), 177–92.

Saunders, P. and Williams, P. (1988) 'The Constitution of the Home: Towards a Research Agenda'. *Housing Studies*, 3(2), 81–93.

SEU (Social Exclusion Unit) (1998) Bringing Britain Together: a national strategy for neighbourhood renewal. London: HMSO, Cm 4045.

Sykes, R. (1994) 'Older women and housing – prospects for the 1990s'. In R. Gilroy and R. Woods (eds), *Housing Women*. London: Routledge, 75–100.

Watson, S. (1986) 'Housing the Family: the marginalisation of non-family households in Britain'. *International Journal of Urban and Regional Research*, 10(1).

Watson, S. (1989) *Accommodating Inequality*. Sydney: Allen and Unwin.

Woods, R. (1996) 'Women and housing'. In C. Hallett (ed.), *Women and Social Policy: an introduction*. London: Harvester Wheatsheaf, 65–83.

6
The Family-Friendly Workplace?
British and European Perspectives

Liz Doherty, Simonetta Manfredi and Hilary Rollin

Introduction

The transformation in urban women's lives as outlined in the accompanying chapters, in terms of their changing roles and expectations within the family, the impact of healthcare and evolving household shapes would be incomplete without an examination of women's workplace experience and attempts to combine paid employment and caring responsibilities. Despite the many advances in women's access to qualifications and employment, the labour market retains gender disparities. Women are still concentrated into relatively low-paid occupations and industries, and earn 20–30 per cent less than men (Doherty and Stead, 1998). While many factors contribute to women's disadvantaged position in the labour market, their primary responsibility for childcare is one of the main barriers to their full integration in all occupations and at all levels of employment. The proportion of childless women in work is considerably higher than that of women with children, yet men's participation is unaffected by having children.

If they are to play their full part in the workplace, women with children need access to affordable, quality, well-located childcare provision, with hours designed to meet their needs. However, 'Sharing the cost of childcare', a briefing paper from the national childcare charity Daycare Trust (1997) shows that the British pay the highest childcare bills in Europe (typically £6000 per year for a couple with two children). Such costs clearly exclude many women from the workforce. European Union sources (European Commission Network on Childcare, 1996) confirm that UK provision compares poorly with that of other member states. Furthermore, the former Conservative government in Britain adopted a policy of deregulation in the labour market and took virtually no independent legislative action to require employers to introduce family-friendly practices. In this context EU policy has been particularly important; without the imposition of directives such as the Pregnant Workers Directive (see below), working women in the UK would now be even less protected than their counterparts in other European countries.

This chapter starts by considering EU policy on childcare and the rec- onciliation of family and professional responsibilities through a review of secondary sources. The European framework is considered in relation to current national policy as implemented by the Labour government (1997–) in the UK. We then present our primary findings from case studies compiled through semistructured interviews with a number of Oxford employers. Despite the gloomy national picture, our research into the family-friendly policies implemented by employers in Oxford and the creativity of initiatives undertaken by individual organisations indicates that positive steps are indeed being taken to facilitate women's integration in the workplace. We conclude by drawing together obser- vations based on good practice among Oxford employers in the context of British national policy and potential developments.

European framework

The key mover behind much of the EU policy framework was the Child- care Network. This was set up in 1986 by the Equal Opportunities Unit of the European Commission, under the Second Community Action Programme for Equal Opportunities (1986–90). It was guided by the EU's commitment to equal opportunities for men and women, and informed and supported policy on issues of equality, gender, children's rights, and the reconciliation of work and family responsibilities for men and women. Its task was defined as 'to monitor developments, evaluate policy options, collect and disseminate information . . . and estab- lishing criteria for the definition of quality in childcare services'. In pursuing these aims it gathered information, analysed trends, drew con- clusions, produced over thirty reports in all the then 12 languages, staged 12 European conferences and seminars, promoted discussion and set up a database. The Childcare Network was among those wound up in 1996 with the reduction of networks to two. European policy has included legally binding law in the form of the Pregnant Worker Directive (1992), the Directive on the Organization of Working Time (1993) and the Directive on Parental Leave (1996). It has also included guidance to member states in the form of the Childcare Recommendation (1992). Each of these is now explored in turn.

The Pregnant Worker Directive (92/85/EEC), adopted in 1992, applies to pregnant workers, workers who have recently given birth and workers who are breastfeeding. The main provisions are the right to a continuous leave period of 14 weeks, which includes a period of compulsory leave of two weeks before and/or after confinement, and protection from dismissal from the beginning of pregnancy until the end of the period of maternity leave. This does not constitute absolute protection as a pregnant worker could be dismissed 'in exceptional cases' which must not be connected with the pregnancy and 'which are permitted under national legislation/practice'. The directive also establishes a pregnant worker's entitlement to time off without loss of pay for antenatal care, entitlement to maintain her contractual rights during maternity leave, and to receive an adequate allowance which should be at least the equivalent of what she would be entitled to under her national legislation in the event of sickness. To avoid endangering the health of the pregnant worker, employers are obliged to carry out health and safety assessments and make whatever arrangements may be necessary, for example temporary reallocation of working hours and duties or early leave.

It is important to note that the legal basis for this directive is found in Article 118a of the EEC Treaty, which is concerned with the harmonization of conditions in relation to health and safety in the workplace. The rationale for treating the maternity rights of pregnant workers as issues of health and safety, rather than as mainstream employment rights, was to enable the Council of Ministers to adopt the directive by majority voting and thus overcome the opposition of the British government. Although the British government's opposition did not prevent the directive being adopted, it did none the less water down its content (Hervey and O'Keefe, 1996). It was necessary to introduce a 'non-regression clause' to avoid any reduction of rights in those member states which already had more generous provision. This was, therefore, a missed opportunity to introduce more radical employment rights for pregnant women.

The Directive on the Organization of Working Time (3/104/EC) laid down minimum hours for daily and weekly rest periods, maximum hours per week (48 hours over a four-month reference period), annual leave and night shifts. It poses practical problems for Britain, running counter to recent policy which has been to introduce flexibility into the workplace through deregulation. Full-timers in Britain work the highest number of hours of all member states (5.1 hours more than Italians and 3.8 more than Germans), and part-timers the lowest (7.4 hours less than Italians and 1.9 less than Germans) (Bercusson, 1994). The Working Time Directive could play a useful part in challenging the 'long hours culture' found in many occupations, and in the UK in particular. This might be significant in enabling more men to take an active role in childcare as there is an indisputable link between working time and men's ability to contribute on the domestic front.

The Directive on Parental Leave (96/34/EC) implements the principle contained in the Community Charter of Fundamental Social Rights, according to which 'measures should be developed to enable men and women to reconcile their occupational and family obligations' (General Considerations, article 4). For this purpose it introduces an individual right to three months unpaid parental leave for working parents which can be taken at any time to care for a child, including an adoptive child, up to the age of eight. Working parents taking parental leave have the right to return to the same or an equivalent or similar job at the end of the period of leave (clause 2.5). As in the case of the 'no regression clause' which it was necessary to introduce in the Pregnant Worker Directive, the Parental Leave Directive contains a provision preventing member states, which already give more generous entitlements, from reducing the level of protection.

The Recommendation on Childcare (92/241/EEC) invited member states to 'take and/or progressively encourage initiatives to enable women and men to reconcile their occupational, family and upbringing responsibilities arising from the care of children', (European Commission, 1992). Among its four key concerns were childcare services, namely the care, education and recreation of young children (up to the age of ten). The recommendation set out principles and objectives for the development of childcare services, including affordability; access in both urban and rural areas, and for children with special needs; the combining of reliable care and a pedagogical approach; the desirability of good relations between services, parents and local communities; diversity, choice and flexibility of services; coherence between services; and by no means least, basic and continuous training for childcare workers appropriate to the value of the work. In recognition of the strategic importance of such training and retraining, and acknowledgement of the status of childcare workers, (hitherto predominantly female, hence low pay, low status) money was made available for this under the NOW (New Opportunities for Women) programme. The three other key concerns were, first, leave arrangements, including the necessary close tie between these and childcare services; second, making the workplace more responsive, hence undertaking an analysis of trends of working parents; and, finally, men's involvement in caring for children, and men as carers. The recommendation identified governments, local authorities, employers, individuals and relevant organisations (e.g. unions) as responsible for promoting family-friendly policies, but omitted to specify their respective roles (European Commission Network on Childcare, 1996). It is noteworthy that EU legislation on childcare was restricted to a recommendation not legally binding on member states.

The national picture in Britain

Following the election of the Labour government in 1997, reconciliation of family and work and the rights of working parents have found a place on the public agenda in Britain. Under the previous Conservative government, combining work with family responsibilities was seen mainly as a matter of private concern (Moss, 1996) as evidenced by the 1996 consultation paper on 'Ideas and Options for Childcare', where it was made clear that the government did not see the provision of childcare as part of its public responsibilities 'except for some specific government initiatives' but expected this service to be developed by market forces 'in response to parents' demands'.

The Labour government which followed has taken a new approach to the question of reconciling work and family life, driven mainly by the need to help lone mothers on benefit to re-enter the labour market through the welfare-to-work programme. Furthermore, the decision of the government to sign the Social Chapter has bound Britain to implement the Parental Leave Directive and the Part-Time Workers Directive. The latter affords more statutory protection to part-time workers and extends to them some of the entitlements, such as paid holidays and access to occupational pension schemes, enjoyed by full-time workers. This measure is likely to be of particular benefit to women since proportionately more women than men work part time.

More specifically, the government has committed itself to a National Childcare Strategy which aims to raise the quality of care and make childcare more affordable and accessible, and to encourage employers to adopt family-friendly policies in the workplace as well as to offer childcare provisions whenever feasible. The strategy requires local authorities to set up Childcare Partnerships to co-ordinate childcare and improve provision in their areas. Funds have been committed to increase the amount of childcare provision, particularly for after-school places (DfEE, 1998, p. 6) and working parents on low income will benefit from childcare tax credits.

This series of measures is complemented by a programme of legislative reforms designed to establish a framework of rights for working parents. The government devoted a section of its white paper, 'Fairness at Work', to family-friendly policies where it spelled out its intention to 'support and reinforce such a family-friendly culture in business' (DTI, 1998, p. 31). It is interesting to note that the Working Time Directive, although introduced by the EU under Article 118a of the EEC Treaty, which is concerned with health and safety in the workplace, has been included in the family-friendly policies section of the White Paper and presented as a measure that 'will enable people to balance better their work and home lives' (DTI, 1998 p. 32). Most of the measures put forward are linked to the implementation of the Parental Leave Directive, and have now been introduced in the new Employment Relations Act 1999 together with the Maternity and Parental Leave etc Regulations 1999. The main provisions of the new legislation are an increase in 'ordinary maternity leave' from 14 weeks to 18 weeks, the introduction of up to 13 weeks unpaid parental leave and a qualifying period of only one year for 'additional maternity leave' (reduced from a two year-qualifying period). By extending maternity leave to 18 weeks the government is remedying an anomaly of the system, whereby women with less than two years continuous employment found their right to return expired after 14 weeks (the minimum period of leave allowed under the Pregnant Worker Directive) even though they were entitled to 18 weeks pay (Fredman, 1997, p. 200). These measures go some small way towards the recommendations on paternity leave and parental leave put forward by the EOC in its review of the Sex Discrimination Act. This proposed the replacement of this legislation by a single Sex Equality Act which should include sex discrimination, equal pay and other relevant legislation, including statutory paternity leave paid at the current rate of Statutory Maternity Pay (SMP) (EOC, 1998).

Although all these developments represent significant improvements for working parents, some important issues remain untackled. For example, as far as the maternity provisions are concerned no attempt has been made either by the government or by the EOC to ensure 'affordability' of maternity leave by all pregnant employees. At present an estimated 20 per cent of pregnant employees earn below the Lower Earnings Limit and therefore do not qualify for SMP (Equal Opportunities Review, 1994, p. 38). Furthermore, the government plans to raise the LEL are likely to exclude even more women in low-paid jobs from paid maternity leave (*Guardian*, 1998).

Another weakness of the current government programme of new legislation and reforms for working parents is that it does not attempt to clarify a situation of uncertainty with regard to the rights of parents to work part time or job share which has been created by case law. Under the Sex Discrimination Act, the notion of indirect discrimination has been successfully used to challenge employers' refusal to allow women returning from maternity leave or with small children to work part time or job share.[1] In these cases women were able to prove that because of childcare responsibilities they could no longer comply with the requirements of full-time work without either the job or the family suffering, as evidenced by the higher percentage of women working part time. Thus, to deny them the option of working part time would amount to indirect discrimination. However, in the case of *British Telecommunications* v. *Roberts* (Equal Opportunities Review, 1996, p. 53) the request to job share on return from maternity leave was not deemed to be 'covered by the cloak of protection which sex discrimination law confers on pregnancy and maternity' (Equal Opportunities Review, 1996). Although the legal basis of this case was alleged direct discrimination, it does nevertheless cast doubt as to the future orientation of employment tribunals in this kind of case.

We are left with a situation where, on the one hand, it is unclear to what extent mothers have a right to work part time or job share and, on the other hand, fathers who wish for more flexible working arrangements are unable to rely on indirect sex discrimination in order to claim reduced hours at work. This state of affairs leaves women uncertain as to whether or not they have a right for their childcare needs to be accommodated by employers and, furthermore, it fails to encourage and enable men to take on a greater share of family responsibilities. It seems that the government has missed an opportunity to encourage changes in gender roles by establishing the right of both parents to work part time in order to accommodate their childcare needs. Further, the fact that parental leave is to be unpaid means that men are unlikely to use it. Where women are the second earners in a family, it is they who will be most likely to take the leave, thereby reinforcing their role as the prime carers in families. Until the law goes further in giving men more parental rights it will be difficult to challenge effectively 'the male bias of existing structures . . . whereby the mother takes primary responsibility for childcare while the father continues to consolidate his position in the paid work-force' (Fredman, 1997).

Why Oxford?

The City of Oxford is particularly interesting from the point of view of women's employment opportunities and the family-friendly policies adopted by employers. Based on the 1991 census, the population of the city is estimated to be 141600 (including 21000 students). The industrial structure of the city has changed over the last few decades, with a marked decrease in manufacturing (the motor industry was once a key employer) and an increase in service industries. The number of people employed overall has fallen from 87000 in 1991 to 83000 in 1996. The statistics indicate that there is a polarisation in the types of occupation carried out. At one end of the scale, there is a higher proportion of professional/managerial groups within the city by comparison with the surrounding county, and at the other end of the scale unskilled groups are also overrepresented within the city. Whilst the city overall benefits from the prosperity of the south-east, parts of it figure among the most deprived in the UK on a range of economic, social, housing and environmental measures (Oxford City Council, 1994, 1998).

Women are generally well represented in service industries and that is also the case in Oxford where women make up 52 per cent of employees compared with 44 per cent in the British workforce as a whole. Figures supplied by the City Council show that in the four largest employment sectors – health and social work, education, public administration and retailing – women predominate. This is an advantage for women because large, public-sector organisations tend to have relatively sophisticated personnel practices as well as being well disposed towards equal opportunities programmes and pressure from trade unions is often strong. When this is coupled with a relatively low unemployment rate in the Oxford travel-to-work area (Oxford City Council, 1996), we might hypothesise that there is considerable pressure on employers competing for female labour to provide a range of family-friendly policies in order to attract and retain women. Furthermore, we might expect professional women in traditionally women-friendly organisations to have exerted collective pressure on their employers to provide facilities to help them integrate work and domestic roles.

Figures discussed in Oxfordshire's Childcare Audit 1998/99 Interim Report (Oxfordshire County Council, 1999) show that the largest number of childcare places provided in the city are in playgroups, which, while good for child development, do little to help working women. Other places are provided by childminders, holiday play schemes, private nurseries, after-school clubs and workplace nurseries (in descending order in terms of numbers of places provided). Virtually all the workplace nurseries within the county are concentrated in the city, presenting a particular advantage to urban women.

We will now proceed to demonstrate that the larger employers in Oxford have indeed developed supportive policies and arrangements which are well ahead of what we could expect to find in the general economy.

Good practice in the case study organisations

Research methods

Information was collected from nine case study organisations based in the City of Oxford. The size of organisation ranged from very large (many thousands of employees) through to medium sized (a few hundred employees). Four of the employers were in the public sector (health, education and local authority), two were related to the motor industry, one was a publisher, one was a large national retailer and one a large charity. In most cases semistructured interviews were conducted with a member of the personnel department or an equal opportunities officer, though in one case the information was gathered through the post, via a short questionnaire.

Women made up the majority of the workforce in all cases except the two organizations related to the motor industry which has a tradition-ally male image. In all cases, women of child-bearing age made up a substantial proportion of the workforce. Although women tended to be crowded into posts at the lower end of the grade/pay hierarchy and several respondents talked about the continuing existence of a 'glass ceiling', women's share of senior jobs has been increasing over recent years.

Maternity and other leave arrangements

All these employers were well informed about legal requirements relat-ing to maternity leave and pay, and all had improved on the statutory minimum arrangements in some way. This had been achieved by extending the equivalent of statutory protection to those with less than two years service and/or by offering more generous benefits than those set down by law. Many had extended the period of full-time paid leave, with two going so far as to provide 18 weeks on full pay. This was often extended by a period of up to 12 weeks on half pay. Several offered unpaid leave as a 'top-up' to give a period of up to one year away from work after the birth of the baby.

There were also one or two innovative approaches. Two employers provided financial incentives to return to work at the end of maternity leave. In one case this involved one and a half times normal pay for the first three months after return, and in another, returners were paid a bonus of £1000 payable in 12 instalments. One employer had introduced ingeniously flexible eligibility rules; these included having worked for a previous employer long enough to qualify for their paid maternity scheme or having had two years continuous employment with any employer in the past by the fifteenth week before the expected week of childbirth.

In the case of fixed-term contracts, most employers simply applied their normal maternity arrangements up to the end of the contract. One employer had gone further than this and introduced an arrangement whereby the maternity leave entitlement continued for up to six weeks after the expiry of the contract.

The majority of employers offered paid paternity leave, five days being the typical allowance. A few employers offered ten days and one offered only one to two days. A couple of employers had extended paternity leave to same-sex partners: these were employers with particularly well developed equal opportunity policies. One employer offered up to 45 weeks unpaid leave to the supporting partners of mothers, although in practice this was hardly ever used. A few had already introduced adoptive leave arrangements, and one or two others were considering this. Two employers provided the same kind of maternity leave and pay to adoptive mothers as to natural mothers. One employer was prepared to consider applications for leave for fertility treatment.

Most of the employers recognised that maternity leave arrangements are difficult to understand and had gone out of their way to present their arrangements and procedures as clearly as possible and in a user-friendly way.

Childcare

All but two of these employers provided workplace nurseries for children below school age. They all accepted babies as young as six months, several accepted three- and four-month olds and two went as low as six weeks. However, in most cases there would be a gap between the end of paid maternity leave and the age at which a baby could be accepted into the nursery. Further, all the nurseries operated waiting lists and several had had to introduce various sorts of criteria for allocating places. Inevitably this meant that not all parents would find places in their workplace nursery as soon as they were needed. One of the employers who did not run a workplace nursery had provided emergency cover by buying one place in a nursery close to the workplace. In addition, the company subscribed to the Childcare Solutions helpline for its employees and their relatives. This provides personal consultations on practical childcare arrangements and parenting issues.

A few of the nurseries were run by private childcare agencies, but most were directly managed by the employer. Most charged a flat rate to all users, though the rate was often higher for younger children. Several employers had attempted to deal with the question of how to enable lower-paid staff to afford the nursery. One employer had a sliding-scale of fees according to family income and another had tried to achieve the same effect by introducing a sliding-scale of subsidy for which users could apply (the subsidy budget was finite and not all applicants would necessarily be successful). However, the problem with this approach was that only users of the workplace nursery could get access to this benefit, yet other low-paid staff might also be incurring childcare costs through private arrangements. One employer had introduced a radical childcare allowance scheme open to all lower-graded staff who incurred childcare costs for children below school age. Staff had to apply for the allowance and clear criteria were set for eligibility. The maximum allowance payable was equivalent to 40 per cent of the cost of a place in the employer's nursery. This scheme could lead to considerable costs for the employer if it were taken up across the organisation.

The majority of employers did not provide any facilities for school-age children. Two ran holiday play schemes for 5 to 14 year-olds and one was about to survey childcare needs across the organisation to gauge the level of demand for different age groups.

A few employers had begun to think about the care of elderly relatives. They tended to believe that their existing arrangements for compassionate and/or dependency leave were sufficient for dealing with this. One employer, however, was in the process of developing a day centre for the adult dependents of employees. This is an innovative development and it will be interesting to see how the project proceeds.

Enabling measures

All these employers claimed to offer some form of flexible working; this included part-time work, job sharing, flexi-time schemes, varied shift patterns, term-time only contracts and phased return after maternity leave. There were different degrees of commitment to this type of provision. In some cases, arrangements were committed to policy (typically job share and phased return after maternity leave), but other arrangements such as part-time working were generally subject to operational requirements and had to be negotiated by individual women. In several organisations interviewees said that implementation of flexible working arrangements was inconsistent and depended very much on the culture of different departments and the perceptions of different line managers. Teleworking was little used, with only one or two employers experimenting with it to any great extent. From the little evidence available, there is reason to think that teleworking may be polarised, being found among senior management staff and relatively junior staff. Compliance with health and safety requirements was cited as one obstacle to extending this form of work.

In practice it was generally felt that women who opted to work part time would not be perceived in an adverse light. However, relatively few women were working in job shares or on a part-time basis at senior levels.

Results of supportive arrangements and areas for future development

All these employers saw themselves as 'family friendly' and the main benefit of their supportive arrangements was that the large majority of women returned to work at the end of their maternity leave. This meant that the employers were able to retain valued expertise, and avoid costly advertising and investment in training new staff. Several acknowledged that the provision of such arrangements was a valuable recruitment incentive.

There was no indication that any of the facilities or arrangements were under any kind of threat in the future; rather, most employers were exploring further developments, for example extended paternity leave and eldercare. The biggest threat to women's employment and eligibility for family-friendly benefits mentioned by several employers was employment insecurity, especially through the increasing use of fixed-term contracts. These strike a double whammy for women: on the one hand the benefits accruing to such contracts (for example, maternity) are limited by the very nature of the duration of the contract, and on the other hand women in precarious employment are disinclined to insist on their existing rights and are unlikely to join forces and press for improved rights.

Conclusions

These Oxford city employers provide a range of family-friendly structures which are more developed than one would expect to find in the general economy. Maternity leave arrangements, on the whole, far exceeded the statutory minimum, and the level of childcare provision in the form of nursery places was exceptional. There are also provisions for career breaks and other forms of unpaid leave, implying that these employers are well placed to comply with the Parental Leave Directive and the 1999 Employment Relations Act.

An imaginative range of flexible working arrangements was available for many women and there were several innovative developments such as the day care centre for adult dependents and the extension of paternity leave to same-sex partners. These developments show how some of these employers have responded to social changes in advance of government policy. The implications of the planned day care centre for adult dependents merit particular consideration. This shows the beginning of an acknowledgement by employers that the reconciliation of work and family is not just an issue for working parents with young children, but for any employee who has caring responsibilities. The number of people in employment with adult dependents (for example, elderly or disabled relatives) is set to increase due to a combination of factors such as an ageing population, longer life expectancy and the reduction of public services. It is noteworthy that the day care proposal comes from a public-sector employer which is in the business of providing caring services and which has a high proportion of women in its workforce. On the one hand this can be seen as a very positive development, but on the other hand we should be aware that, as employers start to provide services which supplement public provision, there is a danger of a widening gap between those who are in paid employment and those who are not.

Even among those women who are in paid employment there appears to be a polarisation in the coping strategies likely to be adopted by different categories of women. Highly paid professional women are more likely to work full time and make use of employer-provided or private childcare arrangements, whereas lower-paid women are more likely to opt for part time working arrangements and avoid nurseries which are beyond their financial reach. This clearly shows the limits of the 1979–1997 Conservative government's 'free market' approach, which left market forces to create services in response to parents' demands. Our findings demonstrate that market forces create services only for parents who can afford to pay market prices. Thus the financial help towards the costs of childcare that the Labour government is committed to provide is going to be extremely important to low-paid women as it will enable more of them to use workplace nurseries and other childcare facilities. It was very clear from the interviews that women themselves want these kinds of arrangements which help them manage their dual role. Whereas large employers have responded in a positive way to women's wishes in this respect, it is very likely that smaller employers with fewer resources at their disposal will be unable to be innovative.

Despite most of the employers in this study offering maternity arrangements far superior to the statutory requirements, Britain nevertheless remains one of the European member states with the least generous provisions for maternity leave. Although the Employment Relations Act aims at simplifying and improving maternity rights, this appears to be more of a tidying up exercise of the existing provisions rather than an effort to upgrade significantly the UK legislation which will continue to lag behind other EU countries. The gap between the end of paid maternity leave and the age when a baby is eligible for a childcare place, whether or not this is offered by an employer, remains a problem. Only two employers had closed the gap by offering nursery places for babies of six weeks to enable women employees to resume work after the period of maternity leave on full, or 90 per cent of full, pay.

It appears from our research that although most of the flexible working time arrangements are open to both men and women, they none the less seem to be aimed primarily at women employees. There is a real danger that if it is predominantly women who take advantage of family-friendly policies, this will reinforce their position as carers and slow-track employees (Purcell and Manfredi, 1997). To ensure further progress it is essential for men to reconsider their role in the family. However, it must be recognized that although employers have an important part to play in shaping cultural and social change, a major role has to be played by the state through social policy and education. The new legislative changes are not going far enough to encourage a more equal division of family responsibilities or challenge the long-hours culture. In particular, it is unlikely that men will take up their entitlement to parental leave as it is unpaid, and it is disappointing that the government has missed the opportunity to introduce paid paternity leave as suggested by the EOC (1998). A helpful policy development would be the introduction of a positive legal right to part-time work for both men and women with caring responsibilities, supported by a policy frame-work which delivered equal rights to full and part-time workers.

At the moment family-friendly policies are part of equal opportuni-ties strategies adopted by employers to improve staff retention, reduce absenteeism and generally increase productivity. There are two issues related to this: first, employers' policies can easily change under pres-sure, and family-friendly policies may no longer be seen as a priority. Second, the effective implementation of family-friendly policies depends on line managers who, as shown by this and similar studies (Lewis and Taylor, 1996), may not favour such arrangements.

Flexibility is often regarded as being family-friendly, but this is not necessarily the case. Some flexible working patterns which have devel-oped as a result of the deregulation of the labour market can be very 'family unfriendly' both from the financial and organisational point of view. Examples of this are the zero-hour contracts and hourly-paid con-tracts which are used particularly, but not exclusively, in the retail sector and education. The implications for family life of yearly-hours contracts and other contracts, such as those designed to ensure the delivery of 24-hour services in the financial sector, should also be considered very carefully by the social partners. Finally, in order to ensure real progress, family-friendly practice must broaden to include other fundamental areas of individuals' daily life such as organisation of schooling, and access to and provision of services.

Note

1 *Home Office* v. *Holmes* [1984] IRLR 299 (EAT); Briggs and North Eastern Education and Library Board [1990] IRLR 181 (Northern Island Court of Appeal).

References

Bercusson, (1994) *Working Time in Britain: Towards a European model, Part II Collective Bargaining in Europe and the UK.* London: Institute of Employment Rights.
Daycare Trust (1997) *Sharing the cost of childcare.* London: Briefing Paper No. 4.
DfEE (1996) *Work and Family: Ideas and Options for Childcare.* London: HMSO.
DfEE (1998) *Meeting the Childcare Challenge.* London: HMSO.
Doherty, L. and Stead, L. (1998) 'The Gap Between Male and Female Pay: What Does the Case of Hotel and Catering Tell Us?' *The Service Industries Journal,* 18(4).
DTI (Department of Trade and Industry) (1998) *Fairness at Work.* London: The Stationery Office.

Eo (Equal Opportunities Commission) (1998) *Equality in the 21st Century, a New Sex Equality Law for Britain.* Manchester: EOC.

Equal Opportunities Review (1994) No. 55. London.

Equal Opportunities Review (1996) No. 70. London.

European Commission Network on Childcare (1996) *The EC Childcare Network: Decade of Achievements 1986–96. Final report*, Brussels.

Fredman, S. (1997) *Women and the Law.* Oxford: Clarendon Press.

Guardian, (1998) 19 March.

Hervey, T. K. and O'Keefe, D. (1996) *Sex Equality Law in the European Union.* Chichester: John Wiley and Sons.

Lewis, S. and Taylor, K. (1996) 'Evaluating the Impact of Family-Friendly Employer Policies: a Case Study'. *The Family-Work Challenge*, London: Sage.

Moss, P. (1996) 'Reconciling Employment and Family Responsibilities: A European Perspective'. *The Family-Work Challenge*, London: Sage.

Oxford City Council (1994) *1991 Census Digest.*

Oxford City Council (1996) *Economic Development Plan 1996/97.*

Oxford City Council (1998) *Economic Development Plan 1998/99.*

Oxfordshire County Council (1999) *Oxfordshire's Childcare Audit 1998/99 Interim Report.*

Purcell, K. and Manfredi, S. (1997) 'Women's Employment and Equal Opportunities in Britain: The Impact of Legislation and Positive Action in a Deregulated Economy. Paper given at European Conference on Equal Opportunities Policy, Amministrazione Provinciale di Genova.

7
Women, Transport and Cities: an Overview and an Agenda for Research

Charlotte Coleman

Introduction

Despite the importance of women, as over half the population, and their increasing mobility, women's travel behaviour and transport needs are not fully understood or properly provided for in our cities. Transport in urban areas raises many issues of direct relevance to women. The design of transport infrastructure, such as bus stops, stations and underground car parks can raise questions of personal safety. Land use policies can also raise questions of equality. The location of new housing, for example, on greenfield as opposed to brownfield sites raises important mobility issues. These are exciting times, given the progress that has been made in developing an understanding of women's travel in the city. The first comprehensive national transport statistics by gender have been produced by government, and national transport policy in the form of the Transport White Paper (DETR, 1998a) has publicly recognised that women do have different transport needs from men, with implications for the provision of city transport infrastructure. However, the subject area of women and transport is still plagued by misunderstandings and stereotypes and a rethink of national policy, while generally welcome, may carry unrecognised gender implications.

The purpose of this chapter is to provide an overview of policy, statistics and issues that relate to women and transport within urban areas. The chapter starts by examining why women's travel is worthy of separate discussion. It then outlines the government's Transport White Paper, 'A New Deal for Transport' (DETR, 1998a) and using the first set of national travel statistics to be broken down by gender illustrates possible flaws in the White Paper. The chapter concludes by identifying an agenda for research.

Why women's travel is important

The roles women (primarily) carry out within the city are different from those of their male counterparts and hence women's travel patterns and transport requirements are different. Since studies in the early 1980s, attempts to understand these differences and their implications for city structure and transport provision have been made. Early studies described women as deprived of access to cars, dependent on public transport, and disabled by their caring and carrying responsibilities (Hill, 1996). Studies during the 1990s, for example Hamilton and Jenkins (1992), attempted to provide a more comprehensive view of women's travel patterns, drawing on available sources of data supplemented, in this case, with statistics from their own study in West Yorkshire. They clearly identified the damaging effect of stereotyping.

> Stereotyping and misunderstanding together with women's traditional role in society as the homemaker and carer has effectively ensured their absence from the transport planning and decision making process. The result has been that city transport systems have essentially been planned by men who have a predominantly male view of how this infrastructure will be used. As consumers of transport provision, however, women have too often been assumed to have identical needs to men's, or simply be unworthy of note . . . the transport world has been slow to see the relevance of women, women's needs or women's issues to the plans and decisions which they make . . . Yet women have travel needs which are as significant as those of men, though radically different in many respects'.
>
> (Hamilton and Jenkins, 1992)

As part of their research they defined the implications for transport planners of women's transport needs (Table 7.1).

Table 7.1 clearly demonstrates why and how women's transport needs are different and hence why separate consideration of women's travel is so important. First, it highlights the difficulties that women may experience from the design of transport infrastructure and city spaces. For example, poor station design can emphasise the vulnerability of women given their physical characteristics. Trench et al. (1992) found that significant numbers of women would not use public transport for personal safety reasons and many others expressed concern over city-centre car parks. Second, Table 7.1 highlights the inadequacy of the transport services that do exist. Many facilities are not well served by public

Table 7.1 Defining women's transport needs: the implications for transport planners

Women as a socially defined category of people, compared to men have

- primary responsibility for childcare and domestic work
- multiple roles, combining paid employment with domestic work
- more constrained opportunities for paid employment and a much greater likelihood of being engaged in part-time and/or casual employment, usually local
- a socialization history which is different from men's
- a smaller physical size

Taken collectively the transport implications of these major features may be outlined as

- women are less likely to be able to afford private transport and hence more dependent on walking and public transport. Even when women can drive and there is a car in the household only a minority have primary access to a car for their own use
- women make around the same number of journeys as men, but a higher proportion of these are local or short distance. The provision of short-distance local transport is therefore of prime importance
- because of women's role as carers, a significant proportion of women's journeys are made primarily to accompany a child or elderly or disabled adults. Such escort journeys are not well catered for by current public transport provision
- shopping for food and other domestic needs is a major component of women's unpaid domestic labour. Heavy loads are again not easily accommodated by public transport
- since many women have to combine two or more roles a substantial proportion of their journeys will be multipurpose. This often results in women's travel patterns being highly complex and does not make them amenable to simple categorization.
- since almost half of women in paid employment work part-time hours it follows that a substantial proportion of their employment related and other trips will be undertaken outside 'peak' travel times
- the division of both paid and unpaid labour along gender lines in our society has far reaching implications for gender differences in journey destinations and purposes. For example, social visits made to ensure the psychological welfare of elderly relatives can be regarded as socially necessary in the same way as trips made to provide physical support
- women's lower social status and smaller physical size render them more vulnerable to attacks and abuse of all kinds, primarily from men

Source: compiled from Hamilton and Jenkins (1992).

transport which raises issues particularly for women's local journeys especially given women's primary responsibilities for shopping and escorting dependents. Third, it highlights the complexity of women's travel patterns. Since Table 7.1 was compiled in 1992 there has been a huge growth in ownership and use of cars by women, with over 35 per cent now owning a car compared to 24 per cent in 1985–86 (Dunning, 1997). Car use has added to the complexity of women's travel and there are still many gaps in policy makers' understanding of women's car use; for example, the relationship between women's car use and their ability to carry out multiple roles, the links between car use and women's perceptions of personal safety, or the role of residential location and car use are not fully recognised.

Women and transport – the growth of a national voice

At a national level women have been actively working to inform and influence transport policy, legislation and provision since the early 1990s. One of the key national initiatives stemmed from a Women's Transport Conference held in Manchester in October 1990. Following the conference a National Working Group was developed which launched the Women's Transport Charter in 1992. This addressed issues of access, safety, planning, information, rural needs and the environment. The charter 'aims to provide for all women's transport needs. This will only be achieved through the involvement of women, including disabled women and black women' (Community Transport Association, 1992). The charter also called for increasing the opportunity for training and employment in design of infrastructure, creation of safe environments and information systems, increasing the awareness of planners and providers, and the development of policy.

Subsequently a key initiative, the Women's Transport Network, was launched by the Conservative government in 1995. Its stated aim is to 'promote transport systems and pedestrian environments that are safe and accessible for all and to encourage women to enter and progress in the transport industry' (DoT, 1995). The network was designed to bring together women working in all aspects of the transport profession, to provide direct input into issues of direct relevance to women (for example, safety for women motorists, crime, social exclusion and transport, and gender audit of women's transport requirements). The network holds general meetings and produces a newsletter; its members come from a diverse range of professions including consultants, local authorities and academia.

The Transport White Paper

The New Labour government, elected in 1997, recognized that 'Government policy can have, and often has had, a different impact on women and men. It is essential, therefore, that Government considers the impact of all policy proposals on women and monitors the effects of that policy' (Cabinet Office, 1998). The Minister for Women and the Women's Unit are working on issues such as childcare, family friendly employment and violence against women. While transport is not as yet a specific issue for the Women's Unit, the aim of integrating the women's perspective into policy is significant. In addition, the stated role of the Women's Unit is to, 'understand and address women's concerns . . . The work of the Women's Unit must be grounded in the current reality of women's daily lives, changing to reflect new priorities as society and attitudes change' (Cabinet Office, 1998). Glenda Jackson, when Junior Minister for Transport emphasised women's travel needs and concerns.

In 1998 the government issued its White Paper on Transport 'A New Deal for Transport: Better for Everyone' (DETR, 1998a), which sees the way forward as an integrated transport policy. For women the White Paper can be viewed as an advance but still flawed. On the positive side the White Paper does make specific reference to the different transport needs of women.

> Women's transport needs are often different. Although they make about the same number of journeys on average as men, these are shorter and they walk and use public transport, especially buses, more. Men are more likely to have first call on the car in a one car household. Many women have concerns about their personal security, particularly when on their own and at night.
>
> (DETR, 1998a)

It then lists seven areas where the New Deal for Transport will be of particular relevance for women (Table 7.2). Further references are made to women throughout the paper in relation to security on public transport, lack of access to cars, taking children to school and accessible buses.

To discuss more comprehensively the significance of the White Paper for women's transport the measures listed in Table 7.2 must be viewed in relation to how women actually travel. Until recently there were no comprehensive national transport statistics that took gender into account. In 1998, however, the DETR produced a new publication *Focus*

Table 7.2　What the New Deal for Transport will mean for women

---

- Greater emphasis on integrated transport, including more accessible buses, better information and safer interchanges
- Safer public transport, including the Secure Stations scheme
- Improving the quality of the pedestrian environment, e.g. making it easier for women with children in prams to get about
- Land use policies to encourage local services, reducing the need to travel by car
- Women's transport needs to be assessed in local transport plans and through auditing transport initiatives
- Safer routes to school initiatives
- Commission for Integrated Transport to take full account of women's transport needs

---

on Personal Travel (DETR, 1998b). For the first time this report provided an analysis of travel patterns by gender in a section entitled 'How and Why Do Men and Women Travel'. A similar publication *Focus on Public Transport* (DETR, 1999) has also produced some analysis by gender, which will be used in the next section.

A new deal for women?

The travel data in this section has been presented in a series of boxes (Tables 7.3 to 7.7) which present data on distance travelled, journey purpose, women as car users, users of the public transport system, and as pedestrians and cyclists. Rather than discuss each box the analysis focuses around areas in which the White Paper has made progress and areas where progress is still to be made. (For more detailed data see DETR, 1998b; for further discussion see Hill, 1996, and/or Hamilton and Jenkins, 1992.)

The car is the main mode of transport for both men and women, but men make more car trips and travel further (Tables 7.3 to 7.5). Women make more of their journeys on foot than men, but make fewer cycle trips (Table 7.7). Women are more likely to use public transport than men, and can be seen to be particularly reliant on local buses (see Table 7.6). Women also have a higher incidence of taxi use, almost certainly a response to concerns about local safety.

Integrated transport, including accessible buses, better information and safer interchanges, is clearly a positive step. Poor design of transport infrastructure, in this case train stations that highlight women's physical vulnerability, is to be tackled by the Secure Stations Scheme.

Table 7.3   Distance travelled and time spent travelling

Distance travelled

- There is little difference between the average number of trips made by men and women but men travel further
- In 1995/97, men made about 4% more journeys per person per year than women, travelling 45% further: on average over 7500 miles per person per year compared to under 5500 miles for women. This was true in every age group (except 17–20), including those in which women made more trips
- Men aged 40–49 travelled about 11 800 miles a year on average, 80% by car as drivers and 8% as passengers. In this age group, women only travelled about 7400 miles, 49% as car drivers and 34% as car passengers
- Over all modes and ages, the average trip length for men was 7.4 miles, compared to 5.3 miles for women, nearly 40% more. Trip lengths were a little higher for every mode, but the significant difference was for car driver trips, averaging 10.1 miles for men compared to 6.1 miles for women

Time spent travelling

- Men spent an average of over 380 hours a year travelling in 1995/97, 16% more than women

Source: Compiled from DETR (1998b) Section 3.

The importance of city structure has been recognised by encouraging more local services that are not dependent on car use for access (this can be viewed as a double-edged sword and will be discussed in more detail below). Local transport plans are seen as the way forward in addressing women's transport needs. Local authorities are responsible for drawing up these plans under consultation with local people, businesses, transport operators and community groups. Accessible, low-floor buses, safer stations, more sensitively designed transport infrastructure and a better pedestrian environment, together with many other initiatives to improve public transport and the walking environment, will benefit many women in the city.

There are however three interrelated aspects of the White Paper that are unhelpful for women in terms of their transport needs and that may actually have serious gender implications.

First, the White Paper continues to call for the increasing reduction in the use of private cars and greater use of greener modes such as walking, cycling and public transport. We have seen that women use cars less, and differently, from men. However, research by the Royal Automobile Club suggested that only 20 per cent of journeys could easily be made by modes other than the car. Short journeys under one mile and car escort trips were found to be the most easily

Table 7.4 Journey purpose

Commuting and business trips

- Over all ages men made 18% of their journeys commuting to and from work in 1995/97, with an additional 5% travelling on business. For women only 13% of journeys were to and from work, and 2% on business. Differences are apparent at all ages, particularly between 21 and 49 when men are at their peak working ages and some women are not working or are working part time because of family responsibilities

Education trips

- Education trips are most important for those aged 17 and under, accounting for just over one-quarter of trips in 1995/97. There was little gender difference at any age in the proportion of trips made for education purposes

Escort trips

- Escort trips are made to accompany another person on a journey. Adult women were much more likely to make escort education trips. At the peak age of 30–39 16% of women's trips were for this purpose, compared to only 3% for men in this age group
- Other than escort education, men and women were equally likely to make escort trips but the pattern varied considerably by age. Escort trips were made mostly by women aged 21–49 and men aged 30 and over. Including escort education women aged 30–39 made over a quarter of their trips escorting someone else

Shopping and personal business trips

- Women made 20% more shopping trips than men in 1995/97 (243 on average compared to 199 for men)
- Men and women made almost the same number of personal business trips
- The relative importance of shopping and personal business increases with age. In 1995/97, men aged 60–69 made more shopping trips on average than women in this age group (315 compared to 302 for women). However, as men in this age group made more trips overall, shopping still accounted for a greater proportion of women's trips
- For women aged 70 and over, nearly 60% of trips were for shopping and personal business

Trip Chaining

- The overall proportion of journeys forming trip chains is the same for men and women, with a minimum of 58% of journeys not returning directly home
- Purpose of journeys not returning directly home is different for men and women. For men 77% of journeys from work are directly home with 9% to another work or business destination and 4% to the shops. For women a similar proportion are directly home with 4% to another work or business destination and 9% to the shops
- Both men and women are more likely to drop off children on the way to work than to collect them on the way home, but shopping is more likely to be done by women on the way home

Source: Compiled from DETR (1998b).

Table 7.5 Women as car users

Driving licence and test

- Men are more likely to pass the practical driving test, but women are better at the new written theory
- 81% of men held a full car driving licence compared to only 57% of women. The difference was even greater for those aged over 50
- The differences between the trip patterns of men and women are declining as more women acquire driving licences and become main drivers

Access to the household car

- Four in five male licence holders were the main driver of a household car, compared to about two in three female licence holders
- Car access was an important determinant of the total distance travelled. For example, women who were the main drivers travelled a total distance of over 9000 miles a year in 1995/97, compared to an overall average (including nondrivers) of less than 6000 miles for all adult women
- Women were less likely to have the main use of a household car, even if they held a driving licence

Car use

- Car was the main mode of transport for both men and women but in all adult age groups car use was higher among men than women
- Women aged 21–59 made more trips as car drivers than as passengers
- Women aged less than 21, or 60 and over were more likely to be passengers
- Overall, people aged 40–59 made the greatest proportion of their trips as car drivers. For women (but not men) this proportion declined sharply for those age 50–59

Source: Compiled from DETR (1998b) *Section 3.*

discouraged (RAC, 1995). It is exactly these short trips that are made primarily by women and it is exactly these car trips that the White Paper seeks to discourage through, for example, the provision of local services and safe routes to school. While such policies appear sensible they are being suggested without a full understanding of the nature of such trips. For example, that women may be combining several journey purposes on the school run (for example, work, food shopping) is generally accepted. But the role women play in household decision making (for example the way tasks are divided within the household) and how it affects their mode of travel is highly complex and not understood by policy makers. Similarly, while more local services are to be applauded there is no guarantee that they will result in a reduction in car use. Research by Headicar and Curtis, investigating the relationship between housing location and car use in Oxfordshire, demonstrated

Table 7.6 Women as public transport users

General public transport use

- Men made around 7% of their trips by public transport, women about 10%
- Public transport journeys showed a ratio of more than three to one in favour of women in the 40–49 age group
- Usage was greatest for those aged 17–20 or over 70. One in five trips by women aged 70 and over were by public transport

Bus use

- Both men and women made more trips by bus than by other form of public transport and buses are particularly important for those aged 17–20 and 60 and over. Middle-aged men made only 2–3% of their trips by bus, but this increased rapidly after retirement, to 10% for those aged 70 or over
- Women of all age groups made more journeys on local buses than men, although there was only a marginal difference in the under 17 age group
- Buses were clearly an important mode of travel for women in full or part-time employment
- In car-owning households women made greater use of local buses than men reflecting the lower proportion of women who were main drivers and their dependence on public transport when the car was not available to them
- Elderly people in the survey sample had difficulties with buses. Women had more difficulty than men in getting to the bus stop, waiting, boarding and alighting and, when on the bus, in getting to or from a seat

Rail use

- Men made around 1.7% of their trips by rail, compared to 1.5% for women. At the peak age of use (21–29) men and women both used rail for 3% of their journeys

Taxi use

- Taxi use was particularly high among young women aged 17–20 who made 28 taxi and minicab trips per person per year (2.5% of their total trips) compared to an all ages average of 12 trips per person per year

Assaults and robbery

- In assaults and robbery of bus passengers both the assaulted and the assailant were often juvenile males, with journeys from school being a source of much of the reported data

Concessionary travel

- Provision was made in the Pension Act 1995 for the age at which women became eligible for concessionary travel schemes to be raised from 60 to 65 over a transitional period from 2010 to 2020.

Source: Compiled from DETR (1998b) and DETR (1999).

Table 7.7 Women as pedestrians and cyclists

Women as pedestrians

- Women made 30% of their trips on foot, compared to 25% for men
- Over a quarter of trips by women aged 21–39 were on foot, declining to just under a quarter for those aged 40–49, before increasing with age to women aged 70 and over, who made just under two trips in five on foot
- For men about one trip in five was on foot. This proportion increased sharply to well over one-quarter for those aged 60–69 and one-third for men aged 70 and over

Cycling amongst children

- Cycle mileage by children fell by more than 40% for 1975/76 to 1993/95. The fall was similar for both boys and girls aged up to 10, but there has been an even larger fall among girls aged 11–15
- For children, boys cycle more, particularly in their teens. At the peak age of 15, young men make about one in eight of their trips by bicycle

Cycling amongst adults

- The peak age for bicycle use was 17–20 for both males and females. Men made four times as many bicycle trips as women in this group. But even at this peak age, only 4% of their trips were by bicycle
- On average men do more than three times the annual cycle mileage of women
- Male casualties outnumbered female casualties by four to one overall and five to one for those aged under 20
- Overall, about one-quarter of cycle stages are less than one mile and another third between one and two miles. Less than one in ten are over 5 miles. Women cycle shorter distances than men; over a third of stages were less than one mile

Source: Compiled from DETR (1998b) and DoT (1996).

that being close to facilities did not necessarily result in a reduction in car use as there were other factors at play, in particular the trade off between cheaper housing and longer commuting distances (Curtis, 1995).

Second, there is no specific acknowledgment of the complexity of women's travel patterns as opposed to those of their typical male counterparts. For example, the White Paper calls for a reduction in car use for the school run through the development of safe routes to school. Such trips are primarily made by women (see Table 7.1) but may be linked into more complex travel patterns that are not easily performed by modes other than the car. Women's lives often involve juggling a variety of roles as worker, carer and housewife, for which a car may be essential.

Women are seen as prime future candidates to boost public transport use. For example, the New Deal states in relation to public transport security: 'this may be worse at night and for older people, women and ethnic minorities... Research has suggested that over 10 per cent extra patronage of public transport could be generated if travellers, particularly women, felt safer in making their journeys'. While safety is a real issue it is important that it is not seen as an 'easy' solution: it cannot be assumed that if public transport were safer more women would use it. For many women public transport is not a viable option given their travel patterns: typically multiple journey purposes and multiple responsibilities within the household. As Hill (1996) highlights, women 'tend to make more complex, encumbered and time constrained journeys... that are more difficult to cater for economically by public transport than are more concentrated journey to work and business flows'. Hill concluded that women's journeys could become the soft target of policies that seek to reduce car use. This is a real concern, as in the White Paper those journeys that are primarily undertaken by women are the targets for reductions in car use, yet these policies have been made with no understanding of the role of transport in women's lives.

Third, the White Paper fails to recognise sufficiently the diversity of women in the city and still focuses on statistical averages and stereotypes (this reflects wider transport planning issues where transport as a subject area is still male dominated). Unquestionably progress has been made in developing our understanding of women's travel needs and transport requirements, but this understanding is often limited and confused. The situation is perpetuated by the use of transport planning jargon to describe certain types of trip, for example 'kiss and ride' and 'escort trips' which can conjure up an unhelpful and stereotypical view of women's travel.

The White Paper is no exception: women are portrayed as vulnerable in their use of the transport system, dependent on lifts and on public transport and making 'escort trips'. This is difficult to get right: for some women the stereotype is the correct picture. However the average figures given in the White Paper can be misleading. For both sexes the car is now the dominant mode of travel (see Table 7.5), but there is diversity among women (and men) in terms of car ownership and use and their general mobility. Many women own company cars and exhibit typical 'male' commuting patterns. Popular myth also exists regarding women's behaviour within the transport system. 'Women drivers' are still stereotyped as incompetent despite evidence that women and men are involved in different types of accident due to their behavioural and physiological makeup and that women are less likely to be involved in serious accidents than men. Conversely, the 1990s phenomenon of 'road rage' has been treated as a predominantly male trait, although recent television documentaries have demonstrated that women can instigate incidents. Little is known about 'road rage' beyond the anecdotal and experts are divided on whether the phenomenon exists, but even less is known about the effects of increased aggression on journeys undertaken by women. Are women being deterred from driving in particular places at particular times?

The stereotypes that appear in the White Paper simply reflect those in many aspects of transport planning and provision. An area of real concern is vehicle design (Stone, 1996), which has been dominated by the requirements of an average-sized driver. Yet women's smaller stature necessitates that they sit closer to the steering wheel, causing them to hit it more quickly in a crash. Seatbelts may not fit shorter women, again increasing their risk of injury in a crash, and the effect of a car crash on pregnant women is still not known (Stone, 1996). Women are more likely to own a small car, often the 'second' car in the household, which is likely to be older than the 'main' car. American research has linked increased female fatalities in car crashes to vehicle age and specification. Stone (1996) also highlighted that different groups of people drive different kinds of miles with different kinds of risks. The most likely explanation for increased female traffic accident and fatality rates relates to the type and location of the miles women drive on a daily basis. More of women's travel takes place in urban areas where the risk of a nonfatal crash is greater.

Hill (1996) points to the increasing polarisation of women's transport which the White Paper fails to recognise. Whilst some women (especially younger), are experiencing transport needs and opportunities similar to those of men, for others, especially lone mothers and elderly women, transport opportunities remain restricted. No mention is made in the New Deal on the effects of income or ethnicity on women's mode choice. Income may affect travel behaviour through housing location. There has been no research the author is aware of that investigates ethnicity in relation to women's travel patterns. Muslim women, for example, are not allowed to expose their bodies and hence may be forbidden to ride a bicycle or even to use public transport due to mixing with unfamiliar men. It is likely therefore that as more is understood about women's travel behaviour we are likely to see increasing polarisation between groups of women.

Conclusions: future research

Women and men travel in different ways and for different reasons. While a clearer picture of these differences has started to emerge over the past decade, and women are taking an increasing role in trying to influence political decision, there is still much to be done. Central government has recognised that

> Despite the vast majority of research collecting information on the sex of the respondent, there is very little robust information readily available on women's attitudes. The absence of a comprehensive understanding of the role of gender in shaping public attitudes is likely to lead to a failure to recognise that women do have different priorities to men and for this to be reflected in government's approach to policy making.
>
> (Cabinet Office, 1998)

The Transport White Paper promises to provide real improvements that will positively affect women's travel, but several key areas remain for further research to inform the policy debate.

The car is now the most important mode for the majority of women. Research is needed that investigates the impact on women of policies that seek to reduce the need to travel by private car. At the same time as women are experiencing new travel opportunities, it is being recognised that the environment can no longer sustain uncontrolled growth in travel and car ownership (Hill, 1996). The White Paper has called for a reduction in car use and an increase in 'greener' modes. Yet it is likely that such policies may work to the disadvantage of women because of their multiple roles (or indeed of men with multiple roles including child rearing) which are often only possible with the use of the car. As local authorities start to produce their local transport plans to move forward the proposals of the White Paper research is needed to understand the possible unequal opportunities that may result.

Second there is an urgent need for further statistical information that could be used to inform policy makers. The information available tends to focus on the types of journeys women are making, their mode, their purpose and distance travelled. Research is needed that disaggregates women's travel and mode choice, for example by household structure, income, location and ethnicity. A women's mode choice for a particular trip will not be made in isolation from the rest of her life. In particular, there is a limited understanding of cultural and religious background on mode choice and travel behaviour. Research is needed to enable a greater understanding of the influence of these elements in terms of travel behaviour, mode choice, and hence access to employment and services.

References

Cabinet Office (1998) 'Ministers for Women'. Fact sheet, London: Cabinet Office.
Cabinet Office (1998) 'Listening to Women'. Fact sheet, London: Cabinet Office.
Community Transport Association (1992) *Women's Transport Charter Resource Pack*. Manchester: Transport Resource Unit.
Curtis, C. (1995) 'Reducing the Need to Travel: Strategic Housing Location and Travel Behaviour'. In *Reducing the Need to Travel: Some Thoughts on PPG13*, Oxford Planning Monographs, 1(2), Oxford: Oxford Brookes University.
DETR (Department of the Environment, Transport and the Regions) (1998a) *A New Deal for Transport: Better for Everyone*. The Government's White Paper on the Future of Transport, London: HMSO.
DETR (Department of the Environment, Transport and the Regions) (1998b) *Focus on Personal Travel*. London: HMSO.
DETR (Department of the Environment, Transport and the Regions) (1999) *Focus on Public Transport*. London: HMSO.
DOT (Department of Transport) (1995) *Women's Transport Network, Terms of Reference*. London: Mobility Unit, Department of Transport.
DOT (Department of Transport) (1996) *Cycling in Great Britain*. London: HMSO.
Dunning, J. (1997) 'Rising Car Ownership Among Women and the Elderly Continues To Fuel Growth in Travel Demand. *Local Transport Today*, 3 January 1997, London.
Hamilton, K. and Jenkins, L. (1992) 'Women and Transport'. In *Travel Sickness, The Need For A Sustainable Transport Policy For Britain*, J. Roberts, J. Cleary, K. Hamilton and J. Hanna (eds), p. 57, London: Lawrence and Wishart.
Hill, R. (1996) 'Women and Transport'. In C. Booth, J. Darke and S. Yeandle (eds), *Changing Places Women's Lives In The City*, London: Paul Chapman.
Royal Automobile Association Foundation For Motoring and The Environment (1995) *Summary, Car Dependence*. London: RAC Foundation For Motoring and the Environment.
Stone, D. (1996) *Patterns of Gender Differences in Highway Safety*. Wisconsin: Wisconsin Department of Transportation.
Trench, S, T. Oc and S. Tiesdell (1992) 'Safer Cities for Women: Perceived Risks and Planning Measures'. *Transport Planning Research*, No 63(3).

8
The Gap between the Spires: Single Women and Homelessness in Oxford, 1890s and 1990s

Caroline Morrell and Karen Kuehne

One of the challenges facing single women in the city is finding somewhere safe, secure and affordable to live. While housing and the home are of central importance in the lives of all women, single women have historically been marginalised, both in housing policy and housing provision. Lack of provision, in combination with their lesser earning power, significantly disadvantages single women in the housing system and leaves them vulnerable to homelessness. However, the problem of female homelessness has been overshadowed by the more visible male problem, and comparatively little attention has been paid to the reasons for, or consequences of, women's homelessness (for exceptions to this see Miller, 1990; Muir and Ross, 1993; Watson and Austerberry, 1986; Brandon, n.d.).

This chapter will examine single women's experience of homelessness in two decades, the 1890s and the 1990s, using Oxford as a local case study. The first section draws on historical research carried out by Caroline Morrell which deals with the housing activities of nineteenth-century women's societies in Oxford, and the second section utilises contemporary research conducted by Karen Kuehne on the position of single homeless women today, focusing particularly on two surveys carried out in Oxford in 1987 and 1996. We have more than an academic interest in the subject. We have both worked in the field of single homelessness in Oxford and were members of the Oxford Women and Homelessness Action Group, the group responsible for carrying out one of the surveys discussed in this chapter. This all-women group took the premise that women's homelessness is a feminist issue which reflects fundamental gender inequalities in society.

We have approached the subject in different historical periods, and from different angles, but certain common themes have emerged which illustrate the continuing connection between the housing system and women's position in society. The widespread poverty and destitution which were such features of working-class life in Victorian Britain have largely disappeared and we no longer see homelessness on the scale on which it once existed. Homelessness is still very evident in our cities, however and, using Oxford as an example, we explore the extent to which this affects women and the changes which may have occurred in the way in which women's homelessness is perceived and responded to. Definitions of homelessness in the two periods, and the historical changes affecting women's housing position, are also discussed.

Housing and homelessness in Victorian Britain

Both the system of housing provision and perceptions of housing need and homelessness were very different in Victorian Britain, and as the historical situation is less familiar to us today, we begin by outlining the background to women's housing position in the earlier period. Those who were comfortably housed in the last century were in a small minority and most working people lived in conditions which, by today's standards, would be considered unfit for human habitation (see RCHWC (1884–5); Wohl, 1973; Stedman-Jones, 1984). Impermanence was also a feature of working-class life to a far greater extent than now. The predominant form of housing tenure was private renting: this was extremely insecure and frequent movement between lodgings was common (see evidence given to RCHWC). The very structure of work dictated that many people followed an unsettled way of life as a number of trades were itinerant or seasonal and involved regular movement round the country in search of work. According to Raphael Samuel

> The distinction between the nomadic life and the settled one was by no means hard and fast. Tramping was not the prerogative of the social outcast as it is today; it was a normal phase in the life of entirely respectable classes of working men; it was a frequent resort of the out-of-works; and it was a very principle of existence for those who followed the itinerant callings and trades. (Samuel, 1973)

This makes the application of the term 'homelessness', as we understand it today, problematical for the period. The term was not often used and references were made to the 'houseless poor' or to vagrancy rather than to homelessness. The 'houseless poor' lived in the casual wards of workhouses, common lodging houses and charitable shelters, all of which by their nature were temporary, occupied on a nightly basis and shared with strangers. A number of people also lived in barns, sheds or in the open air; the Population Census of 1911 counted 10 694 females in such situations. The Departmental Committee on Vagrancy (DCV) appointed in 1904 estimated that the number of people with no settled home varied between 30 000 to 80 000, depending on fluctuations in the economy, (DCV, 1906, I:22). Women were recorded in all the places where homeless people were to be found, but were invariably outnumbered by men. In 1905 a national census of persons in common lodging houses, casual wards and elsewhere (refuges, shelters and sleeping out) counted 59 743 men, 8118 women and 2907 children (DCV, 1906, p. 21). Because of the low numbers recorded, women's homelessness was considered to be 'comparatively unimportant' (DCV, 1906, p. 112). However, these figures do not reflect the true picture of women's homelessness because, as we shall see, much of women's housing need was concealed.

The dominant ideology of the period held that women's place was firmly in the private realm of the home and assumed a domestic role for women as wives, mothers and homemakers. Women of all classes were generally housed by virtue of their relationship to men. However, census figures show that single women made up one-third of all adult women in the period. The housing situation of single women of the working classes was very different from both that of their married counterparts and from that of single women of higher social status. Large families, overcrowding and poverty meant that most working-class girls had to leave home at an early age in order to earn a living. Contemporary evidence showed that women's work was low skilled, low status, low paid and often subject to seasonal unemployment. Zimmern (1912 p. 43) wrote that 'women's wages amount, roughly speaking, to one half of those of men'.

This placed working women in a very disadvantaged position in the housing market and those who did not live in generally subsisted in the cheapest lodgings (see Higgs and Hayward, 1910). Most working-class single women secured a roof over their heads by going into domestic service, the largest source of employment for women up until the Second World War. Workers in the dress trade, the second largest occupation for women, also lived in their place of work, as did those employed in the shop trade, a growing source of employment for women over the period.[1] Occupation dictated housing for women in the last century, thus the situation was precarious: the worker who lost her place also lost her home.

The only statutory provision for homelessness was the workhouse and there is ample evidence that most people would go to great lengths to avoid this degradation. The Royal Commission on the Poor Laws stated that 'the workhouse and everything within its walls is anathema excepting to the very dregs of the population' (RCPL, 1909, p. 15). If dismissed without a character reference, women workers were extremely unlikely to find another position. Returning to parents was not an option for most as the overcrowding and poverty of working-class homes meant that their families were unlikely to be able to take them back in again. For domestic servants who came from the workhouse, as many did, there was no home to return to. Many young women turned to prostitution in order to survive (see Butler, 1869; Higgs, 1906).

While little official attention was paid to the question of women's homelessness, concern about prostitution, the 'great social evil', permeated Victorian and Edwardian society. William Gladstone said that the problem of fallen women was 'the chief burden of his soul' (quoted in Walkowitz, 1980, p. 32), and Mrs Pankhurst wrote in 1913 that 'the problem of prostitution' was 'the greatest evil in the civilised world' and 'perhaps the main reason for militancy' (*Suffragette*, 8 August 1913, quoted in Rosen, 1974, p. 208). There were also fears about the existence of an organized white slave trade which lured young women into prostitution. The National Vigilance Assocation (n.d., *c.* 1900, p. 16) made specific links between the living-in system and this trade.

Middle- and upper-class women responded to the plight of working women in the city, their 'poor friendless sisters', by setting up societies to help and befriend them. As part of this mission they provided accommodation lodges for young women of respectable character and rescue homes and penitentiaries for 'fallen women' – and it is evident that elements of surveillance were implicit in this provision. Bodies such as the Girls' Friendly Society set up in 1875, the Metropolitan Association for the Befriending of Young Servants in 1873 and the Ladies' Associations for Befriending Girls in the 1880s organised on a national scale to provide a system of safe lodgings and supervision for young working women, and by the 1890s there were few towns which did not possess such facilities. It was said in 1893, 'for the hundreds of preventive and rescue homes, industrial schools, convalescent homes and homes of rest, the women of England seem to be almost exclusively responsible' (Sellars, 1893).

This was very much women's work for women and it can be seen in the context of the early women's movement. Women were coming together to campaign for the vote and for rights to employment and education. Women were reaching out to women here across the class divide and the language of sisterhood was consciously used. It can also be seen in the context of the social purity movement of the time. Unattached women in the city were perceived both to pose a threat to sexual morality – hence the need to supervise them – and to be vulnerable to sexual exploitation – hence the need to protect them. The way in which women organized in Oxford acts as a local exemplar of the national situation.

Oxford in the 1890s

Oxford at the end of the nineteenth century was a small university city with a population of just under 50000. The census figures for 1901 show that out of 17157 unmarried women over the age of fourteen, 7126 were engaged in waged work. Of these 3696 were employed in some form of domestic service, 1291 were employed in the dress trade and 219 worked in drapers' shops (*Census of England and Wales*, 1901, Tables for the City of Oxford, pp. 41–51). Over half the single working women in Oxford then worked in living-in trades and thus were dependent on their employment for their housing. Oxford, with its large population of single young men, was also a magnet for prostitutes and there were large numbers of them living in the common lodging houses in the poor parts of the city (Engel, 1979–80).

There were five charitable lodges for women in varying degrees of housing need in Oxford in the 1890s. At the top end of the scale were the Young Women's Christian Association (YWCA) and the Girls' Friendly Society (GFS), two societies which housed young working women of 'unblemished character'. The Oxford Ladies' Association for the Care of Friendless Girls (OLACFG) catered for those of less respectable character who were at risk of homelessness, and the Oxford Female Penititentary and House of Mercy (OFPHM) and the Oxford House of Refuge (OHR) provided rehabilitative accommodation for fallen women. Between them these hostels, or lodges, housed some 90 women; they were always full and each recorded that they had to turn women away.

Significantly, the Oxford Penitentiary for fallen women was the largest of these organizations. It was begun in 1832 in a small house which took six women, but by the 1890s it had moved to Holywell Manor and was accommodating 40 women. These women were prostitutes, described in the annual reports as living in 'houses of sin'. There were no equivalent institutions for men of course but, interestingly, penitentiaries were generally managed by all-male committees. The OFPHM was managed by a committee of college dons and clergymen, but it was women who actually ran the home. It was staffed by Anglican sisters and a number of Oxford ladies took a kindly interest in the inmates, visiting the Penitentiary and providing gifts of clothes and food.

The women in the Penitentiary were not from Oxford, but were sent there from other towns because it was thought 'absolutely necessary to separate the girls who have been acquainted with one another before entering the refuge' (OFPHM, 1891). They stayed there for two years until they were deemed 'to be sufficiently restored in character to face the temptations of life' (OFPHM, 1891), and then were generally found places in domestic service. As the name suggests, the women were there to do penance for their sins and they were subject to a strict regime of work and prayer. They earned their keep by doing laundry and thus metaphorically 'scrubbed away their sins'. 'Let the young women realise throughout the sin of their fall', it was said, 'sin can only be realised through suffering' (Mrs Creighton, 1901). However, there was also kindness there. The annual reports quote letters from old inmates talking about the 'dear old home' and mention that women regularly came back for visits. Some of the women never left the Penitentiary but stayed on and became workers themselves (OFPHM, 1882) which perhaps indicates the paucity of alternatives available to them.

We have little information on the individual women or how they came to the Penitentiary, but in 1865 it was reported of four young women who applied for admission, 'these poor creatures were vagrants in a great state of destitution' (OFPHM, 1865). In 1883 it was said of one 15-year-old inmate, 'C is only fifteen . . . mother is insane, "father shut me out and said he couldn't afford to keep me"' (OFPHM, 1883). In 1886 we hear of girls 'begging for admission' (OFPHM, 1886). So while some of the women may have come to the Penitentiary in a genuine state of repentance, it is equally possible that they were destitute and desperate and would accept the regime in exchange for a roof over their heads and an escape from the life of the streets.

The second organization which worked with fallen women in Oxford, the House of Refuge was set up in 1874 and took women directly from the streets or from brothels, either those who were sought out by rescue workers or women who came asking for admission for themselves (OHR, 1900). Like the Penitentiary the House of Refuge was managed by a committee of men but run by Anglican sisters and a group of lady visitors. We do not know how large the Refuge was, but in 1879 it was recorded that 44 women had passed through the home in that year and that to some it was 'the first and only *home* they had ever known' (OHR, 1900), which reinforces the suspicion that the underlying cause of these women's way of life was homelessness. Again, there is little information about the women who came to the Refuge, but it appears that some of them were very young. In 1884 a 12-year-old was admitted and the report for that year commented sadly, 'we used to deal with women, then with girls, now it is with children' (OHR, 1884).

The Oxford Ladies' Association for the Care of Friendless Girls (OLACGF) was an organisation which aimed at preventive as well as rescue work. It aimed to help 'any girl in Oxford who either needs a helping hand, or who is desirous of giving up a sinful or unworthy life' (OLACFG, 1893). The Association ran a training home for domestic service, lodgings for girls considered as 'doubtful cases', and a home for unmarried mothers and their babies from the workhouse. Unmarried mothers were in a very vulnerable situation and without the help provided by women's societies faced a great struggle for survival. Official reports commented that the deaths that occurred in childbirth in the workhouse were mostly due to illnesses which arose from the state of exhaustion and misery in which the poor women were admitted, 'the depressing conditions associated with shame and its serious consequences' (Local Government Board, 1882, p. xiviii).

Six young women passed through the training home in 1883, its first year of existence, and 25 in its second. In 1908 it moved to a house which could take 16 girls. In 1894 it was said that 'the training home continues to give loving shelter to a good many girls from our work-house who are entirely without a home of their own' (OLACFG, 1894). It was also recorded that destitute girls were received into the training home free, so a number of them must have been literally homeless. Sexual abuse was recorded in some instances: in 1892, for example, there was a note that a little girl of eleven was rescued from bad surroundings and boarded out in the country (OLACFG, 1892); in 1893 two girls were taken from 'immoral surroundings'; in 1894 one was rescued from 'a terribly bad father in Oxford' (OLACFG, 1894). Contemporary evidence indicates that then, as now, sexual abuse played a significant role in female homelessness. The records of the first Salvation Army shelters for homeless women in London show that in the late 1880s four in ten of the girls and young women who came to them cited sexual abuse, either by parents or employers, as their reason for seeking refuge (see Hendessi, 1992).

We now come to the first of the societies which were set up for prevention only – the Girls' Friendly Society. It was organised within the structure of the Anglican Church and worked only with women of 'unblemished character'. The Society was initially aimed at domestic servants between places, but as different types of work began to open up in the cities for women, in offices and shops, it extended its mission accordingly and opened its lodgings to all (respectable) young women in need of housing. Its founder, Mrs Mary Townsend, said, 'the Society owes its origin to the fearfully prevalent and increasing sin of impurity, secondly to the conviction that "prevention is better than cure"' (Townsend, 1882, p. 6).

Accommodation lodges formed part of the Society's armoury against sin, and by the 1890s there was a comprehensive network of lodges, not only in Britain but also overseas. Lodges existed in over 60 British towns and in 1905 it was said that 'a GFS member may now travel from Paris to Odessa, or from Biarritz to St Petersburg and be safe in the care of the GFS all the way' (Money, 1905). The Oxford lodge opened in 1891 and at first only took four women. By 1897 it had moved to larger premises, and in that year 123 residents passed through the home, including girls being trained for service, servants between places and several young women who had been taken in late at night through missing trains or 'other emergencies' (OGFS, 1897). Supervision was the key aim and young working-class women were deemed to be in need of firm 'mothering' in order to ensure that they did not go astray. The GFS also provided a servants' employment registry, a scheme for meeting girls at the station and a range of wholesome activities – classes, choirs, reading groups – to ensure that their leisure time was fully occupied.

The other women's organization in Oxford which worked with girls of unblemished reputation, the YWCA, took women of a higher social standing than the GFS – 'young women of good character who are employed in business or teaching in this city' (Oxford YWCA, 1885). Like the GFS it was an Anglican organization, and the provision of accommodation was part of its wider mission to young women. In 1884 the YWCA provided lodgings for five young women and in 1886 it moved premises to a house which could take 16 lodgers. This was still not enough to meet the need; the report of 1898 talks of the Committee's sorrow at continually having to turn girls away, and in 1902 its provision was extended to 22 beds. 'Even with increased accommodation', the report for that year said, 'every bed in the dormitory is engaged' (Oxford YWCA, 1902). The record of continued expansion of all these forms of accommodation attests to the housing need of young women in the city, and the provision of the YWCA in particular reflects the growing numbers of young women of the lower-middle and middle classes entering employment or education over the period.

Oxford was no large industrial town in which a housing problem might have been expected, but a small university city, and the existence of these facilities indicates that female homelessness was widespread. Neither were these activities unique to Oxford. The YWCA and the GFS were large national organizations with many local branches, Ladies' Associations for Befriending Young Girls existed in 120 towns and penitentiaries and refuges for prostitutes were to be found all over the country (Sellars, 1893). Clearly there was a great need for lodgings for women which was not being met by the commercial housing market, and the activities of these women's societies went a long way towards saving women from homelessness and making life more tenable for them in the cities. There are many questions about the elements of social control involved, and about the intersection between class and gender. The priorities of the lady organizers who provided the lodges might not have been those of the working-class women who used them. Prostitution and the sexual vulnerability of young women in the city were what preoccupied these societies and the question of housing tended to be subsumed under the heading of social purity. However, it is an example of women recognising, and responding to, the problems which arose from the lack of housing for single women, and acting in a very practical way to meet that need.

Housing and homelessness in the 1990s

We now move forward a hundred years to Oxford in the 1990s. The social and economic context, the housing system and the position of women are very different in some respects from the situation of the 1890s, although there are also continuities. The level and nature of homelessness in the city of Oxford is discussed using the results of a survey carried out by the Oxford Women and Homelessness Action Group in 1987 and repeated in 1996 by Karen Kuehne as a project for a Master's degree.

Housing standards have improved beyond recognition over the last hundred years, state welfare provision has greatly reduced absolute destitution, and although homelessness has by no means disappeared, its scale is much-educed. A number of changes have affected the housing position of women in particular. Perhaps most importantly, domestic service has virtually disappeared, and with it the living-in system, outside a few specialised sectors. There are now far more occupational opportunities open to women, and higher pay enables many more women to live in independent housing. Motherhood outside marriage is no longer disastrous and lone mothers are among the priority groups for local authority housing – which paradoxically has led to their being stigmatised in some quarters as 'queue jumpers'.

However, there are also a number of parallels between the two periods. Women continue to be paid less than men, government housing policy and provision continues to be aimed at the family, and the needs of single homeless people are generally left to the voluntary sector. Single women have less access to owner occupation or good-quality rented accommodation than do single men. Analysis of the National Child Development Survey, a large-scale birth cohort study, showed that in 1982, holding other factors constant, women with partners were an astonishingly 100 times more likely to be in owner-occupation as women who were single (Munro and Smith, 1989, p. 9). For men, having a partner had no direct effect on tenure attainment (Munro and Smith, 1989). The domestic ideology constructed in the last century is still an important force in shaping women's lives, and the belief that women (should) relate primarily to the home and the family has by no means disappeared (Hakim, 1995). Violence and sexual abuse remain features of family life, and the lack of access to alternative safe housing and financial dependence upon a partner mean that often women remain in intolerable situations because there is no real alternative (Lander, 1997). Hidden homelessness is still a significant factor and this makes quantifying the numbers of homeless women very difficult. Comprehensive statistics for single homelessness are not available either nationally or locally (Oxford Housing Rights Centre, 1995). Research carried out by Shelter shows that there are more than 70 000 single people forced to stay in bed-and-breakfast hotels alone, and that many more have to sleep on friends' floors or sofas, or find other forms of temporary shelter (Holmes, 1999). This is remarkably close to the 70 768 people without a settled home recorded in 1905.

The definition of homelessness also remains problematical. While it may seem at first sight that the meaning of homelessness is clear, the debate about the meaning of the word is central to the difficulty in determining both the extent of, and the appropriate response to, the problem. Under legislation introduced in the Housing Act 1977 and under Part III of the Housing Act 1985 only those single people found to be 'vulnerable' receive assistance from local authorities. Vulnerability includes mental health needs, escape from violence, young people at risk, and other community care needs. Most single homeless people fall outside these categories (Leigh, 1994, p. 23). CHAR (Housing Campaign for Single People) advocates a definition incorporating all possibilities of 'rooflessness' which, although very wide, seems more realistic:

> Single homeless people include those who sleep rough in open air sites . . . those who reside on a temporary basis in hostels, night shelters and similar accommodation . . . those who reside with friends or relatives on a temporary basis because they are unable to find separate accommodation. Single women living in women's refuges and hostels should be included.
>
> (Foster, 1994)

Homeless women are not a homogenous group. As Milburn and D'Ercole (1991) point out, 'homeless women vary in their race, age, marital and parental status, access to temporary housing, and duration of homelessness, and in their paths into and out of homelessness'. However, large-scale studies have found certain common characteristics among homeless women. The Centre for Housing Policy at the University of York carried out a survey of homeless single people in 1991 on behalf of the Department of the Environment (DoE, 1993). They found that a large percentage had no educational or vocational qualifications, which would correlate with unemployment and low earning power, and that a high proportion had spent some time in an institution, such as a children's home or in foster care, which mirrors the situation of girls leaving the workhouse in the last century.

Oxford in the 1990s

Of the five hostels for women in Oxford in the 1890s, only the YWCA and the GFS remain. The Penitentiary has long closed, the Oxford Ladies Association for the Care of Friendless Girls dissolved itself in 1921, and the Refuge turned into a mother-and-baby home after the Second World War, remaining in existence until the early 1990s. Homelessness has not gone away, however. There is an acute shortage of affordable accommodation in the city and a very visible population of homeless people. Oxford also has a well-developed network of facilities for single homeless people. There is a mixed night shelter and three direct access hostels for homeless people in the city which between them have some 150 beds. One of the hostels is men only, and women are always in a small minority in the other three.

The Oxford Women and Homelessness Action Group (OXWHAG), concerned about the lack of provision for homeless women, came together in the early 1980s to campaign for the provision of a women-only hostel. It was argued by housing providers in the city, in terms reminiscent of the Departmental Committee on Vagrancy's comments of 1906, that the low numbers of women in the hostels showed that there was not a significant problem for women. However, OXWHAG believed that the predominantly male population of these hostels was intimidating to women and deterred them from seeking admission, and that there were far more women in housing need in the city than those to be found in these hostels. In 1987 the group carried out a survey (OXWHAG, 1987) to discover the level and nature of homelessness among women in Oxford.

Questionnaires were sent to all relevant organizations in Oxford with a request to fill one in for every homeless woman who asked for advice or shelter in a four-week period. Fourteen agencies responded and returned questionnaires on 77 different women. Fifty-five women were found to be actually homeless, that is, staying in one of the homelessness hostels, and 22 were found to be potentially homeless, that is, they presented to advice agencies with acute housing problems but did not materialise in the provision made for homeless people. The age range of the women was from 16 to 67 with 61 per cent of the women being under 30. In terms of length of homelessness, those women in the older age range were more likely to be long-term homeless. A wide range of reasons for homelessness was found. The overall themes identified were unemployment, pregnancy, ill health, family breakdown and alcohol problems, as well as breakdown of tenancy. These themes seemed to be contingent on age, with teenagers likely to be homeless because of pregnancy or leaving care, and women in their twenties due to marital breakdown, health and alcohol problems or unemployment. Women over 40 were often homeless due to alcohol or mental health problems or to leaving tied accommodation following illness or retirement. The survey showed conclusively that homelessness affected significant numbers of single women in Oxford, and that that the provision made in the homelessness hostels was not acceptable to many of them.

The 1987 survey was repeated in 1996 to ascertain any changes in the nature and level of homelessness among women. Fewer agencies responded, six as opposed to 14, but the number of homeless women identified, 54 as opposed to 77, was relatively higher. Approximately the same proportions fell into actual or potential categories of homelessness. The age range was the same, from 16 to 67, and the same reasons for homelessness were identified.

A number of new trends were found, however. First, alcohol and drug problems were listed as the reason for homelessness for a higher proportion of the group (although this may have been affected by the fact that the majority of the returns were made by a medical centre for homeless people). Second, many of the women had multiple reasons for their homelessness, such as alcohol problems, mental health problems and relationship breakdowns. Third, the women being seen were increasingly younger, with over one-third being under 25. The age difference between those who were short- or long-term homeless had also disappeared, and young women were as likely as older women to be classed as long-term homeless. One young woman was listed as being homeless due to sexual abuse, but this is not likely to be an accurate representation of the problem. The number is probably closer to the ratio of four in ten found by Hendessi in the research she carried out with homeless women in 1991. One of her findings was that workers seldom asked the women if they had been sexually abused, although many of the women wished they had been asked (Hendessi, 1992).

Some of the differences between the findings of the two surveys may be a product of the smaller range of agencies which responded in 1996 as compared to 1987, and of the medical orientation of the agencies in the second survey. However, it is worrying that the women identified seemed to be younger, and that more young women were deemed to be long-term homeless. The range of additional problems, such as alcohol and drug abuse, is difficult to separate out as contributing causes, or conseqences, of homelessness, and more research is needed in this area. It is clear that, despite our belief that poverty and the lack of affordable housing are the fundamental issues in women's homelessness, we must accept the fact that many single homeless women have a range of support needs. The fact that single women's homelessness has not improved in the intervening nine years suggests that this problem will not simply go away, nor is it only related to economic cycles.

We have presented two snapshots of women's homelessness in different periods in one small British city, but the themes which emerge have resonance for the national scene. It is clear that over the time-span covered the underlying reasons for women's homelessness have, to some extent, changed. However, women remain economically disadvantaged in the labour market, and hence the housing market, housing provision is still aimed at the family, and single women are still marginalised in the housing system. Homeless women are less visible than men on the streets or in hostels, but it is clear that much of women's homelessness is concealed.

Responses to the situation of homeless women have certainly changed. Homelessness is no longer considered as primarily a moral problem, and the major need is seen as housing rather than supervision and 'mothering'. However, it is still the case that it is women's organizations who are most concerned with women's homelessness. It has been salutary to recognise that the women and homelessness group with which we were involved in the 1980s went through many of the processes which the women-only groups of Victorian Oxford did. We also consisted of middle-class women with different, but equally preconceived, ideas of the sort of provision which homeless women needed. Different times and different circumstances, but the same basic issue of women's homelessness and of their exclusion from provision, set against a period of feminist organisation, resulted in a very similar response.

Finally, it is notable that, with few exceptions, the research into single homelessness fails to include definitions of homelessness given by homeless women themselves. The historical material contained in this chapter consists of the reports of the lady organisers of the accommodation lodges and their perceptions of the young women who came to them; the contemporary surveys contain the interpretations of the agencies of the situation of the women on whom they reported. Watson and Austerberry (1986) interviewed women who had become homeless, and it worth ending with their quotation of one woman's definition of homelessness:

> Homelessness is nowhere to put your personal belongings – things mean a lot to a single person. You can't express yourself in your furnishings as an individual. It's an affluent age and you feel you're on the outside looking in. (p. 98)

Note

1   The occupational figures contained in the decennial censuses of the population are a useful guide to where women lived. The 1911 census showed that domestic service, textile manufacture and dress work accounted for 57 per cent of all occupied females over the age of ten (*Census of England and Wales, 1911*, (1913), Cd 7018 lxxviii, 321, p. 159).

   Clara Collet's analysis of the 1901 census showed that domestic service was not only the largest employer of women but, with a total labour force of 1 748 954, was the largest single industry for either men or women (Clara

Collet, *The money wages of indoor domestic servants*, Parliamentary Papers, 1899, XCII I, p. 3). The numbers of those living in as shop assistants is more difficult to establish from the census, but the Interdepartmental Committee on the Truck Acts, appointed in 1906, heard evidence that the total number of shop assistants was about 750 000 and that between 400 000 and 450 000 of them lived in. No sex breakdown was given but, as shop work employed approximately equal numbers of men and women, we can assume that some 200 000 women were living in as shop assistants (*Report of the Interdepartmental Committee on the Truck Acts*, 1908, p. 136).

References

Brandon, D. (n.d.) *Women without homes*. London: Christian Aid.

Butler, J. (1869) *Women's work and women's culture*, Basingstoke: Macmillan.

Census of England and Wales, 1901 (1902) City of Oxford, Cd 1332.

Census of England and Wales, 1911 (1914–16) Cd 7018.

Clara Collet, *The money wages of indoor domestic servants* (1899) XCII, I.

Creighton, Mrs (1901) Address to the Oxford Ladies' Association for the Care of Friendless Girls, 5 February 1901, reproduced in their annual report.

DCV (Departmental Committee on Vagrancy) (1906) I–III, Cd 2852, 2891, 2892, ciii I.

DoE (Department of the Environment) (1993) *Single homeless people*, London: HMSO.

Engel, A. J. (1979–1980) 'Immoral intentions: the University of Oxford and the problem of prostitution, 1827–1914', *Victorian Studies*, 23, 79–107.

Foster, S. (1994) *Single homelessness: a short guide to local research* London: CHAR (Housing Campaign for Single People).

Hakim, C. (1995) 'Five feminist myths about women's employment.' *British Journal of Sociology*, 46(3), September, 429–55.

Hendessi, M. (1992) *4 in 10: report on young women who become homeless as a result of sexual abuse*, London: CHAR (Housing Campaign for Single People).

Higgs, M. (1906) *Glimpses into the abyss*. P. S. King & Sons.

Higgs, M. and Hayward, E. (1910) *Where shall she live? The homelessness of the woman worker*, London: P. S. King & Sons.

Holmes, C. (1999) *Guardian*, 24 February, 2–3.

Interdepartmental Committee on the Truck Acts (1908) I–III, Cd 4442–4.

Lander, A. (1997) 'Prioritising pipe dreams', *Housing*, July/August, p. 11.

Local Government Board 1882 Eleventh annual report.

Leigh, C. (1994) *Everybody's baby: implementing community care for single homeless people*. London: CHAR (Housing Campaign for Single People).

Milburn, N. and D'Ercole, A. (1991) 'Homeless women: moving towards a comprehensive model', *American Psychologist*, September.

Miller, M. (1990) *Bed and breakfast women: women and homelessness today*. London: Women's Press.

Money, A. (1905) *History of the Girls' Friendly Society*. London: Hatchards.

Muir, J. and Ross, M. (1993) *Housing the poorer sex*. London: London Housing Unit.

Munro, M. and Smith, S. (1989) 'Gender and housing; broadening the debate.' In *Housing Studies*, 4(1).

National Vigilance Association (n.d., *c.* 1900) *In the grip of the white slave trader*. London: C. Arthur Pearson Oxford Housing Rights Centre Report, 1995.

OFPHM (Oxford Female Penitentiary and House of Mercy) (1865, 1881, 1883, 1886, 1887, 1891) Annual Report.

OGFS (Oxford Girls' Friendly Society) (1987) Annual Report.

OHR (Oxford House of Refuge) (1884, 1900) Annual Report.

OLACFG (Oxford Ladies' Association for the Care of Friendless Girls) (1892, 1893, 1894) Annual Report.

Oxford YWCA (Oxford Young Women's Christian Association) (1885, 1902) Annual Report.

OXWHAC (Oxford Women and Homelessness Action Group) (1987) Survey.

RCHWC (Royal Commission on the Housing of the Working Classes) (1884–5) I and II, XXX.

RCPL (Royal Commission on the Poor Laws and Relief of Distress), (1909) *Minority Report*, Cd 4499.

Rosen, A. (1974) *Rise up women*, London: Routledge and Kegan Paul.

Samuel, R. 'Comers and goers'. (1973) in H. J. Dyos and M. Wolff (eds), *The Victorian City: images and realities*, London: Routledge and Kegan Paul.

Sellars, E. (1893) 'Women's work for the welfare of girls.' In Burdett-Coutts, A. (ed.) *Women's Mission: a series of congress papers on the philanthropic work of women by eminent writers*. London: Sampson Low, Marston & Co.

Stedman-Jones, G. (1984) *Outcast London: a study in the relationship between classes in Victorian Society*, London: Penguin.

Townsend, M. E. (1882) *An appeal to the mistresses of elementary schools from the Girls' Friendly Society*, GFS pamphlet, London: Hatchards.

Walkowitz, J. (1980) *Prostitution and Victorian Society: women, class and the state*. Cambridge: Cambridge University Press.

Watson, S. and Austerberry, H. (1986) *Housing and homelessness: a feminist perspective*. London: Routledge & Kegan Paul.

Wohl, A. (1973) 'Unfit for human habitation'. In H. J. Dyos and M. Wolff (eds), *The Victorian City: images and realities*. London: Routledge & Kegan Paul.

Zimmern, D. (1912) 'The wages of women in industry.' *Proceedings of the National Conference on the prevention of destitution*. London: P. S. King & Sons.

9

Regen(d)eration: Women and Urban Policy in Britain

Sue Brownill

Introduction

Urban policy, or its 1990s manifestation as urban regeneration, has been a major feature of British social policy for 30 years transforming large areas of our towns and cities.[1] Yet the absence of debate on women and urban policy in theory and practice is striking. Most major texts (see, for example Atkinson and Moon, 1994) make no reference to women and within the more policy-focused literature only recently have a few publications seriously addressed the issue (Brownill and Darke, 1998; May 1997; Riseborough; 1997). Elsewhere, where gender is raised it is often due to concerns about young men rather than to any sense of what the issues for women may be. This chapter seeks to address these silences by critically reviewing the evolution of urban policy from a feminist perspective and by initiating debate about key issues for intervention within current policy and practice.

While ostensibly taking a chronological review of urban policy, the aim of this chapter is to underline some key issues and themes including conceptions of women within the 'urban problem', women's relationship with urban space and women's access to power and influence in the governance of urban policy. The purpose is not just to list and categorise, but also to look at how we might achieve an urban policy that challenges and transforms a woman's place in the city. First the chapter discusses different theoretical and political approaches. It concludes by highlighting areas for further action and analysis.

Perspectives on women and urban policy

It is possible to identify a variety of perspectives on women and urban policy. May (1997), for example, refers to two: 'gender blind' and

114

'gender aware'. It can be argued, however, that such a dichotomy over-simplifies the issues. This chapter, while arguably not overcoming all the problems associated with categorization and simplification (for a fuller discussion see Brownill, 1997), identifies five approaches, briefly summarised as: 'problem' focus, gender blind, liberal, essentialist, and 'thinking difference'. Each not only has particular theoretical under-pinnings but also carries with it certain policy implications.[2] This section briefly summarises each approach, while examples of how they have materialised within urban policy itself follow.

'Problem focus' and gender blindness

Turning to the first two of these perspectives, there is a recurring theme within urban policy of problematizing women's role in the inner city or 'areas of deprivation', underpinned by theories of social pathology or the underclass. As we shall see, at a variety of points in history it is women's role as mothers, and especially as 'bad' or single mothers, that is seen as an indicator of 'problem' areas and a contributory factor to the social malaise and poverty with which policy is confronted. Thus policy does not have to be gender blind to have a negative impact on women in the urban environment, a point missed if May's (1997) dichotomy is followed.

For other approaches to the urban problem the term gender blind may ostensibly be more appropriate. In the 1970s and 1980s the primacy ascribed to the economic as the causal factor in inner-city decline from both the Left and the Right led to the exclusion of gender from the urban policy agenda and a failure to recognise any differences within the populations who would supposedly benefit from such policies (Green and Chapman, 1992; Brownill, 1993). In the 1990s there was a similar tendency to use buzzwords or slogans such as regeneration, partnership, empowerment and social exclusion as universalistic terms without thinking through the different experiences, expectations and impacts they hold for different sections of the population. Yet these policies and strategies carry major implications for women and operate within a society in which sexism and discrimination still operate. Both these approaches fail to recognise and take into account gender rela-tions in the analysis of the urban policy.

Alternative perspectives

Approaches that do seek to address the gender dimensions of urban policy have come from a variety of areas indicating that the 'gender aware' category is itself differentiated. In writing about feminist geography McDowell (1993a, 1993b) lists three currents of thought: rationalist or empiricist feminism; antirational or feminist standpoint theory, and postrational or postmodern feminism (see also Harding, 1987), here translated, maybe somewhat loosely, into liberal, essentialist and 'thinking difference' respectively.

Within liberal feminism a body of literature has developed based on the analysis that the spatial reflects and reinforces social relations, including those of gender (see, for example, McDowell, 1983, 1993a, 1993b; McDowell and Sharp, 1997; Booth, Darke and Yeandle, 1996; Little, Peake and Richardson, 1988; Matrix, 1984). Studies showed how the structure and governance of the built environment affect women. Women's differential use of space and therefore the impact, for example, of transport policies and housing based on the separation of home and work, have been well documented in such studies. The predominance of the nuclear family norm in housing design, urban policy and access to housing has been shown to discriminate against women (Roberts, 1991). Women's safety in the city has also been highlighted (Valentine, 1989). Given the spatial focus of urban policy, the importance of this analysis is clear despite the fact that most of the literature has chosen to ignore it (but see LGIU, 1994). Such feminist critiques have shown how women are included in urban policy through their involvement in action around such issues as housing and play space and yet also excluded from power and influence by the ways in which consultation, decision-making bodies and policy processes operate (Brownill and Darke, 1998; Riseborough, 1997; Gilroy, 1996). Such grassroots involvement by women challenges the assumptions made in much of the academic and policy literature that the community is undifferentiated and that there are no gender dimensions to power relations either within the community or between the community and outside agencies.

Translated into policy, this approach can be linked with attempts largely at the level of urban local government to devise and implement policies that recognise and address women's needs in the built environment, such as the establishment of women's committees and specific initiatives, for example safe estates for women. Politically, emphasis has been also placed on widening consultation and funding women's organisations to ensure women's voices were heard within the city. This basically liberal approach rests on a belief in the power of the State to change women's position and a discourse based on needs, inequality and rights. It has had a limited impact as major change was precluded both by the unwillingness of central government to act on equal opportunities, and by inertia and opposition within the local State itself (Brownill and Halford, 1990; Wainwright and Macintosh, 1987). In addition, the confidence that 'women' can be spoken of as an undifferentiated category was criticised by women of colour and women outside academia. Pateman (1988), in outlining the masculinist assumptions behind liberal political theory, questioned whether reform using existing political structures was possible. Out of these critiques developed new approaches.

The first of these, feminist standpoint, rather than seeing women's relationship with the built environment as signifying the inferiority of women, turned it on its head and celebrated the 'feminine'. Thus women's experience in the city can be seen as liberating (Wilson, 1991) and the basis for the reconstruction of communities (Campbell, 1993). Furthermore, the absence of women from policy making has been used by feminists as an explanation for the fact that planning and other policies have ignored women, with the implication that women's involvement in these structures will change matters (Greed, 1993, 1996). Such approaches can be criticised for being oversimplified and essentialist; however, they have also raised important issues such as the long tradition of women organising within and around the community with their emphasis on the personal being political, and the attention to the process of policy and action, not just the outcomes.

The final strand of thought identified by McDowell (1993a, 1993b) relates to what has been termed 'postmodern' or 'thinking difference'. Such an approach argues against the search for historical certainty and explanatory categories in the face of the recognition of diversity and difference. Taken to its extreme this would preclude the use of a category such as gender (along with class, race and capital); instead the focus should be on 'multiple differences, none of which are theoretically privileged' and the 'replacement of the subject woman with a new notion of partial and fractured identities' (McDowell, 1993b, p. 310). However, feminist writers and theorists have been keen not to throw the baby out with the bathwater; thus writers have insisted on the retention of some notion of gender while simultaneously exploring the differences between women and the interconnections of gender with other relations in the urban environment (McDowell, 1993a, 1993b). The challenge is to translate this approach into the policy arena to suggest strategies for change. Sandercock (1998) has made an interesting start to this within the field of urban planning and later sections of this chapter discuss the beginnings of such an approach within urban policy. In the following section I provide a chronology of urban policy and indicate how, when and where these different approaches have had a bearing on urban policy and the lives of women in cities.

A chronology of women and urban policy

It is possible to distinguish four phases of urban policy, as detailed below. Historical accounts of urban policy are not new (see, for example, Atkinson and Moon, 1994) but none has attempted to trace the gender dimensions to this history. It is not intended to imply that we are seeing a linear progression to a more acceptable policy but rather to trace the impact, challenges and limitations of different theories, ideologies and policies.

The beginnings of urban policy: 1968–77

A distinctively urban policy did not emerge in Britain until 1968 with the announcement of the Urban Programme and the Community Development Project (CDP). At this time society was undergoing its cyclical rediscovery of poverty but discussion was of 'pockets of deprivation' within specified urban areas rather than of a general problem. Behind these programmes was a social pathology interpretation of the reasons for poverty. People were not poor because of structural issues within society but because of their own failings and characteristics. A 'cycle of deprivation' existed caused by ill health, children suffering from deprivation, consequent delinquency, unstable marriages, ill health and the cycle starts again (CDP brief, quoted in Green and Chapman, 1992). They therefore had to be helped to 'pull themselves up by their bootstraps' and get themselves out of poverty.

As already noted, according to this problem-focus perspective, women and especially single parents contributed to the decline of inner urban areas by being poor mothers and transmitting poverty to their offspring. The percentage of one-parent families was one of many indicators used by the DoE to identify 'deprived' areas. As with race, the complexities of gender in the urban environment were passed over in favour of a simplistic labelling.

Alternative perspectives at the time unfortunately only added to the marginalisation of women. The CDP involved 12 action research projects in defined areas of Britain. They rejected the social pathology interpretation of the causes of inner-city decline in favour of a structural analysis of economic decline. Heavily influenced by Marxist economics, the CDP argued that economic restructuring and not the people in those areas caused the problems of the inner city. But as indicated above, this concentration on the economic was to the exclusion of gender relations; instead, women's position was seen through the blinkers of a strict political-economy approach. Thus women's roles as workers and as trade unionists were seen as appropriate areas for action while one CDP banned work on play and related issues as 'soft and uncontentious'. Nevertheless, even though women workers were acknowledged, it was the largely male world of manufacturing industry that was the focus of attention and policy. The call for the creation of 'real' jobs often ignored sectors of employment employing women. Women's organising in the community, for example around housing issues, was marginalized in favour of those issues deemed 'structural' and amenable to political action by organised (male) labour (Green and Chapman, 1992).

Yet there were some openings, for example the concentration on social pathology within urban policy offered some benefits for women. The Urban Programme, the other urban experiment at that time, provided local authorities in areas of need (which as we have seen were partially determined by the numbers of single-parent families within them) with funding for capital and revenue projects. This enabled significant funding of local voluntary organisations, among which were organisations either run by women or which aimed to provide resources and facilities to meet their needs. Thus, in the late 1970s and early 1980s, projects like the Surrey Docks Childcare Campaign gained funding not only for facilities but also to work with local women in raising confidence and consciousness. On the ground, alternative definitions were emerging.

1977: the White Paper on the inner cities

In 1977 the first White Paper relating exclusively to the inner city was published. It reflected the shift to the economic interpretation of urban problems initiated by the CDP and given weight by other government studies. Four reasons were cited for inner city decline – and none of them contained a gender dimension. The result was a shift in funding from social to economic projects. Although projects such as the Lewisham and Haringey Women's Employment Projects were still funded by the Urban Programme it is likely that this shift disproportionately affected women's groups.[3]

A further change from 1977 was in the governance of urban policy, from local authorities to 'partnerships' between central and local government. Formal partnership committees were established in key areas representing a centralisation of power that was to be taken further in the agency structures of the 1980s. As we show later, such shifts in local democracy have major implications for the involvement of women in the formulation and implementation of urban policy.

Urban policy in the 1980s: privatisation and alternatives

The 1980s witnessed a plethora of different, sometimes conflicting, approaches to urban policy, all with their own implications for women. At a national level, with the election of a radical rightwing government the urban problem was reinterpreted as a result of the crowding out of private-sector investment by public-sector activity. What was needed was to sweep away the red tape of local authority bureaucracy and replace it with a style of governance that would encourage private-sector led regeneration. Benefits from this private sector activity (usually speculative property development) would then 'trickle down' to an undifferentiated local population. If this did not work the problem was one of a population unwilling to become part of the enterprise economy. At the local level, alternative approaches were being carried out, which included policies and processes specifically aimed at women. This section will focus on two manifestations of these approaches: the London Docklands Development Corporation (LDDC) and the Greater London Council (GLC).

The LDDC was one of the first Urban Development Corporations (UDCs) set up in 1981. UDCs were the flagship of government regeneration and, although little has been written about the gender implications of UDCs (but see Brownill,1990; Docklands Childcare Project, 1996; Women in Docklands, 1994), it is possible to use them as illustrative of the impact of the New Right urban policy concentrating on two main issues: overall strategy and governance.

UDCs began the trend of what has been termed 'entrepreneurial governance': short-lived, single-issue agencies run by government appointees (not elected politicians) with a 'can-do' as opposed to a red-tape mentality. Du Gay (1996) has pointed out the negative implications for equality of such structures. The fact that the 12 LDDC board members only ever included one woman at any one time and often none shows how women are disadvantaged in appointments through patronage. Whether or not a lone woman board member is seen as speaking for women she clearly cannot represent the variety in women's interests and her presence does not guarantee power and influence. Women's input is also reduced when consultation is no longer required by law and is curtailed by the necessity of speed. The LDDC operated with a view of the community as a homogenous 'other' not structured along lines of gender, race or class, resulting in consultation policies that did not explicitly set out to seek women's views unless a specific worker made it a priority.

The overall LDDC strategy was initially one of physical regeneration – the transformation of the inner city through flagship property developments. This accelerated the trend we noted earlier of downplaying social projects and strategies, which had in the past provided an opening for women's organising in the inner city. The strategy of attracting private-sector, corporate investment also led to the marketing of development opportunities in particular ways. Thus images of (male) executives windsurfing in their lunch hours while clutching a mobile phone and the development of a 'businessmen's' (*sic*) airport in the Royal Docks were promoted. The property professions are dominated by men (Greed, 1993): this too helps explain why 1980s regeneration ignored women's needs.

The transformation of space into the 'man-made world' of the bright, new, shiny Docklands is worth noting. The 'thrusting' tower of Canary Wharf leaves little to the imagination in terms of the links between men and corporate power and their domination of the landscape. (Indeed, it is nicknamed the winking finger by local people due to the flashing lights on the top to warn aircraft.) The privatisation of space, with little public open space, dependence on private transport (women have less access to cars), the lack of social facilities and the reliance on housing for sale (as women have lower incomes in general, households headed by women are more likely to be excluded from areas of high owner occupation) all served to underline this.

Yet there were contradictions in the UDC. From the late 1980s there was a shift towards a more social remit with investment in community projects and a greater attention to community investment. Within this, space for women was opened up. For example, the LDDC's Community Services Division began to provide childcare and other facilities in the area. However, rather than indicating a shift in strategy or a redefinition of regeneration, these issues remained marginal to the overall programme (Brownill, 1993). The attention to mixed development in flagship developments held within it the possibility of creating environments where work, home and facilities are close by, thus breaking down the separate sphere of women's place in the home which some writers have referred to (see, for example, Mackenzie, 1989). Finally, notwithstanding the question of whether property speculation represents an effective way of reviving local employment, one spin-off of property development was largely service-sector and office-based employment, a sector of the economy employing disproportionate numbers of women and replacing the male world in the docks.

This echoes recent writing that has been keen to show the positive aspects of the inner city for women (for example, Bondi, 1991; Warde, 1991; Wekerle, 1984). These writers, echoing a standpoint or essential-ist view, show that inner-city areas can offer more suitable environ-ments for women not fitting the suburban family norm (for example, Duncan et al., 1991, have shown large numbers of single women living in inner London) and seeking to combine working with family respon-sibilities. Although it is arguable that the movement of such households into the inner city represents gentrification rather than regeneration and may be displacing other, less affluent women, this is an example of the reversal of the view of the inner city as being a threat to women and stresses the positive role of women within regeneration.

Alternative voices in the 1980s

As indicated earlier, local government at this time was actively pursu-ing alternatives. Often these approaches took as a strategic starting point women's differential experience of the urban environment referred to earlier. For example, the GLC publication *Changing Places* (GLC, 1986) saw gender as a land-use issue. The report aimed at transforming urban space from a women's perspective through policies relating to transport, shopping, the environment and housing. 'Women in London live in a city built by men for men and have little opportunity to shape or influ-ence the urban environment. Planning policies . . . can go a long way towards changing this' (p. 2). Attempts were made to open up the struc-tures and processes of local government to women through women's committees, widening consultation processes and confronting and hopefully changing the attitudes of officers and members alike. Initia-tives such as popular planning, the promotion of bottom-up policy for-mation and recruitment policies were also seen as ways of increasing women's power and influence.

While the possibilities opened up by this approach cannot be under-estimated, the limitations should be pointed out. Wilson (1991) sees such a narrow approach as repeating the paternalism of traditional town planning. Another example from Docklands serves as a further illustra-tion. The People's Plan for the Royal Docks was intended as an alter-native 'bottom-up' plan to the proposed 'businessmen's' airport, but women working on the plan came up against the same problems of mar-ginalisation and trivialisation of women's issues (see Brownill, 1990). It was, in the words of one women involved, the male, macho stuff in the docks that grabbed the attention. In terms of processes of popular planning, the pyramidal hierarchy of the GLC and the need to meet manifesto commitments clashed with the ways in which women and others were organising in the community, making links between the local, the personal and the political. While I have argued elsewhere about the dangers of setting up a dichotomy between formal/masculine and informal/feminine forms of political organising (Brownill and Halford, 1990) this area of women's political organising in the city remains to be adequately understood and supported by policy.

The 1990s: empowerment, partnership and social exclusion

The 1990s represent a very different urban policy environment yet many of the trends we have already noted remain. A new consensus is emerging centred on buzzwords such as partnership, empowerment and social exclusion. Potentially, this can open up space for women, but what are the implications of these developments in practice? On the one hand we can see a return to a gender-blind approach in much of government policy, practice and research on urban policy. However, there are also attempts to put gender more centre stage and to think through difference and diversity.

The aims of national urban policy initiatives in the early 1990s, such as City Challenge and the Single Regeneration Budget (SRB), included 'holistic', that is, not solely physical regeneration. Objectives of strengthening community capacity and meeting the needs of ethnic minorities appeared as a welcome change from the 1980s, but again there was no specific reference to gender. Since the change of government in 1997 the emphasis has shifted to social exclusion, but this is discussed in universal terms and the gender dimension is largely ignored (Darke and Brownill, 1999). Urban policy is characterised by 'target fetishism' (Gray, 1997) and is output driven. This concentration on the tangibles, such as numbers of jobs, can down-play the importance of the intangibles such as the processes and relationships of regeneration and leads to the favouring of 'hard' economic targets as opposed to 'soft' social ones, again with a disproportionate effect on women.

When we look at another mantra of 1990s regeneration – partnerships – the same invisibility holds true. Partnerships are the new form of governance for urban policy, bringing together the public, private and voluntary sectors. Government guidelines for 'effective partnerships' make no mention of the need to ensure that the make-up of partnership boards and the consultation they undertake reflects the composition of the local population (DoE, 1997). Women are still underrepresented on partnership boards, although they are present in greater numbers than on UDCs (Riseborough, 1997). The way power operates in partnerships is also important. For example, Gilroy (1996) states that while outsiders saw a community development trust board she studied as an attempt to meet as equals, for community representatives it was characterised as patronage. This was overlaid by gender relations as the public- and private-sector representatives were mainly male and those from the community women. As one community representative said, 'there is something about men in suits which makes me fall silent'. Thus the forms of governance of urban policy in the 1990s raises serious implications for the power and influence of women within urban policy which are being largely ignored.

As with policy, a plethora of policy-oriented research aimed at improving the policy and practice of area regeneration has been produced which takes no account of gender relations. For example, Stewart and Taylor (1996), in a review of this literature, comment on 'the invisibility of gender as an issue in estate empowerment, despite the fact that many of the leading activists are women' (p. 43), thus illustrating the impact of the naturalisation of women's role in the urban environment. Yet neither they nor others seriously challenge this invisibility: in their own review of empowerment as a concept informing current theory and practice, gender (and race) are not considered in the discussion on barriers that result in differential access to power. Thus within the literature on estate and urban regeneration the significance of gender is implicitly recognised, yet it is omitted from the analysis, policy recommendations and research.

There are examples of where gender and regeneration are being considered, again from a variety of perspectives. Power and Tunstall (1997), studying various estates which experienced riots in the early 1990s, state that 'the special characteristic of these areas concerned the economic and social status of the inhabitants, and in particular, the young men' (p. ix). Again there is a 'problem focus' to the gender analysis but the primary concentration is on the behaviour of young men rather than a comprehensive account of gender relations within these. We also have a recurrence of the social pathology thesis in that the authors quote contributory factors as 'poor quality parenting', 'depression and irritability in mothers', 'lack of adequate mothering' as well as a lack of male role models within the family. Once again women as mothers are seen as part of the problem of our cities and not as part of the solution. As Kleinmann (1998) points out, many ministerial statements on social exclusion use similar underclass references.

Campbell (1993) approaches the same events and estates from a different perspective. For her men and women react to the situation they find themselves in on the estates in different ways: men respond with crime and destruction and women with survival and solidarity and notes that 'the redoubts of active citizenship on these estates were run by women' (p. 247). She thus challenges the negative assumption that lone parents are part of the problem and depicts them rather as the glue that keeps the areas together. She argues that the underclass and associated theses are 'anti-feminist', blaming the women for not managing men, and notes how women activists, with little or no access to the political elite, are let down by the policy and political system which does not know how to support their attempts to change their areas. While some have criticised Campbell for being essentialist – women = good, men = bad – women are at least put on the map in her analysis and issues of women's organising raised.

We can also see in the 1990s some initial attempts to think through urban regeneration, taking as a starting point the diversity of experiences and expectations of issues such as regeneration and exclusion (Gilroy, 1996; May, 1997; Brownill and Darke, 1998). May (1997), for example, points out how women's experience of poverty and living in regeneration areas has its own dimensions. Gilroy (1996) takes this idea of recognising the diversity in the community further. She cautions that 'outsiders' view a community in terms of 'place' and assume all residents share the same values and concerns, while the reality is very different. In talking about empowerment she shows how there can be different routes to power for different sections of the community. In the community she writes about, job creation and job-related training were seen as a strategy favoured by and directed towards men, while women were often taking a lower-key path. For them, the need for self-esteem was paramount and she quotes the example of activities which started around the local nursery school where an enlightened head encouraged and set aside space for parents to get together. From this, community businesses developed and an active group involving men and women around parenting. There are also 'general lessons about nurturing different capabilities and forms of governance'.

Brownill and Darke (1998), through an analysis of both gender and race in urban regeneration, have attempted to build strategies for inclusive regeneration based on a similar recognition of diversity within regeneration areas. As with empowerment, they argue, regeneration should not be seen as a monolithic goal but as one that has multiple goals with different routes to them. Far from leading to fragmentation, they show how such a strategy can be made central to regeneration through a number of steps, including: making sure baseline information includes gender-specific data; applying equal opportunities conditions to partnerships; ensuring capacity building involves all actors, not just the community; involving local people in the processes and delivery of regeneration; setting gender-specific targets, monitoring these and ensuring national policy takes a more central lead in promoting gender issues – in effect, mainstreaming them.

These developing approaches are making more explicit the analysis and practice that has been emerging during the 30 years of urban policy in the UK. While still in their formative stages and not immune from some of the same criticisms made of other initiatives, they show that gender relations and diversity within the community are important, not just for analysing what happens in these areas but also as a basis for structuring policy and governance.

Conclusions

The above discussion has revealed a variety of perspectives on women and urban policy. In the conclusions I want to build on this by briefly outlining a number of issues which deserve further exploration in terms of extending the positive in existing work.

First, we have seen how a variety of approaches to women and regeneration have operated both in the past and present. At the level of theory, while this article outlined an initial framework there is still much work to be done to refine and develop this. It is important that urban policy analysis and evaluation moves from the current lack of engagement with the gender dimensions of regeneration to highlight the implications for women of policies, processes and outcomes. May's (1997) suggestion of a gender audit of national regeneration policy would be a significant step in this direction.

Second, there is a need to recognise the diversity that exists within the community and the urban environment. Communities are not homogenous, nor indeed are categories such as 'women'. An emphasis on diversity recognises the role women play within regeneration and challenges the view within urban policy which sees women only as 'problems'. That spatial policy is dealing with an urban environment itself influenced by gender relations has to be made clear along with the fact that for different localities the ways in which social relations and politics are gendered will have an impact on policy formation and implementation.

Third, there must be a critical engagement with the structures and processes of urban policy governance. The contradictory potential of the impact of 'entrepreneurial governance' and the short-life, partnership agencies which now proliferate within urban policy on equal opportunities has been noted. Ways of promoting the inclusion of women and minimising the exclusion and the reinforcement of gendered inequalities in power and influence must be considered.

Fourth, policies themselves need to be more attuned to difference. Concepts such as 'regeneration' need to be examined for their implications and meanings for diverse groups in the community. An important aspect of this is the recognition of different routes to empowerment and regeneration, as Gilroy points out (Gilroy, 1996). Talk of 'unleashing the potential' (Taylor, 1995) can only be meaningful when it is recognised that people will have different aspirations as to what their potential is, different ways of reaching it and different demands for support, action and policy along the way. Attention to process as opposed to the current output fetishism could be an important starting point.

And finally, while it is a well-used conclusion that putting gender at the centre can transform theory and practice in ways not solely limited to women, in the case of urban policy it is one which is worth repeating.

Notes

1 No universally accepted definition of urban policy exists; however, in this chapter the term refers to spatially bounded policies aimed at 'turning round' particular urban areas deemed to be in decline or suffering from high levels of deprivation.
2 I am grateful to my colleague Jane Darke for initial ideas towards such a classification. As ever, any problems with the end results are mine alone.
3 Munt (1994) shows clearly how the shift from social to economic funding reduced the funding of ethnic minority groups by the urban programme.

References

Atkinson, R. and Moon, G. (1994) *Urban Policy in the UK*. London: Macmillan.
Bondi, L. (1991) 'Gender Divisions and Gentrification: a Critique'. *Transactions, Institute of British Geographers*, 16, 190–8.
Booth, C., Darke, J. and Yeandle, S. (1996) *Changing Places*. London: Paul Chapman.
Brownill, S. (1990) 'The People's Plan for the Royal Docks; Some Contradictions in Popular Planning'. In J. Montgomery and A. Thornley (eds), *Radical Planning Initiatives*, Aldershot: Gower.

Brownill, S. (1993) *Developing London's Docklands*. London: Paul Chapman (2nd edn).

Brownill, S. (1997) 'Regen (d)eration: Women and Urban Policy in the UK'. Paper presented to the Women and the City Conference, Oxford, September 1997.

Brownill, S. and Darke, J. (1998) *Rich Mix: Strategies for Inclusive Regeneration*. Bristol: Policy Press.

Brownill, S. and Halford, S. (1990) 'Understanding Women's Involvement in Local Politics'. *Political Geography Quarterly*, 9(4), 396–414.

Campbell, B. (1993) *Goliath*. London: Virago.

Darke, J. and Brownill, S. (1999) 'A New Deal for Inclusivity?' Paper presented to Planning Research Conference, Sheffield, March 1999.

Docklands Childcare Project (1996) *How To Plan for the Under-Fives and Their Parents*. London: Docklands Childcare Project.

DoE (Department of the Environment) (1997) *Effective Partnerships: A Handbook for Members of SRB Challenge Fund Partnerships*. London: HMSO.

Du Gay (1996) 'Organising Identity: Entrepreneurial Governance and Public Management'. In S. Hall and P. Du Gay (eds), *Questions of Culture and Identity*, London: Sage.

Duncan, S., Eyles, J. and Baigent, M. (1991) *Gender divisions of labour in Britain*. Working Paper 77, University of Sussex Centre for Urban and Regional Research, Brighton.

Gilroy, R. (1996) 'Helping to Build A New Framework'. Paper presented to ACSP/AESOP (American Collegiate Schools of Planning/Association of European Schools of Planning) Conference, Toronto, July 1996.

Gray, A. (1997) 'Contract Culture and Target Fetishism'. *Local Economy*, February: 343–57.

GLC (Greater London Council) (1986) *Changing Places*. London: GLC.

Greed, C. (1993) *Women and Planning*. London: Routledge.

Greed, C. (1996) 'Urban Spatial Policy: A European Gender Perspective'. *European Spatial Research and Policy*, 3(1), 47–61.

Green, J. and Chapman, A. (1992) 'The British Community Development Project; Lessons for Today'. *Community Development Journal*, 27(3), 242–58.

Harding, S. (1987) *Feminism and Methodology*. Milton Keynes: Open University.

Kleinman, M. (1998) 'Include Me Out? The New Politics of Place and Poverty'. CASE paper 11, London: London School of Economics.

Little, J., Peake, L. and Richardson, P. (1988) *Women in Cities*. Basingstoke: Macmillan.

LGIU (Local Government Information Unit) (1994) *Women and Urban Regeneration*. London: LGIU.

McDowell, L. (1983) 'Towards an Understanding of the Gender Division of Urban Space'. *Environment and Planning D*, 1, 59–72.

McDowell, L. (1993a) 'Space, Place and Gender Relations: Part 1. Feminist Empiricism and the Geography of Social Relations'. *Progress in Human Geography*, 17(2), 157–79.

McDowell, L. (1993b) 'Space, Place and Gender Relations; Part II. Identity, Difference, Feminist Geometries and Geographies'. *Progress in Human Geography*, 17(3), 305–18.

McDowell, L. and Sharp, P. (1997) *Space, Gender and Knowledge*. London: Arnold.

Mackenzie, S. (1989) 'Women in the City'. In R. Peet and N. Thrift (eds), *New Models in Geography, 2*, London: Unwin Hyman.

Matrix (1994) *Making Space: Women and the Man-Made Environment*. London: Pluto.

May, N. (1997) *Challenging Assumptions: Gender Assumptions in Urban Regeneration*, York: YPS.

Munt, I. (1994) Race, Urban Policy and Urban Problems. In H. Thomas and V. Krishnarayan (eds), *Race Equality and Planning: Policies and Procedures*, Aldershot: Avebury.

Pateman, C. (1988) *The Sexual Contract*. Cambridge: Polity Press.

Power, A. and Tunstall, A. (1997) *Dangerous Disorder*. York: Policy Press.

Riseborough, M. (1997) *The Gender Report: Women and Regional Regeneration in the West Midlands*. Birmingham: Centre for Urban and Regional Studies.

Roberts, M. (1991) *Living in a Man Made World*. London: Routledge.

Sandercock, L. (1998) *Towards Cosmopolis*. London: Wiley.

Stewart, M. and Taylor, M. (1996) *Empowerment and Estate Regeneration*. York: Policy Press.

Taylor, M. (1995) *Unleashing the Potential*, York: Policy Press.

Valentine, G. (1989) 'The Geography of Women's Fear'. *Area*, 21, 385–90.

Wainwright, H. and Macintosh, M. (1987) *A Taste of Power*. London: Verso.

Warde, A. (1991) 'Gentrification as Consumption'. *Environment and Planning D: Society and Space*, 9, 223–32.

Wekerle, G. (1994) 'A Woman's Place is in the City'. *Antipode*, 16(3), 145–53.

Wilson, E. (1991) *The Sphinx in the City*. London: Virago.

Women in Docklands (1994) Unpublished discussion paper to Docklands Forum, London.

10
Servicing the City: Women's Employment in Oxford

Satya Kartara and Hilary Simpson

Introduction

Slap in the middle of England stands the city of Oxford, on an ancient crossroads, where two rivers meet to form the Thames, the site of one of the world's oldest and most famous universities. In this lies a paradox for women in the city. On the one hand it can be taken as a national paradigm for the position of women in the labour market. Women work in all the usual occupations and as such contribute enormously to the city. Yet when it comes to the academic sphere, a large minority of women are much more highly qualified than the national average.

So, what role does women's employment play in a city such as Oxford? One type of answer can be provided by simply imagining for a moment the impact that a withdrawal of labour by working women would have on the local economy and the local community. It is unlikely that any primary school would be open, and most secondary schools would also be forced to close. The city's hospitals would be shut, together with a high proportion of health centres and other healthcare services. Old people's homes, nursing homes and day centres in the city would be left unstaffed. The public and academic libraries would shut their doors. Most shops, banks, hotels and restaurants would be closed. The fire service and possibly the police service would be able to function only in respect of their emergency roles – and they would probably need to, since public order would be in danger of breaking down.

Those who were not involved in the strike – including the vice-chancellors of the two universities and most of their professors, the majority of the heads of colleges, the chief executives of the City

Council, the County Council and the city's healthcare hospitals and services, and the leaders of most of the city's institutions and businesses – would find Oxford an eerily quiet place on such a day, so heavily does the infrastructure of the city now depend on the services provided by working women. (To imagine the additional consequences of a simultaneous withdrawal of women's domestic labour is beyond the scope of this essay.)

Such a fantasy makes it clear that women run a city such as Oxford in the sense of keeping it going and enabling it to function. It is equally clear that women do not run it in the sense of holding the key symbolic and decision-making positions. Women are essentially responsible for servicing the city.

Labour market trends and characteristics in Britain

The 1990s saw the biggest increase in women entering employment in Britain. During this decade the proportion of the workforce who were women reached 50 per cent (Briely, 1996). During the recession in 1993 there was a 2.8 million fall in the number of men in work, while there was a 2 million rise in the number of women in work. Future predictions are that the trend of women's growing participation in the labour market is set to continue. Despite these encouraging statistics regarding the rise of women in the labour market, inequality persists as the majority of women remain in low-paid, low-status jobs (Walby, 1990; Cockburn, 1991).

The disadvantage faced by women entering the labour market is levied on them by discriminatory forces inextricably linked to patriarchy. Walby (1990) defines patriarchy as a 'system of social structures and practices in which men dominate, oppress and exploit women' (p. 20). This system of patriarchy is based on gender power relations whereby men assume a right to control women. Much of the continued disadvantage is the direct result of everyday policies and practices within organisations, where a complex web of myths and outdated beliefs about the appropriate roles of women and men has perpetuated the belief that women are not suited to positions of power and influence. These traditional beliefs include notions of women as nurturers and carers who are suited to household tasks and men as the breadwinners in the institution of the family (Scott, 1994). These ideas also include images of women as the objects of men's desire, so that women are dichotomised as madonnas or whores. Neither lends itself to the concept of powerful, influential, decision makers.

Cockburn (1991) claims that patriarchy is not just a word used by feminists to rebuke men, nor is it a term which is outdated. She states that 'It is an important dimension of the nature of modern societies, whether capitalist or state socialist. It is a living reality, a system that quite observably shapes the lives and differentiates the chances of women and men' (p. 18). Thus patriarchy continues to discriminate against women in the workplace through the unequal division of labour. Women are subjected to both horizontal and vertical occupational segregation. Horizontal segregation sex-types jobs into masculine and feminine jobs. Through gender segregation different values and remuneration are attached to men's jobs and women's jobs. Most female-dominated occupations are characterised by low status, low pay and limited access to skills acquisition, promotion or training (Meehan, 1985). Some women's jobs are 'economic ghettos', where low pay and few benefits are expected as the norm. Women's aspirations are blocked and their talents are wasted because their choice of occupation is limited to a subset of options (Wilson, 1995; Ledwith and Colgan, 1996). Vertical segregation occurs when men are in higher grades within an occupation and women are segregated into lower grades. This happens despite the fact that women may have the same or higher qualifications as men doing similar jobs. Universities provide a clear example, as will be seen below.

Scott (1994) argues that economic changes such as increased participation in the labour market, and changes in family structure such as increased divorce rates and single parenthood, have done little to change attitudes about women's and men's roles. The essentialist beliefs about gender, embodied in the notions of strength, dexterity and sensitivity, play a fundamental role in the sex-typing of jobs which is sustained by tradition as much as by the rational strategies of individual employers and employees.

Organisations are part of wider society and thus organisational cultures reflect traditional views and values about the appropriate role of women. Organisational cultures are defined in terms of the symbols, language and practices which determine the 'shared values (what is important), and beliefs (how things work) that create behavioural norms (the way we do things around here) which guide the activities of organisational members' (Itzin and Newman, 1995). The cultural norms in organisations are gendered, and deeply imbedded beliefs and values discriminate against women in terms of the way they are structured and organised: for example, working practices such as senior managers being expected to work hours that are incompatible with most women's domestic responsibilities, lack of opportunity for women to enter senior positions within organisations (sometimes there is positive obstruction to women doing so), stereotyping within interview processes and job segregation. Gendered organisational cultures operate on an informal basis; there are no written rules or regulations. They are not articulated in verbal or written form; the actual discrimination is almost invisible because 'it is the way it is' (Barrett, 1988; Walby, 1990). These processes are powerful because they are regarded as perfectly natural, yet they stop women from achieving their potential. However, women play a fundamental role in the labour market.

This paper explores women's experience of the labour market in Oxford, a city made up of a mosaic of women from different cultures, and different social and educational backgrounds. Women from these different communities have similarities as well as differences. Most women face some form of inequality within the labour market. But it can take different forms and affects different women to different degrees.

Women's employment in Oxford

In numerical terms women are not a minority group in the city's labour market. However, a recent survey conducted by a local women's organisation shows that women's participation in the labour force is differentially represented across the sectors. Table 10.1 clearly demonstrates a high degree of job segregation within the Oxford labour market (Hoare, 1998). The majority of working women are located in caring jobs or in the service sector. The national trend is replicated through vertical just as it is through horizontal segregation, as few women work in management positions in Oxford (Hoare, 1998).

One explanation among others for women remaining in low-paid, low-status jobs is to do with women's lack of qualifications. This is one area where Oxford is atypical. Recently, a household survey conducted by Oxford City Council (1999) found that Oxford's population was far better qualified than the national average, for both women and men. In the case of women in 1998, 26 per cent had a degree or higher qualifications, while nationally only 8 per cent obtained qualifications at this level. Fifteen per cent of women in Oxford as compared to 10 per cent nationally were qualified to diploma level. These figures arise because Oxford has a large proportion of residents with academic connections. However, there are some groups in the city who are less well qualified and those figures are more consistent with national trends. For example,

Table 10.1   Women's employment in Oxford

Employment sector	Women employed %
Construction industry	8.3
Manufacturing	6.4
Printing	28.7
Publishing	62.0
Information technology	43.4
Research and development	35.8
Healthcare	85
Retail and service sector	55
High street retail	81.6
Construction products retail	33.3
Public transport	8.9
Security	6.5
Financial services	50.2
Education and public sector Administration	58.8
Film, video and design	18.2

Source: survey conducted for Oxford Women's Training Scheme (Hoare, 1998).

the 1996/97 General Household Survey (Office for National Statistics 1996/97) found that 36 per cent of the national population had no formal qualifications, whilst in 1998 the Oxford Household Survey showed that 29 per cent of Oxford's citizens had no formal qualifications.

In many ways Oxford is a divided city with the university and people connected with it on one side and the 'local residents' on the other. There are people facing poverty and disadvantage living in the shadow of affluence and privilege. Areas such as Rose Hill, East Oxford, Blackbird Leys, Barton and St Clements have been identified as areas of high deprivation. All have been the subject of successful bids for the Government's Single Regeneration Budget. Oxford has 2000 lone mothers living on income support, many with few or no formal qualifications. These women face the dilemmas of remaining at home and looking after children or taking the step of going out to work and falling into the poverty trap. The real dilemma starts when women are faced with the reality that low levels of qualifications attract low-paid work. Then there is the problem of childcare: most women find that little or no affordable childcare is available in the city. Most women in these circumstances have little choice but to remain on state benefits and hence in poverty. The New Labour government is beginning to make some provision to help women stuck in the benefit trap through the New Deal for Lone Parents programmes. Nonetheless, most women find that the transition from benefits to work is difficult, that childcare is one of the biggest barriers to taking that step and the lack of affordable, quality childcare is one of the biggest barriers.

Ethnic minorities

One fact about Oxford which many people living outside the city find surprising is the high concentration of people from ethnic minority communities. A recent survey conducted by Oxford City Council shows that 10.6 per cent of the city is of African Caribbean or South Asian descent. In terms of employment women from ethnic minority communities are more likely to be unemployed than their white counterparts; the national unemployment rates for ethnic minority women (combining all groups) aged 16 and over are 18 per cent compared to 8 per cent for white women (Cabinet Office, 1999).

The employment patterns for women in Oxford show that 53.7 per cent of South Asian women were economically active while 65.7 per cent of white women were economically active (Oxford City Council, 1998). However, these figures may not be giving the whole picture. The South Asian community in Oxford is a mosaic of diversity. It includes people of different religions, people who speak different languages, eat different food, people from different class and caste systems and those who have varying degrees of exposure to the white community. Many South Asian women are subject to cultural and religious values which constrain them from working outside the home. Anecdotal and observational data shows that much higher numbers of South Asian women may be economically active within the city than appears in official statistics. One of the reasons for the discrepancy is the tendency for South Asian women to work for the family business.

South Asian communities on the whole have a preference for self-employment. The reasons for this vary from the immigrant minorities desire to do well in a new country to their preference of self-employment as a reaction against the barriers and blocks they face from the dominant society. Jenkins (1984) termed this 'the reaction model', with ethnic minority self-employment being looked at as a reaction against racism and blocked avenues of occupational mobility, a survival strategy for coping on the margins of the white-dominated mainstreams of the economy (p. 231).

The majority of businesses run by South Asians in Oxford are located in the small business sector, such as grocery shops and newsagents, with the major area being restaurants. Most of the women who work in the these businesses work mainly behind the scenes; back of house rather than front of house. The women will be engaged in tasks such as book-keeping, stock taking, shelf filling after hours, cleaning, cooking for the business, etc. Although these are skills which could attract remuneration in the labour market most of the women tend not to gain recognition for their contribution to the business, at least not in the public sphere. From the traditionalist's perspective it is not seen as appropriate for women to be seen as being involved in economic activity, which is perceived as a male domain. One must point out, however, that class distinction plays a major role in the way that women are perceived by the myriad traditions and difference in culture within and among the South Asian community itself.

Anecdotal evidence also identifies home working to be prevalent among South Asian women. Many of these women work long hours sewing soft toys and working on tedious tasks such as threading fish tackle with fishing wire for very little money. Although the work is mundane and tedious, with little financial reward, there seems to be a big demand for home working within the community. Many of the women in this group may have difficulties with the English language and may be unable to access work outside the home as well as facing opposition from family about going out to work. Yet South Asian, women like any other women, want some form of financial independence, and home working provides this without women having to break tradition or be unemployed and looking for work.

However, there is an ever-growing number of South Asian women who are engaging in work outside the home. The majority of these women tend to lack formal qualifications or have qualifications from their native countries which may not be recognised in Britain. These women tend to work in low-status jobs such as cleaning in hospitals and university colleges, which are major employers in the city. Furthermore, Oxford has now its second and third generation of migrants from South Asia. The younger generation of South Asian women are not subjected to the same levels of cultural constraints as their mothers and are taking up jobs outside the home. Again, the majority of these women are working in the unskilled and low-paid sectors, mostly in retail and the service industry.

Part-time workers

Of the 43 500 women employed in Oxford, 55 per cent work full time and 45 per cent work part time. This is in line with the national percentages for women's full- and part-time employment. In contrast, only 15 per cent of male employees in Oxford are part time (although this figure is above the national average).

Part-time work is the pragmatic solution adopted by almost half the working women in Britain to the unresolved dilemma of reconciling their paid work with their domestic (particularly childcare) responsibilities. In this respect the UK is significantly different from other European labour markets. Employed mothers have the second shortest working hours in Europe; the opposite is true for working fathers, who work the longest hours in Europe (Brannen et al., 1997 p. 94). This pattern is linked to the historic lack of formal, affordable childcare in Britain.

The prevalence of part-time working among women in the UK and its impact on the labour market has been well documented; for example in Rubery and Fagan's 1994 study for the Equal Opportunities Commission, which concluded that 'part-time working has now been found in a range of studies to be associated with occupational downgrading and indeed with more segregated employment' (p. 35). The dilemma inherent in the widespread take-up of part-time work by women in Britain is explored at length by Hewitt (1993) where she writes:

> Part-time and flexible employment . . . may do little to improve women's exclusion from the most responsible and rewarding opportunities at work, and even less to challenge men's absenteeism from the home. But the alternative – that women should adopt male working hours and employment patterns – simply does not meet the aspirations of most women. (p. 63).

Very few management-level posts are available on a part-time basis. Nationally, less than 10 per cent of all working women are in management positions and these are mostly full time. It is presumed by employers that higher-level (that is, managerial) jobs cannot be conducted by part-time workers (Hansard Report, 1990). This is largely due to the unwillingness of many employers to explore changes in their organisations which will enable women to move up the hierarchy. The difficulty is that as long as women continue to carry the major responsibility for domestic life they will continue to suffer restrictions put upon them in achieving their full potential in the workplace. Through part-time work women balance paid work with domestic responsibility, but it carries both financial and career disadvantage. Research shows that up to 30 per cent of women's life-time earnings can be lost after having children, mainly due to the return to work part-time (Hansard Report, 1990).

Service sector, service jobs

As well as a typical division between full- and part-time working, women's employment in Oxford also shows a strong concentration in certain key sectors – or, to put it another way, a high degree of segregation. The Annual Employment Survey reveals that eight out of ten women who work in Oxford are employed in the service sector. Nearly a quarter (24 per cent) are working in health and social work; the next most significant sectors are education (17 per cent), public administration (17 per cent) and retail (12 per cent). These four areas of work between them therefore employ seven out of ten of the women working in the city. Men's employment in the city, on the other hand, is more evenly distributed among the various sectors, with the largest groups working in education (16 per cent), public administration (15 per cent) and the car industry and related businesses (12 per cent).

Virginia Woolf, writing 70 years ago, speculated, in *A Room of One's Own* that in a hundred years time women would 'take part in all the activities and exertions that were once denied them. The nursemaid will heave coal. The shopwoman will drive an engine' (Woolf, 1929, p. 61). But the movement of women into the types of jobs traditionally held by men has not materialised to the extent that Woolf and others predicted, partly because the traditional jobs have themselves declined so dramatically in number. The areas in which women are employed still tend, at the beginning of the twenty-first century, to be extensions of their traditional roles within the family: the education of the young, the care of the sick and elderly, and the provision of household goods and services. Women are still, in the main, nursemaids and shopwomen rather than heavers of coal or drivers of engines. The now decimated automobile industry was once the largest employer in Oxford, with women's work there being mainly in the traditional female occupations such as sewing car upholstery, and clerical and canteen work.

A second source of information about women's employment patterns is the census, although the data relates only to women living in Oxford rather than to women working in Oxford, a large proportion of whom commute from outside the city. The 1991 census shows that, among working women resident in Oxford, the largest single group (43 per cent of the total) were employed in professional, administrative or managerial occupations. A further 22 per cent were employed in clerical and secretarial occupations; 12 per cent were employed in occupations such as catering, childcare and cleaning; and 8 per cent were employed in retail and sales, with the remaining 15 per cent spread across a range of other occupations.

At first sight it may appear encouraging that 43 per cent of working women living in Oxford were employed in rather grand-sounding professional, administrative or managerial occupations. However, this is a very broad occupational classification covering virtually all white-collar jobs above the clerical level, with the exception of sales jobs.

Of the large proportion of women in Oxford employed in professional, administrative or managerial occupations, the majority (41 per cent) fall into the subcategory of 'associate professional and technical occupations'. This covers a range of 'support' jobs, including technicians and support workers in health and social welfare. The next largest group (34 per cent) are the professional occupations, which include a number of female-dominated occupations such as nursing, teaching, social work and library work. The smallest group (25 per cent) are the managers and administrators. Women in Oxford, therefore, not only work overwhelmingly within the service sector, they also work predominantly in service roles.

Women in the universities

Given the key role played by the two universities in the life of Oxford, it is revealing to examine women's participation at the two extremes of the academic spectrum – professors on the one hand and contract research staff on the other.

In 1995/96 only 8 per cent of university professors in the UK were women (Griffiths, 1997 p. 19). The opportunities for advancement which the academic world appeared to offer to women of Woolf's generation have never been realised. Within Oxford as a whole the overall percentage of women professors was 10 per cent, but this hides a significant discrepancy between the position at Oxford University and the position at Oxford Brookes, the 'new' university which, until 1992, was Oxford Polytechnic. Oxford Brookes had 52 professors, of whom 14 (27 per cent) were women. This was the second highest proportion of any university. Oxford University, on the other hand, had

232 professors, of whom only 15 (6.5 per cent) were women, placing it 46th in a league table of 68.

At the other end of the academic spectrum are the staff employed to carry out Oxford University's highly rated research in the sciences and social sciences and who are increasingly employed on fixed-term contracts. There are approximately 1300 contract research staff employed by Oxford University (plus several hundreds more in arts subjects who tend, within the Oxford University system, to be employed by the individual colleges). When Virginia Woolf wrote *A Room of One's Own* (Woolf, 1929) such posts were just beginning to become available to the new women graduates, and the possibilities seemed exciting.

Twenty-years ago, a two- or three-year research contract was generally a stepping-stone to a tenured academic position for people who had completed, or were completing, a higher degree. Since then, the amount of research undertaken by universities has increased dramatically and the number of research staff employed on fixed-term contracts has risen accordingly. However, there has been no corresponding increase in lectureships for these staff to progress to, and there now exists a large body of research staff in Oxford whose employment is characterised by a high degree of insecurity.

In 1995 the Oxford University branch of the Association of University Teachers carried out a survey of contract research staff employed by the university which reveals some interesting gender differences. Overall, 56 per cent of the survey respondents were men and 44 per cent were women. However, the majority of male respondents were in the younger age groups, whereas there were significant numbers of women respondents in their thirties and forties, and some in their fifties. This suggests that, for many women, research posts on short-term contracts have become a permanent, if somewhat precarious, way of life.

Of course, academic staff at all levels depend on a large number of support staff: administrators, librarians, secretaries, cleaners, catering staff, nursery workers and so on. These are typically low-paid occupations and show a high degree of occupational segregation and, not surprisingly, are female dominated.

Women's expertise, men's power

In addition to experiencing insecurity women may also pay a price in terms of marginalisation and exclusion from the real sources of organisational power and decision making. One of the major reasons for women's continued lack of power within organisations is due to gendered cultures and the male dominance that exists in organisations. Cockburn (1993) argues that male dominance is not casual but systematic, not incidental but historic. Power, she says 'is always organised', it is organised through men's influence which is embedded in the rules and procedures of an organisation. It is embedded in the structures over which only men have influence and which women are not permitted to penetrate. Even if some women climb to the higher ranks of the organisation they are prevented from using their authority and power. This continues because of the historical acceptance within organisations that only men have the characteristics (aggression, forcefulness, competitiveness) required to succeed in positions of power and authority (Green and Cassell, 1996). Women, on the other hand, are seen as soft and nurturing, and lacking competitive confidence.

Recently, some of the positive aspects of feminine qualities have been recognised as potentially useful management tools. The future is a listening, sensitive manager with highly developed interpersonal skills (Green and Cassell, 1996). Green and Cassell argue, however, that these so-called feminine qualities are slotted into devalued management jobs. Coyle (1993) considers that these feminised management positions are becoming a low-paid ghetto for women whose earnings as managers are below even average female earnings. Restructuring of management jobs has meant that new management positions where more women might be employed do not carry the authority and control previously associated with management. This holds true in Oxford as more women in the service sector take up management positions, yet the real power and authority is still held by men as women's management roles are given less status.

Conclusions

In this discussion of women's employment in Oxford we have seen that despite the high level of academic achievement among women there, their employment in the city fits the national paradigm of women's work. Women are the silent servicers of the city and if they were to down tools Oxford would truly come to a standstill. Yet paradoxically, as elsewhere, with a few exceptions, Oxford women continue to face high levels of inequality, with limited opportunities to access a wider range of jobs and occupations or to achieve positions of influence and authority. An important factor here is the part-time nature of much women's work, which in Britain is to do with women's need to balance paid work with their caring, family responsibilities.

The majority of part-time workers are women, and much of this is to do with women's need to balance paid work with their caring responsibilities such as childcare. Although part-time working is one solution to this dilemma, it comes at a price. Most part-time workers remain in low-paid work and have little training and development opportunities. Recently, assumptions that higher-level posts cannot be carried out by part-time workers have been challenged by both the public and private sectors. More jobs with high levels of responsibility are conducted on a part-time and job share basis. However, the change is slow and in the meantime capable, qualified women, especially those who work part time, continue to be trapped in low-status, low-paid work (Buxton, 1998).

Male dominated organisational cultures which Itzin and Newman (1995) call the 'traditional culture', tend to be based on the sexual division of labour in two ways; hierarchically, with women at lower grades; and by reflecting traditional views about the appropriate jobs for women and men. Hence women remain in the service roles as the helpers of men.

Nationally, the huge rise in women's presence in the labour market has involved a major social shift. This change has come about because of economic demands, not because of changing attitudes towards women's roles. The shift has been remarkably rapid and has left the attitudes, norms and institutions behind. Unless there is change in traditional attitudes to women's roles and the gender relations of power within the wider social context, women will continue to struggle to achieve recognition, influence and authority in the workplace.

References

Barrett, M. (1988) *Women's Oppression Today*. London: Verso.

Brannen, J. et al. (1997) *Mothers, Fathers and Employment: Parents and the Labour Market in Britain 1984–1994*. London: DfEE.

Briely, S. (1996) *Women in the Workplace*. Edinburgh: HMSO.

Buxton, J. (1998) *Ending the Mother War: Starting the Workplace Revolution*. London: Macmillan.

Cockburn, C. (1991) *In the Way of Women*, Basingstoke: Macmillan.

Cockburn, C. (1993) 'Men's Stake in Organisations'. In *Organisations, Gender and Power: Papers from an IRRU Workshop*, Warwick: Warwick University.

Coyle, A. (1993) *Organisations, Gender and Power: Papers from an IRRU Workshop*. Warwick Papers in Industrial Relations, Warwick: University of Warwick.

Green, E. and Cassell, C. (1996) 'Women Managers, Gendered Cultural Processes and Organisational Change'. *Gender Work and Organisation*, 3(3), 168–77.

Griffiths, S. (1977) 'The Struggle for Equality'. *Times Higher Education Supplement*, 6 June, p. 19.

Hansard Society for Parliamentry Government (1990) *The Report of the Hansard Society Commission on Women at the Top*. London: Hansard Society.

Hewitt, P. (1993) *About Time*. London: Rivers Oram Press.

Hoare, P. (1998) 'A survey of women's employment in Oxford'. Oxford Women's Training Scheme.

Itzin, C. and Newman, J. (1995) *Gender, Culture and Organisational Change: Putting Theory into Practice*. London: Routledge.

Jenkins, R. (1984) 'Ethnic Minorities in Business: A Research Agenda'. In R. Ward and R. Jenkins (eds), *Ethnic Communities in Business*. Cambridge: Cambridge University Press.

Ledwith, S. and Colgan, F. (1996) *Women in Organisations: Challenge Gender Politics*. Basingstoke: Macmillan.

Meehan, E. M. (1985) *Women's Rights at Work, Campaigns and Policy in Britain and the United States*. London: Macmillan.

Office for National Statistics (1996/97) *General Household Survey*. London: The Stationery Office.

Oxford City Council (1998/1999) *Economic Development Plan*.

Oxford City Council (1998) *Household Survey*. Oxford: Oxford City Council.

Rubery, J. and Fagan, C. (1994) 'Occupational Segregation: plus ça change?' In R. Lindley (ed.), *Labour Market Structures and Prospects for Women*, Manchester: Equal Opportunities Commission.

Scott, A. M. (1994) *Gender Segregation and Social Change*. Oxford: Oxford University Press.

Walby, S. (1990) *Theorizing Patriarchy*, Oxford: Basil Blackwell.

Wilson, F. M. (1995) *Organisational Behaviour and Gender*. Maidenhead: McGraw-Hill.

Witz, A. (1993) 'Women at Work'. In D. Richardson and V. Robinson, *Introducing Women's Studies*, London: Macmillan.

Woolf, V. (1929) *A Room of One's Own*. London: Hogarth Press.

11
The Role of Women in Tenant Management: the Case of Kensington and Chelsea[1]

Jane Darke and Verna Rowland

Introduction

> Good [people] will always get there . . . Positive discrimination is
> such a lot of trouble.
>
> (Baroness Hanham, Leader of the Council, Royal Borough of
> Kensington and Chelsea)

Equality with respect to gender, ethnicity or other attributes, is
not a hot political topic in the Royal Borough. Kensington and
Chelsea (K&C) is one of the ten richest districts in Britain (in per
capita income), is under permanent Conservative control, yet it also
ranks among the worst districts for poverty, with pockets of multiple
deprivation in North Kensington.[2] Sixteen per cent of the population have minority ethnic origins, including a considerable variety of
groups.

Thirteen per cent of households are tenants of housing owned by
the local authority and these are, uniquely for Britain, under the management of a board where elected tenants have a substantial majority.
This chapter will attempt to describe and account for three phenomena: first, the fact that a radical initiative in tenant management has
arisen in a traditionally minded local authority; second, the relatively
high participation of women in the tenant management organisation
(TMO), and, third, the complex situation with respect to equal opportunities. Different participants of both genders hold polarised views on
this issue.

Before discussing how the TMO [then] came about in K&C we outline
some background on social housing in Britain for those unfamiliar with
this, and describe how K&C is an unusual case among local councils.

The housing policy context

Council housing was born out of the failure of private landlords to provide affordable housing to adequate standards, at points in time when those affected had sufficient power to bring about legislation for state support. All major political parties during the twentieth century have at times supported the idea that local authorities should be subsidised to build and manage housing for working-class households, although the Labour Party has been the strongest advocate. There were high rates of building of council housing in the years after each World War and in the 1960s. This tenure housed 30 per cent of households in England at its numerical high point in 1978, and 20 years later houses 16 per cent. Council housing is numerically most significant in big cities: in 1998 it provided 31 per cent of the housing stock in inner London, but only 13 per cent in K&C where political preferences (see below) have led the council to support housing associations rather than build directly.

Part of the reason for Margaret Thatcher's election victories in 1979 and 1983 was her promise that council tenants would be able to purchase their homes at a discount, thereby transferring to the higher status of home owner. From 1980, central government severely constrained the freedom of action of local government, including reducing the amount they could spend on their housing, and initiated a series of moves designed to attenuate their role as owners and managers of housing. Among these were the 'Tenants' Choice' proposals in 1988 to encourage alternative landlords to take over the stock, subject to a tenants' ballot, followed in the early 1990s by proposals that local authorities must go to compulsory competitive tender (CCT) for their housing management functions.

Whilst there are some poorly managed housing departments, the general view was that CCT would involve expense and bureaucracy in pursuit of savings and efficiency gains that might never materialise. The proposals were perceived by most tenants and housing authorities as heavy handed. Actual transfers of ownership or management have been negligible, with the exception of some local authorities which have transferred their stock to housing associations ('large scale voluntary transfer') in order to escape public spending constraints. This requires the assent of tenants in a ballot.

The Royal Borough of Kensington and Chelsea

K&C is one of almost 400 housing authorities in England. It was created from smaller boroughs when London local government was reorganised in 1965. It has always been under Conservative control, with (except for a short period from 1968) an opposition Labour group. Currently there are 39 Conservative and 15 Labour councillors, with no other party represented. No wards (electoral districts) are regarded as marginal. The wards to the north of the borough, which have a greater proportion of council tenants and of ethnic minorities, regularly return Labour councillors; those in Chelsea in the south and the centre of Kensington, including some of the highest-status residential areas of London, are invariably Conservative, despite having some council estates and council properties among other housing.

There is not only stability in the party in control: many councillors have served for repeated terms, including some who pre-date the 1965 reorganisation. As usual in positions of elected authority, men predominate, comprising 82 per cent of Conservative and 53 per cent of Labour councillors, although during the research period and at the time of writing the leader is a woman, Joan Hanham. The council has a stated commitment to equal treatment (and must in any case comply with legislation) but has no monitoring or implementation procedures for equal opportunities. The assumption is that opportunities are available to all.

The political stability of the council makes it unique among inner London boroughs. Only two other inner London boroughs have been consistently Conservative in recent years: Wandsworth (since 1982) and Westminster, but both these have been perceived as more vulnerable to electoral change. Unlike K&C, both were praised by Thatcher as flagships of the radical right, whereas K&C is more traditional in its Conservatism. Its local politics were the subject of a classic study by Dearlove (1973) which shows features still recognisable today. The political norms in the borough include:

- avoidance and dislike of sudden or rapid change;
- a belief in a minimal role for government, avoiding unnecessary costs and bureaucracy;
- a belief that local politicians know better than central government what is best for the borough;
- an expectation that people can and should be self-reliant and take responsibility for their own lives rather than looking to the State;

- a reluctance to define their administration as political; rather their approach to decision making is seen as applied common sense.

Elected members were thus predisposed to favour passing control of their housing stock from a local government bureaucracy to tenants, provided the latter could be seen as competent and responsible.

The development of tenant involvement

Tenant power has developed steadily since 1980, but at the time of Dearlove's 1973 study tenants were beyond the political pale. The area was notorious for exploitative or neglectful private landlords and for squalid and overcrowded housing, but the council was reluctant to intervene. O'Malley (1977a, 1977b) describes women, including many from minority ethnic backgrounds, taking a major role in campaigns to press the council to take action. There was redevelopment of some areas with scant consultation with or sensitivity to existing residents. Tenants and residents resorted to demonstrations, false bidding at property auctions and lock-ins of councillors to try to publicise their plight and shame the council. Councillors were thereby able to dismiss the problems, believing that tenants were being manipulated by agitators and troublemakers (Dearlove, 1973, pp. 156, 195).

A change in the late 1970s came from four 'stakeholders', and women were instrumental in bringing this about. A new tenant leader, Doris Besant, organised in what was perceived as a responsible manner, breaking with agit-prop tactics and avoiding party politics. Joan Hanham became chairman of the housing committee and, according to her recollections, thought 'blow me, I am going to talk to them'. This break with the previous practices of her Conservative colleagues shows the capacity for independent views described in Campbell's (1987) study of Conservative women. Martyn Kingsford, the newly appointed deputy director of housing (now chief executive of the TMO) was told to 'stop the fighting'. He brokered an agreement between Mrs Hanham and the opposition housing spokesman, John Keys, that both sides should refrain from using housing issues to gain party advantage: a norm still adopted in the TMO.

The rapprochement with tenants led to the setting up of a tenants' consultative committee (TCC) in 1980, with representatives from tenants associations throughout the borough. The TCC commented on all reports before they went to the housing committee, which has never rejected their recommendations. After some stormy early meetings a high degree of trust and respect developed. When the Tenants' Choice proposals were published by the newly re-elected Thatcher government in 1987 the tenants made it clear, through a petition organised by Doris Besant, that they wished to remain with the council. In a defining moment, the council accepted the tenants' preference, rather than the line favoured by the Conservative government. It was resolved to retain the stock unless and until tenants chose otherwise.

The structure of tenant involvement was elaborated and developed, with area committees to channel estate views to the centre and a small advisory committee working closely with the directorate. In the early 1990s CCT was perceived as a threat, as the borough's location could have attracted bidders for housing management whose agenda would not prioritise the interests of tenants. An alternative appeared late in 1992 in the form of a new policy, the Right to Manage, which the government envisaged being used by tenants associations on individual estates incompetently run by leftist councils. However, the legislation empowered K&C tenants to declare a Right to Manage all the council housing in the borough, a step they took in 1993, supported by both parties on the council.

This decision was supported by a preliminary ballot of tenants, and was followed by elections to the shadow board and a training programme. After a confirmatory final ballot the TMO took over in 1996. Under the Right to Manage legislation the council cannot rescind this transfer of power although tenants have the opportunity to vote for a change every five years. The K&C TMO remains much the largest example of tenant management in the country, with around 10000 homes, and the only one managing the whole stock of a housing authority: a radical development in the governance of council housing.

Accounting for tenant control

We have discussed elsewhere the question of how far tenants really are in control.[3] The view of all councillors interviewed and of most tenant activists and officers is that they are indeed in control, exercising their functions competently and thoughtfully and taking a somewhat more hands-on approach than the councillors used to. The research supports this conclusion and elsewhere we have outlined how their input has made a difference and countered the views of sceptics who assume that the tenants can easily be manipulated to suit the convenience of officers.

The puzzle remains: to explain the emergence of the only example of borough-wide tenant management in one of the few Conservative-run housing authorities. In fact the TMO accords well with the local political culture outlined above. By becoming a TMO the borough avoided a sudden change that CCT would have caused. Passing responsibilities from the council to tenants meets the objectives of minimising (local) government's role and of encouraging self-reliance in a group perceived by Conservatives as tending to overdependence (Waldegrave, 1987). A senior housing officer recalled being impressed by the words of a councillor at a meeting with tenants at the time the TMO was under consideration: 'You tell us what power you want, what you want given across to you, when you are ready for it and we will empower you. We will give you that power. It will be passed from the housing committee to you.'

The belief in localised decision making has been mentioned. The depoliticisation of housing issues remains the norm: most tenants interviewed avoided mention of party politics; others stated their respect for other actors whose politics they did not share: 'I think we have got some brilliant councillors. I know they are Tories and we have Labour too ... At the end of the day that is what politics is about. At the housing committee they get on fabulous. Basically at housing committee you just say what you think' (woman activist representing tenants and leaseholders).

Gender and political representation

Despite the persistent tendency for women to be under-represented in political roles, particularly more senior ones, it is only in recent years that this has been seen as requiring explanation. What research there is has tended to focus on women reaching Parliament rather than less formal settings (although the formal/informal dichotomy is arguably unhelpful: see Brownill and Halford, 1990). Women's involvement in community-based activities has also been rather under-researched (but see, for example, Mayo, 1977; O'Malley, 1977a; Hood and Woods, 1994) but much of this work, like research on tenant participation, has been predicated on a view that activism is a manifestation of class struggle and hence to privileged forms of collective action based on an ideal type of organisation at the point of production. This has led researchers to overlook particular issues and to fail to notice existing forms of organisation by women (see discussions in Green and Chapman, 1992; Campbell, 1993; Brownill and Darke, 1998).

Studies of women in Parliament and in local government may be helpful in examining other settings in that the reasons for women's absence or presence may be constants. Despite the election of an unprecedented number of women MPs on 1 May 1997 it remains the case that women are seriously underrepresented at all levels of formal political activity. The 120 women MPs represent only 18 per cent of the total, this a doubling of the percentage after the 1992 election and compared to much lower figures in earlier years. The percentage of women among local councillors is slightly higher but men still dominate in positions of power and influence as leaders and chairs of major committees (Wilson and Game, 1994).

Women in Kensington and Chelsea Council and in the TMO

Kensington and Chelsea is typical of local authorities in having a male-dominated elected council (74 per cent, close to the national average; see Wilson and Game, 1994 p. 212). As noted above, the Labour group is closer to gender equality than the Conservatives. However, men and women councillors have equal chances of becoming chair or vice-chair of a committee: about 50 per cent of councillors occupy such roles.

In the TMO the grassroots are female dominated. The tendency nationally is for more women than men to be living in council housing, due to the greater likelihood of their being in housing need through poverty or caring responsibilities (see Darke, 1996), so the high numbers of women may be no more than proportionate. Among office holders (chairs, vice-chairs, secretaries and treasurers) in tenants' and residents' associations in K&C, 62 per cent are women, but they are far more likely to act as secretary (71 per cent) or treasurer (78 per cent) than chair or vice-chair (43 per cent).

The proportion of women declines as higher tiers of involvement are reached: five of the 13 tenant and leaseholder members of the TMO board are women, including the chairman,[4] Doris Besant MBE. Mrs Besant was unanimously re-elected as chairman in 1997 and 1998. There appears to be a mix of ethnic groups on the board roughly proportional to that of tenants in K&C (one-quarter of whom have minority ethnic origins) but we have not asked board members to define their own ethnicity. There is representation from other groups commonly included in equal opportunities policies: disabled and gay persons, and representatives range in age from the thirties to retirement age.[5] Although women are still somewhat under-represented it would be hard to find a governing body that was more representative of its members and service users.

Women's participation in the TMO, although not equal to men's, shows much less gender polarisation than in most of local government. The under-representation of women is clearly not a concern for housing staff or tenant activists: the replies given to a question on equal opportunities and under-represented groups showed no consistent perception of who was disadvantaged, although many groups were mentioned. Martyn Kingsford is aware that women are somewhat under-represented on the TMO board but anticipates that this will improve over time as new board members are recruited from the more representative lower tiers, such as the area review boards or TCC, and as initiatives for tenant training take effect.

If women's participation is greater than in most political arenas, to what can this be attributed? Might the style of policy making in the TMO be 'feminine' rather than 'masculine'? We now attempt to relate the K&C case to other writings on women's participation in the political system and on how far policies are geared to equal opportunities issues.

Authors have differed on how to explain the under-representation of women in politics, and indeed on whether explanation is required. Stacey and Price (1981) suggest, rather, that the figures represent a notable advance, given that women were fully enfranchised in Britain only in 1928. Some writers have argued that women do not need political participation because they have compensating power in other spheres, such as the home and their own informal networks (although it is also argued that women are subject to patriarchy in the private as well as the public sphere – see Stacey and Price, 1981; Walby, 1990). Walby (1997, p. 139) has further suggested that we should analyse how far the content of policies is directed at transforming gender relations rather than the gender of legislators. However, if we do wish to account for the low numbers of politically active women, we may wish to consider a range of possible explanations.

It could be that women are (or used to be) socialised to accept male dominance in the political and other spheres as 'natural' (Pateman, 1988). Politics is seen as a dirty business, an arena where women would not feel comfortable. Next, it has been argued that the mechanisms for selection of candidates, particularly at national level, are biased (Campbell, 1987; Norris and Lovenduski, 1993). Selectors operate with stereotypes of candidates supported by an admiring wife, or attribute antiwoman prejudice to the voters, or are themselves under pressure to vote for their associates from male-dominated networks in clubs or trade unions. A further explanation would concentrate on the material barriers: the long and unsocial hours for women who have or want children, the lack of childcare provision in Westminster or in most town halls, the difficulties of adequately replacing their labour in the home (Norris and Lovenduski, 1993, pp. 380–1). It is possible that women may choose not to put themselves forward because they dislike the confrontational style of political culture, the personal jibes, heckling, the boys' school mode of jocular and ritualised competitiveness. This could be a significant way in which the Kensington and Chelsea TMO differs from other political arenas (see below).

It seems to the present writers that all these accounts have partial validity and that the style of political conduct could be presented in terms of two polar types:

Masculine	*Feminine*
confrontation	co-operation
winner takes all	reasonable compromise
process an end in itself	aimed at positive outcomes
aim of belittling others	respect and dignity

Just as Walby (1997) reminds us that the gender of politicians may be less interesting than their policies, so the above polarities do not necessarily map on to actual gendered actors. Thus former Prime Minister Margaret Thatcher could be regarded as a 'masculine' politician and current Prime Minister Tony Blair a 'feminine' one.

It is certainly the case that the conduct of the TMO would place it, too, in the 'feminine' category. The values of respect and dignity for all participants pervade proceedings: meetings are courteous and participants take care not to show impatience towards those less familiar with procedures. Co-operation and compromise are inherent in tenant management: where there is bargaining over resources such as a programme of improvement works, it would clearly be damaging to future working relationships if one group were to gain a disproportionate share. In our research observations, tenant committees were seen to attempt to be fair to all groups rather than maximising gains for individual estates.

Our research notes on meetings observed include many further instances where the atmosphere is in marked contrast to that typical in council committees, or in Parliament. Meetings are characterised by friendly laughter and sometimes larking about, with no division into political camps. In a TCC meeting tenant A attempted to raise an issue about the lack of a meeting room on his estate, but was politely told by the chair that this was not an appropriate issue for this meeting. Leaseholder B (male) commented, and was criticised by A for interfering in his tenants' association. Tenant C (female) attempted to mediate and suggested that the general issue of associations with no meeting place be discussed at a future meeting. A further member (female) made a conciliatory comment designed to smooth feelings so that the meeting could continue in a friendly atmosphere. At another meeting a leaseholder was puzzled about why she had to pay a service charge and a contribution to capital costs of improvements. An explanation was given (by a man), together with information on how leaseholders can get involved in the TMO. Asking what an area review board was for, she was told 'we listen and support each other'. These meetings were described by the observer as friendly and well conducted; there was a relaxed but purposeful atmosphere.

The conscious norm of valuing and listening to all participants is practised and promoted in the training programme organised by the tenant participation support staff. The joy of a tenant activist who had been applauded after plucking up courage to give feedback in a training session was still vivid when she was interviewed for the research several months later, and her personal growth in confidence was very apparent.

The style of debate, then, is conducive to women's participation, with the 'feminine' style of political conduct being practised by both men and women. It could be suggested that as women are socially constructed as homemakers, their participation in housing policy making at local level is not perceived as anomalous or remarkable. Women's involvement in a TMO is thus assumed to be 'natural'. Potential participants may be encouraged by the frequent emphasis on equal opportunities in tenants' newsletters and other literature. The other issues discussed above, the barriers of time and the conflict with other duties such as childcare, undoubtedly make it difficult for many participants, particularly as (unlike MPs) tenant activists are unpaid, but our observations suggest that much of the work as a representative is done from home or at least around the estate, and that many of the men who are activists have caring responsibilities too.[6]

Equal opportunities

Equal opportunities (EO) are built in to the constitution of the TMO, and all board members have had training and competency assessment in equal opportunities (EO). EO training is a prerequisite for the employer functions they carry out, such as grievance and disciplinary hearings. Some of the tenant and leaseholder board members are conscious of the scope for improvement on EO and have set in place arrangements to bring this about. For example, the cultural barriers inhibiting the participation of Asian women have been recognised and the TMO is sponsoring a social and education group in Chelsea to take the TMO direct to them. It is hard to imagine such an initiative being taken by the Royal Borough.

The need to broaden recruitment and skills development for tenant activists is being tackled in part through mentoring. This takes place at many levels in the organisation and allows less experienced or skilled members to observe their more experienced peers and to discuss their role with them. At K&C there are other training initiatives from single sessions to year-long certificated courses. In all training activities, equal opportunities forms a part of the content and of the process: for example, mentoring is seen as aimed at developing confidence and competence in those who would otherwise be reluctant to participate.

The priority given to EO in the TMO stands in stark contrast to its absence in the council. It was noted earlier that K&C, whilst claiming to have an equal opportunities policy, has refused to take measures that would enable the council to ensure that its legal obligation to equal treatment was being discharged, or to follow policies to combat specific forms of disadvantage. The scepticism expressed by Joan Hanham's words at the start of this chapter is typical. Martyn Kingsford's commitment to equal opportunities at the time when he was still within the council as director of housing was seen as excessive: 'For years I have pushed at the (equal opportunities) door and was notorious for it. I was the only department to train staff in community development and ethnicity issues. The TMO has normalised it.'

It would be wrong to give the impression, however, that all participants would see the TMO's performance on EO in a positive light. The EO subcommittee is not well attended and some tenant activists have little interest in or sympathy for the issue. A woman tenant board member said, 'I have switched off on equal opps. I think the TMO has gone overboard like everybody else ... These things have financial implications ... At the end of the day tenants will pay extra rent and could well do without this'. A male councillor, one of the minority of non-tenant board members expressed similar views. He recognised the right of the TMO to take EO further than the council did, but was concerned that this might in turn create demands on the council. By contrast a male tenant representative on the board cited EO as an example of how the TMO had made a difference but was concerned that only one woman board member took an interest in women's issues.

Equal opportunities in service delivery could still be perceived as falling short of best practice. Ethnic monitoring of allocations and other aspects of the service, and ethnic and gender monitoring of the workforce, are only just beginning. The chair of the EO committee spoke of 'appeasement' and feared that equal opportunities was not seen as a priority.

Conclusions

We have argued that the tenant management organisation at Kensington and Chelsea represents a radical and unique departure for council housing. At a time when local authorities are being asked to rethink their relationship with the publics they serve, K&C can stand as an example of what is achievable when tenants, councillors and officers are determined to bring about change. Tenant empowerment appears to accord well with Conservative values, but space prevents discussion of another intriguing question: the absence of equally radical initiatives in councils controlled by other parties.

It has also been shown that women are already well represented in the TMO and that structures are in place to further develop their involvement. Increasing women's participation may involve not only formal equal opportunities policies and procedures, but also a change in political culture and in style of operation. The absence of confrontation in debate, and the ethos of mutual support, contribute towards empowering those who are less confident. The respect tenants are accorded provides reassurance, and training increases their understanding and effectiveness.

The TMO has chosen to give equal opportunities a much higher profile than was (and is) true of the council, and the board is close to being representative of the diversity among tenants. Elsewhere we have discussed how far the K&C example could be replicated in other housing organisations, suggesting among other prerequisites for success a high degree of commitment on all sides, and a long lead-in time in order to develop trust, experience and skills (see Darke and Rowland, 1998).

Positive examples are rarely flawless and often seem to generate overzealous attempts to find fault. Although it is possible to discern an gap between rhetoric and reality both in the extent to which tenants are making significant decisions and in equal opportunities procedures, any such criticism should consider how far most local authority housing departments would stand up to such scrutiny. Judged by this standard, the TMO at Kensington and Chelsea represents a very considerable innovation in the governance of housing and in the empowerment of women.

Notes

1   The research, to study the origins and first few months in operation of the TMO, took place in 1997–8, and was supported by a small grant from the School of Planning at Oxford Brookes University. The authors gratefully acknowledge this assistance.
    The research methods are the characteristic case study ones of semifocused interviews with key participants, observation at meetings and analysis of documentary sources such as council and TMO minutes. The Royal Borough and the TMO have been exemplary in facilitating research access and are thanked for their co-operation. The authors would like to thank all the people in Kensington and Chelsea who assisted the research with interviews and estate visits. Jane Darke would particularly like to thank three past students on the Certificate in Tenant Participation, Jill Brown, Cy Ford and Joanne Kelly, who alerted her to the fact that something exceptionally interesting was happening in K&C.
2   Gordon and Forrest (1995, pp. 75, 79, 83) rank Kensington and Chelsea as ninth from top (out of 366 districts) on income. At the same time the Royal Borough ranks 12th worst on the Townsend Deprivation index and 24th on poverty.
3   Briefing paper available from the authors; other papers in preparation.
4   This is the title used both in the TMO and in the RBK&C.
5   Information volunteered by board members in the course of discussions on equal opportunities.
6   The researchers know of male activists who care for a disabled relative.

References

Brownill, S. and Darke, J. (1998) *'Rich Mix': Inclusive Strategies for Urban Regeneration.* Bristol: Policy Press.
Brownill, S. and Halford, S. (1990) 'Understanding women's involvement in local politics'. *Political Geography Quarterly*, 9(4), 396–414.
Campbell, B. (1987) *Iron Ladies*. London: Virago.
Campbell, B. (1993) *Goliath*. London: Methuen.
Darke, J. (1996) 'Househunting'. In C. Booth, J. Darke and S. Yeandle, *Changing Places: women's lives in the city*. London: Paul Chapman.
Darke, J. and Rowland, V. (1998) 'It can be done: Tenant Management at the Royal Borough of Kensington and Chelsea'. Briefing paper available from the authors.

Dearlove, J. (1973) *The politics of policy in local government: The making and maintenance of public policy in the Royal Borough of Kensington and Chelsea.* Cambridge: Cambridge University Press.

Gordon, D. and Forrest, R. (1995) *People and Places.* Bristol: School of Advanced Urban Studies.

Green, J. and Chapman, A. (1992) 'The British Community Development Project: Lessons for today'. *Community Development Journal,* 27(3), 242–58.

Hood, M. and Woods, R. (1994) 'Women and Participation'. In R. Gilroy and R. Woods (eds), Housing Women, London: Routledge.

Mayo, M. (1977) *Women in the Community.* London: Routledge & Kegan Paul.

Norris, P. and Lovenduski, J. (1993) ' "If only more candidates came forward": Supply-side explanations of candidate selection in Britain'. *British Journal of Political Science,* 23, 373–408.

O'Malley, J. (1977a) *The politics of community action.* Nottingham: Spokesman.

O'Malley, J (1977b) 'The housing struggles of two women'. In Mayo, M., *Women in the Community,* London: Routledge & Kegan Paul.

Pateman, C. (1988) *The sexual contract.* Cambridge: Polity Press.

Stacey, M. and Price, M. (1981) *Women, power and politics.* London: Tavistock.

Walby, S. (1990) *Theorising Patriarchy.* Oxford: Blackwell.

Walby, S. (1997) *Gender Transformations.* London: Routledge.

Waldegrave, W. (1987) Speech to the Institute of Housing Annual Conference. Reported in *Inside Housing,* 26 June 1987, p. 3.

Wilson, D. and Game, C. (1994) *Local government in the United Kingdom.* Basingstoke: Macmillan.

12
Women and Popular Music Making in Urban Spaces

Mavis Bayton

Introduction and context

It has been suggested that music is the core activity which shapes modern social life (Finnegan, 1989). It is certainly true that music, mainly popular music, pervades modern urban social space. It emanates from car stereos, Walkmans, clothes shops, hairdressers, cafés, pubs, clubs and house windows. It provides the soundtrack to the city both on film and in everyday life. Setting up bands and playing music is a popular pastime in the city. It is, however, a predominantly male one. One would expect a random distribution of the sexes among music-making groups of all kinds. But this clearly is not the case (Finnegan, 1989; Cohen, 1991; Bayton, 1998). Women are positioned within the world of popular music largely in consuming, decorative and support-ive roles. Whilst there has been a longstanding position for women as vocalists in bands, there is a striking absence of women instrumental-ists. High-profile women performers tend to be singers. The Spice Girls in the 1990s, just like Madonna in the 1980s and the Supremes in the 1960s, are important role models for girls, certainly, but not ones which get them into playing instruments. Although there has been a gradual increase in the numbers of female instrumentalists since the watershed of punk, and despite the seemingly stronger female presence in the British music charts in the 1990s, they are still massively outnumbered by men. There are no biological reasons to explain this; women are just as musical as men. Therefore my research has investigated the social factors involved and also examined the ways in which women have, against the odds, managed to become music producers as well as merely music consumers.

Research methods

My findings are based on extensive ethnographic research undertaken in two periods – the early to mid 1980s and the mid 1990s – providing comparative data. I began with participant observation as a member of Oxford's first all-women band (The Mistakes), at gigs, rehearsals, in the studio and on tour. Later, I broadened the scope of my fieldwork by undertaking in-depth interviews with women musicians at various career stages: starting out, semiprofessional and fully professional. In all, I carried out 105 interviews (most over two hours in length). They were structured by a schedule containing over 200 questions and recorded on tape. Additionally, I undertook observation at women's music workshops and carried out innumerable brief informal unstructured interviews with men and women working in the record business, in recording studios, on music magazines, with sound engineers, and so forth. Lastly, clutching notebook and camera, I went to gigs, hundreds of them. The main questions that concerned me were as follows. First, why were so comparatively few women playing instruments in bands? Second, what was special about those rare individuals who were doing it? Third, what were their experiences in playing music and how did their careers work?

Whilst I included vocalists, sound engineers, music teachers, administrators and participants at women's music projects/workshops, a record distributor, a band manager and a studio manager amongst my interviewees, the majority played instruments in bands. Although I interviewed some famous female performers, the main focus of my research was on local music making, amateur and semiprofessional bands, about which very little has been written in Britain outside of biographies and autobiographies. I diversified my sample in terms of career stage, geographical location, type of music and instrument played. Recent feminist scholarship has rightly been careful to take account of the differences between women which in the late 1960s and early 1970s were obscured behind the monolithic category 'woman'. Therefore, in selecting my interviewees, I also made a point of including a wide variety of women in terms of ethnicity, social class, sexual preference and so forth. Ageism operates strongly in local music making, keeping women over thirty in the small minority, but I deliberately included interviews with some of them. Most of my interviewees were white for the simple reason that there are few black women (or men) in rock/indie music, but I made a point of interviewing seven non-white women, including several high-profile performers. However, what stands out, above all, is that despite these differences in identity, structural location, style of music or instrument played, there are strong similarities in the stories that women told. Although ageism, racism, homophobia and classism affect them differently, women of all ages, colours, classes and sexual preferences have in common the fact that they are women. Their separate individual experiences are linked, since sexism and sexist practice impact on all of them, albeit with different inflections.

Theoretical framework

Women's local music making has been largely ignored and published scholarship in the area is limited. Thus, there was no obvious body of theory relating directly to my work that I could turn to in order, initially, to structure my research or, later, make sense of my findings. As an ethnographer this did not worry me too much and I have largely developed my own theory, grounded in everyday reality, incorporating women's daily experiences from their grass-roots accounts. However, I have been strongly influenced by two sources. First, Simon Frith. Earlier subcultural theorists (Hall and Jefferson, 1976) took for granted young people's ability to choose what to do in their leisure time and thus merely addressed the question of how their choices should be interpreted. In contrast, Frith (1983) argued that different leisure patterns are a reflection, not so much of different values, as of the different degrees of opportunity, restriction and constraint that are afforded to different individuals and social groups. A particular leisure pursuit may be made easy or difficult for an individual according to their social structural position, gender being one aspect of such societal location. Frith's argument was that, for everyone, leisure, consumption and style involve a relationship between choice and constraint. I believe that such constraints are crucial to the explanation of women's absence from rock/indie bands. I chose to conceptualise these in terms of the material and the ideological, although in reality, of course, these two are closely interrelated. (For instance, lack of access to equipment is an important material constraint, but one of the reasons for its denial is ideological.) Material constraints operating on potential female instrumentalists include lack of money and time, lack of access to equipment and transport, the regulation of female leisure/play (by parents, boyfriends, husbands), and exclusion by male musicians. The main ideological constraint is the hegemonic masculinity of rock music making: the perceived masculinity of the musical discourse itself and that embedded within rock instruments and associated technology.

Feminist ideas have been another influence. Although it is not the case that each and every woman is oppressed by each and every man, it is clear that the local music world (like the wider world) is organised in such a way that men as a group are privileged over women as a group. Some women musicians did indeed have excellent support from some men but it is still the case that women musicians as a group suffer from myriad sexist assumptions, comments, harassment, prejudice and so on from men as a group in the rock world, which works to undermine their confidence and impede their musical careers. This does not mean that women are simply 'victims' or passive in the face of this oppression because the very shared knowledge of that oppression can be, and often is, the source of empowerment and change: there is both 'agency' and 'structure'.

Research findings and analysis

A full analysis of my findings can be found elsewhere (Bayton, 1998). This chapter focusses mainly on one aspect. The concept of space (both material and metaphorical) has been recently utilised by a number of academics in the field of gender and sexuality (for example, Bell and Valentine, 1995; Duncan, 1996; McDowell and Sharpe, 1997) and I intend to use urban space as a lens through which to focus on the world of popular music making.

The urban spaces within which rock exists are populated overwhelmingly by men and culturally saturated with a masculinist value system which operates, at every level, to exclude women. The whole rock world is constructed by and for men, such that women are positioned as 'out of place' within its boundaries. But women have challenged the utilisation of rock spaces, have resisted the classification of rock spaces as 'masculine'-coded domains. I shall examine these patterns of domination and resistance, illustrating my points by drawing on qualitative data from my field research. Insofar as the distinction is meaningful, the focus will be on public and semipublic space (pubs and clubs) rather than private space, even though inequality of private space within the home is certainly an important factor in its own right *vis-à-vis* women's opportunity to engage in music making.

So-called 'public' space is actually colonised by men. Young males dominate in the playgrounds, parks, sports facilities and the city streets. Thus, it is no surprise that when music-making facilities are on offer these too are controlled by young males. Girls are hesitant, embarrassed, feel out of their depth and need positive encouragement from a committed teacher or youth worker who understands gender dynamics, as was stressed to me by a number of women who have been involved in running music workshops and projects. Playing supposedly 'masculine' instruments serves to undermine girls' femininity and they feel unsure of themselves. Leila, working at the West London Women's Music Project, told me: 'Music facilities in youth clubs are nearly always dominated by boys. There's a lot of facilities available in community halls, community centres, that's supposedly available to mixed groups but it's dominated by men. It just doesn't work.'

Boys at school tend (consciously or not) to keep girls out of the available music-making spaces. Like other school student bands in the late 1980s, The Frantic Spiders, who started when they were fifteen, were the only female band in their school and were distanced from the boy musicians:

> When I first got an acoustic guitar, there was a group of people who would every lunchtime all go and play electric guitar in the music room. They were all boys. 'Cause I really wanted to go and do that and I felt completely intimidated because they were so arrogant about it. If you were a girl, the only way you could join in their little music group was if you were really sexy and could sing, 'cause that's all the girls were thought to be good for was being singer in their band. So it was just horrible. I just kept out of the way.
>
> (Charley)

If girls do manage to gain access to music-making facilities they may have difficulty keeping their privacy. In the 1990s the Eynsham band, Frances Belle, used to have boys hanging around outside their practice space all evening, banging on the windows. 'And then we'd come out and tell them to bugger off, and they'd say "you sound really shit" or something' (Hannah Collett, of Frances Belle). If a women's band is to survive, then, male outsiders must be excluded in its early stages, especially boyfriends or husbands, while it is particularly necessary that male musicians are excluded because they can be threatening and judgmental.

Women musicians will also need to acquire musical equipment, which necessitates entering a highly male-defined space. Both the customers and assistants are usually men. In any of these shops you can observe the confident and assertive way in which young males try out the equipment. Young women, however, typically find trying out equipment a severe trial. Because they are scared of showing themselves up and being patronised or put down by the assistants, they are inhibited in what they perceive to be a male arena. Nearly all of my interviewees, in both the 1980s and the 1990s, had these feelings, for example Aimee Stevens (the 16-year-old guitarist of Frances Belle):

> I feel very intimidated. Especially going to ask – they're all stood behind the counter, these massive metal blokes. Well, that's what they look like, judging by their image. I go up and go, 'Can I have a top E string?' because I don't know the proper names or anything, so it's even worse. And they go, 'What gauge? What sort?' And I'm like, 'I don't know'. So I don't like going in and looking at guitars or anything in music shops. . . . When you're trying they're just staring at you, if you don't know much as well – and then they pick it up and go (*imitates complicated guitar playing*) and you're going, 'Oh no, I'll just take that'.

Even experienced players relayed tales of condescension and patronisation, for example Fran (bass player in various female bands in Nottingham – Sub Rosa, Mothers of the Future, The Very Good Rock 'n Roll Band):

> You go in and all the blokes are sitting in one corner talking about some riff that they came up with last night, totally ignoring you. They are very patronising. They see that you're a woman and they think, 'How did you dare come in our music shop?'.

Being in a band requires women's presence out of the home for long periods at night. A gig may end at eleven o'clock or midnight but the hidden aspect of band work means that musicians may not get away until one or two o'clock. There may then be a long drive ahead. For young women, in particular, this poses many problems: transport, parental restrictions, but particularly the dangers of the city streets at night. Extensive empirical research since the late 1970s has shown the prevalence of actual physical and sexual violence, harassment and verbal abuse (Hanmer and Saunders, 1993; Hall, 1985; Stanko, 1985; Hanmer and Maynard, 1987; Hester et al., 1996). However, it is the omnipresent possibility of sexual violence that affects all women, regardless of class, age or ethnic group, because more than actual attacks, fear of violence is a crucial constraint on women's freedom, limiting what they can do, where they can go, when and who with.

Although, in reality, women are far more likely to be attacked in their home and by someone they know, large numbers of women are afraid to go out alone at night. Indeed, concern about violence determines the leisure patterns of women, especially after dark and where transport is poor (Green, Woodward and Hebron, 1990). Public space – the streets, the bus, the tube, the train – are viewed as alien, hostile (male) space.

This in itself helps to explain the lack of women in bands (as well as the lack of female street buskers), but probably the main issue concerns the more limited space of the venue. If the world of leisure poses threats for women, that is particularly true of pubs – one of the main sites for the performance of popular music. This phenomenon has been most fully explored by Valerie Hey who states that public houses have never actually been public for women, but are 'male "playgrounds" to which women are "invited" on special terms' (Hey, 1986). Women who go to pubs alone risk being the subject of endless sexist joking, intrusive staring and being pejoratively labelled. Sexual harassment, on a continuum from the subtly oppressive or dismissive to the overtly violent, transforms the potentially neutral space, the gigging environment – the venue – into a male terrain. Moreover, the amenities provided and not provided and the material working conditions of rock all reflect an unquestioned assumption of the masculinity of bands. Women are made to feel out of place because the places are designed for men.

Gigging in the early 1980s

There isn't a changing room. There's beer spilt all over the place. You're gonna get gobbed on. Maybe, climbing into a van, without being able to change, and driving to somewhere where you're gonna sleep on someone's floor. Bad conditions. The lack of care. The lack of tenderness, warmth . . . the whole kind of macho thing of having to survive on a shoestring and heroic treks through the bloody snow to get to a gig on time, or whatever it is. I think it's really awful.

(Vi Subversa of Poison Girls)

And a rehearsal room in the 1990s

The floor's an ashtray and there are beer cans everywhere and it stinks and it is cold and the guys don't clean up after them. So on two or three occasions I've gone down to the desk and said, 'Would somebody come and clean it up before we work in here?'.

(Vanessa, bass player in Birmingham band
The Fabulous Jam Tarts)

The important factor, here, is not so much the physical conditions per se as the value system which romanticises and sustains them. As rock venues are organised entirely around the notion that rock bands are male, inadequate dressing-rooms are a particular bugbear for women. Well-known and prestigious venues often lack even minimal facilities. When the Mistakes played at The Rock Garden in London the only place to change was a tiny toilet which smelt of Jeyes fluid since the official changing room was dirty, contained dozens of beer kegs and a thirteen-piece male band. It is not simply a question of clubs failing to provide reasonable facilities for performers: by smashing up the facilities male bands create an environment which works to exclude women.

> At the Greyhound one time they did up the dressing-room and it was quite nice. It had a basin and sink and a few chairs and it was quite reasonably decorated. And there was a toilet next door. Gradually over the months it deteriorated and deteriorated. They didn't bother to clean it up properly. And the bands who used it must have been really shitty, because there was graffiti all over the walls and the sink was permanently blocked. They never bothered to put soap or towel out anymore. And it was just awful in the end: the chairs were broken, the toilet smashed up. I hate that kind of thing. Men seem to be much more like that than women.
>
> (Hlison Rayner of Jam Today)

The world of rock does not have to be like this; many women musicians try to change it. Every Woman, for instance, a vocal-dance act from Sheffield, insist on 'two dressing rooms with lockable doors, wash basin, hot and cold water, table and chairs, adequate heating and lighting, toilets, full length mirrors'. On the other hand, a band would find it hard to obtain these conditions on the indie and rock circuits until they were successful enough to play really big venues. Moreover, other bands criticised Every Woman: 'Who do you think you are expecting such conditions? Superstars?'

I believe that male musicians accept bad conditions because they endow masculinity, making the life of a rock musician one which most women would not choose. It is, then, another way of excluding women, as is language which a single woman in a male band may find herself under pressure to use in order to become 'one of the lads'. Both the female members of indie band Ms45 had done this.

One of the earliest camouflage devices that I learned being a girl in a band with guys is to become a foul-mouthed crass bastard, simply so that I wouldn't have a separate language for the 'treehouse' and then when the girl came in. On the other hand, it's sad that I had to change myself that way. But, on the other hand, I didn't want to feel that marginalised because everyone was being polite around me.

(Shareen)

However, the most significant clash between women's needs and the masculine code of rock gigs revolves around children. Women still have responsibility for the vast majority of childcare in our society and this impedes their involvement in the music-making world because rock venues do not usually accommodate children. Many gigs take place in pubs, from which environment children are legally barred. Gigs are typically unsuitable for children from the point of view of health and safety, being dirty, cramped and full of potential dangers such as electrical cables and leads. Aside from these physical dangers, the audience poses a possible threat. Thefts and fighting may occur. A baby could not be safely left in a changing room. Indeed, there is usually no safe place for a baby or young child. Some venues, even reputable ones, lack dressing rooms; they certainly do not cater for children. Furthermore, babies, nappies and breast-feeding are anathema to the protagonists of the 'heroic' vision of rock 'n roll life.

Alison Rayner (of 1980s feminist jazz-rock band Jam Today), determined to challenge the assumption that musicians are male and the public–private division, detailed the problems her band faced and how they organised to overcome them:

Gigs vary. Some gigs are fine and some are extremely difficult. If there's a dressing room – at the moment he's very young, he's only a few months old – if he's not asleep, then we have to have somebody come and sit with him while we're playing When I book gigs now I have to remember, that's another thing to mention . . . I have to say, 'Right, the other thing is that we have a baby. And is there a suitable room? And if the baby's asleep will there be somebody who can sit with the baby? Sometimes, like a pub, you just get a kind of blank look and they say, 'Oh, it's nothing to do with us'.

Some women managed to incorporate their children into their performances. Once Ali Smith, a local Oxford musician, had three little children, she knew she just had to go on playing in order to stay alive, so she always took her young children to gigs where kids are allowed. I have even witnessed her playing the sax with her baby on her hip at the same time. On the other hand, Ali stresses how difficult this juggling act is: 'You're a mother first and a musician second, always'. This makes it extremely difficult for such women to turn their hobby into a career and become professional. In contrast, male musicians' children tend to be cared for by their wives and girlfriends.

The gig, whether it be in a pub or club, is peopled mainly by men. Audiences are still predominantly male, as are promoters, lighting crew and so forth. But it is not only the predominance of men that defines the gigging space as male. Even more, it is the way that men typically assert authority over that space. Probably the most rampant sexism is encountered in interaction with technicians. Sexist attitudes of the sound crew lead to women's bands being undersold on time and attention.

> People tend to take you less seriously. It's all very well for boys to be in bands; that's what they've always done. But if you're a girl – oh, you're doing it because your friends are doing it, or because the person you are going out with is doing it. Therefore you are not taken seriously. Like, if you're talking to the PA they ask the men what sound they want. They don't ask you what sound you want. There have been many times when I've said, 'We want a sharper sound on the bass' or 'Take more off the bass drum', and the PA men turn round and look at you and think, 'How can she know about this? What does she know?'.
>
> (Veronica, keyboard player in a 1980s Oxford band)

My recent research suggests that the increased visibility of women musicians in the 1990s has not changed attitudes. Interviewees told me of being deliberately blinded by techno-talk, constantly patronised and ignored, while some had even experienced sabotage. Most women musicians had encountered some kind of problem, even commercially successful ones.

> A lot of sound engineers think you don't have a clue what you're doing with equipment and stuff. It's like, 'I'll do that. I'll do that.' I think, 'God! Do I have a brain?' And that gets to me quite a lot sometimes.
>
> (Manda Rin, of professional Scottish band, Bis)

Women musicians have, of course, retaliated. In particular, the strong female performers in the 1990s have used their power to tackle this problem unreservedly.

> There was one particular roadie who definitely was having a problem with the fact that I was female. . . . He came up and he pinched my arse. And a few days later, he was fiddling around with a case and there were quite a few blokes looking around, I just went up to him and I squeezed his bum really hard. And he jumped out of his skin and walked out and he didn't touch me again. That's the way I deal with the things if I do get it.
>
> (Katherine Garrett, based in Oxford and keyboard
> player in pro band, The Mystics)

When a sound engineer patronised Debbie Smith (of Echobelly) and then messed up her equipment during the course of a gig she simply hit him with her guitar.

Understanding the complex, technical world of PA can give a feeling of power to those with this 'superior' knowledge. At big gigs sound technicians stand in their own little physical enclosures into which few people are allowed. I have often watched 'outsiders' attempt to enter this territory, inching their way over and being edged back again by the crew who patrol its boundaries. It is a male space in which a woman mixer is often simply denied any form of access to the desk.

> They were making this awful balls-up of the sound. It was terrible. But they wouldn't let me be on the mixing desk. They didn't actually give a verbal reason. Just two men. Just consolidated themselves at the desk. They basically ignored me and I gave up in the end, totally frustrated.
>
> (Gina, London-based 1980s sound engineer)

Female musicians also often face sexism from male musicians who may resent the popularity of a women's band. Frances Belle told me that local musicians, despite initially helping them, were relieved when their band split up, while some of the 'help' was patronising, taking the form of boys storming on stage during a gig and, unasked, altering their amp and microphone levels. There can even be violence, as in these instances.

> A very ambitious band . . . abused us, put our guitars out of tune before going on stage, ripped off our equipment. Because they were

very competitive and they wanted to blow us off the stage. That's happened a lot.

(Vi Subversa of Poison Girls)

Atomic Candy entered a rock open competition and their success elicited violence from male bands competing against them.

We won first heat, knocking out Scunthorpe's main contingent. The next heat came along and we knew they were going to be trouble. We had various phone calls telling us not to turn up, that we were going to get into trouble when we got there. And we thought, 'Fuck that, we are going to go and hopefully we are going to win it!'

We got in there, started playing and some of our equipment got nicked off the stage even though there was security round the stage. We were halfway through one of the numbers and beer glasses started getting thrown at us. And we didn't win – surprise, surprise. . . . These lads had just got it into their heads that no woman was going to win the competition over them and it got really out of hand.

(Fran of Sub Rosa)

Lastly, women's bands have to contend with sexism from audiences, which comes in a variety of forms, one manifestation being the way that audiences typically expect women to be less competent than men. The most common form of harassment is verbal abuse of the 'show us yer tits' variety, evaluation being based as much on the size of the musician's breasts as on her guitar playing, and such comments are meant to be heard by the performers. It can be startling and off-putting for the novice band to be told to strip. Singers and frontwomen are harassed more than instrumentalists, and younger women tend to get more abuse. But women in the 1990s have been retaliating strongly actively drawing the audience's attention to the perpetrator and confronting him. L7 like to suggest that the man saves his breath for blowing up his inflatable sheep when he gets home. My interviewees suggested a number of effective one-line retorts, for instance:

You come up here and get your trousers off and we'll get our tits out.

(J.W. Myhill of Valley of the Dolls)

It's all right. I remember what it was like when I had my first drink.

(Caroline Scallon of Soul Devotion)

Loads of people would say, 'Sit on me face' and I'd say, 'Why? Is your nose bigger than your dick?'

(Mandy of Ms45)

The area in front of the stage (the 'moshpit') is highly male dominated. It is difficult to just stand there as a woman because the men are dancing forcefully. Feminist bands have often encouraged women to come down the front into that space, but men may react aggressively.

A lot of students from the Poly came down – male students. And the women had done what they quite often used to do in those days. They'd formed a semicircle in the front and were dancing with linked arms. And the blokes linked arms behind them and were dancing, kicking their legs up and were actually kicking the women and children. They were just being hateful. They were making fun of them. They just couldn't understand what was going on.

(Terry Hunt, of 1980s band Jam Today)

Dramatic incidents are rare, but nonovert violence and general harassment were commonplace and taken for granted in the 1980s.

There's always either a comment or some uneasy atmosphere or something. Every gig there'll be some little something that has to be dealt with. (But) a lot of women just have that experience happen to them so much of the time that they block it out. And it's the victim syndrome. It's like almost that you draw that kind of attention to yourself, that somehow women are responsible for those things. Or, 'Oh, it's not serious, dear. It doesn't matter'. We're so used to being harassed.

(Terry Hunt, Jam Today)

Even in the 1990s such remarks were so routine that they barely required comment. Practically every woman musician I interviewed had experienced them.

Conclusion

Women instrumentalists are rare in the pubs and clubs of our cities. The reasons for this are manifold. Here I have chosen to focus mainly on the gendered politics of urban space. The fact that rock/indie is mainly peopled by men and, moreover, permeated with a masculinist value system strongly limits women's involvement in playing instruments in bands. I have shown how men sometimes actively exclude women from participating in this world. A further inhibiting factor is women's main responsibility for childcare in this society.

The situation is not static. The more sympathetic response to popular music within schools is giving girls an increased opportunity to learn rock instruments. However, this in itself is not enough. As Lucy Green's recent research on music in schools has shown, there is often a collusion between teachers and pupils which perpetuates the taken-for-granted gender politics of music (Green, 1997).

It often takes great courage for a girl to challenge 'common sense' and she will need support in the process. Active intervention is crucial. When gender issues are seriously addressed, the effects can be dramatic. Just one enlightened, sensitive teacher or youth worker who challenges the gendered musical status quo can have an immense effect in a particular locality, radically increasing the number of girls playing in bands. For example, in the mid 1990s, with only a handful of all-women bands in the whole of the city of Oxford, the nearby village of Eynsham was sporting two female teenage bands. This was the result of one (male) youth worker's efforts in encouraging 15-year-old students to learn to play. He paid for and arranged tuition for them from Oxford band members, provided free rehearsal space and access to equipment, and set up prestigious gigs for them in Oxford.

A women-only context in which to learn musical and technological skills has been of central importance for many female musicians, all of my evidence pointing to the importance of providing some male-free, protected spaces (in schools, community centres, youth clubs) in which young women can be supported in learning to play. Women's music projects are still rare. The gender-blind norm serves to maintain patriarchy.

It is clear that many community schemes have been doing admirable work but have been operating on a shoestring. Women's music projects are notoriously underfunded. They have had trouble finding buildings, and have often only kept going by the voluntarily unpaid labour of highly committed tutors and administrators. Outside London, such projects often face local opposition. However, where these projects do exist, they provide a safe atmosphere in which young women can learn to play traditionally 'masculine' instruments. Such projects offset material constraints by providing free or cheap access to equipment, space in which to be noisy, and music tuition by women who also act as role models, showing that it is perfectly possible for them to play rock. In particular, these projects confront technophobia and give women both skills and confidence in dealing with equipment.

Consequently, this research suggests that separatism can be effective as a temporary strategy for increasing the number of young women musicians. Since the 1980s, local councils in Britain sought to alleviate local youth employment problems in urban areas by financing music projects. Insofar as they have done this without addressing the sexism of rock, they have in practice been funding *men's* music making. My research findings suggest that one important way in which the local state has been able to challenge male hegemony is to subsidise women-only learning environments. Women's music making must be supported and given a higher profile if more role models are to become available: woman as sound engineer, woman as music programmer, as well as woman as drummer and guitarist. It is beginning to happen, but there is a long way to go before the percentage of women in popular music-making reaches 50 per cent.

References

Bayton, M. (1998) *Frock Rock: women performing popular music*. Oxford: Oxford University Press.

Bell, D. and Valentine, G. (1995) *Mapping Desire: geographies of sexualities*. London: Routledge.

Cohen, S. (1991) *Rock Culture in Liverpool: Popular Music in the Making*. Oxford: Clarendon Press.

Duncan, N. (ed.) (1996) *Bodyspace: destabilizing geographies of gender and sexuality*. London: Routledge.

Finnegan, R. (1989) *The Hidden Musicians: Music Making in an English Town*. Cambridge: Cambridge University Press.

Frith, S. (1983) *Sound Effects: Youth, Leisure and the Politics of Rock'n'Roll*. London: Constable.

Green, E., Woodward, D. and Hebron, S. (1990) *Women, Leisure, What's Leisure?* London: Macmillan.

Green, L. (1997) *Music, Gender, Education*. Cambridge: Cambridge University Press.

Hall, R. (1985) *Ask Any Woman: a London Inquiry into Rape and Sexual Assault*. Bristol: Falling Wall Press.

Hall, S. and Jefferson, T. (1976) *Resistance Through Rituals: Youth Subcultures in Post-War Britain*. London: Hutchinson.

Hanmer, J. and Maynard, M. (1987) *Women, Violence and Social Control*. Basingstoke: Macmillan.

Hanmer, J. and Saunders, S. (1993) *Women, Violence and Crime Prevention: a West Yorkshire Study*. Avebury: Avebury Publishing.

Hester, M., Kelly, L. and Radford, J. (1996) *Women, Violence and Male Power*. Buckingham: Open University Press.

Hey, V. (1986) *Patriarchy and Pub Culture*. London: Tavistock Press.

McDowell, L. and Sharpe, J. P. (eds) (1997) *Space, Gender, Knowledge: Feminist Readings*. London: Amold.

Stanko, E. (1985) *Intimate Intrusions: Women's Experience of Male Violence*. London: Unwin Hyman.

13
Organising Rural Women Migrants in Beijing[1]

Cecilia N. Milwertz

At a lively event of talks, singing and accounts of heartbreaking individual life stories some two hundred young rural women gathered on 6 April 1997 in Beijing to celebrate the first anniversary of their organisation – the Migrant Women's Club.

Two developments in Chinese society have been particularly important in leading to the setting up in 1996 of the first formal organisation for rural migrant women in Beijing. First, restrictions on temporary migration have been significantly relaxed since economic reforms were initiated in 1978 allowing for individually or family motivated migration to supplement previous mainly state-initiated migration (Davin, 1999; Mallee and Pieke, 1999). A host of new employment opportunities have been provided for a rural population whose labour had for more than two decades been underemployed and underutilised, and it is estimated that between 40 and 100 million rural inhabitants had migrated to urban areas by the mid 1990s (Solinger, 1998).

Second, many forms of nonstate and semistate organising have emerged or re-emerged in China since 1978 (White, Howell and Shang, 1996). Among these are women's organisations. The transition from planned to market economy has had numerous negative political and economic impacts especially on the lives of women, but has simultaneously opened up opportunities for the establishment of a plurality of women's organisations that challenges centralised, state-sponsored women's organisations (Zhang Naihua, 1995; Jaschok, 1998). During the first 30 years of the People's Republic of China, one organisation, the All-China Women's Federation, was mandated by the Communist Party to represent women.[2] Together with many other groups, networks and organisations set up on the initiative of women the Migrant

Women's Club is a manifestation of the multiple forms of organising that now exist, albeit under precarious political conditions.

In some cities migrant women are joined in informal networks based on place of origin to facilitate exchange of experiences and mutual assistance with the aim of improving living and working conditions and wages (Solinger, 1995, pp. 27–9; Zhang Junzuo, 1994, p. 88). The Migrant Women's Club is engaged in the more far-reaching objective of creating a change in urban-rural and gender hierarchies.

This chapter aims to document and analyse the values and practice of self-initiated activism for the improvement of women's lives by exploring the background and structure of the Migrant Women's Club and discussing the club's representation of the interests of rural migrant women in urban Beijing during the first 15 months of its existence from April 1996 to August 1997.

Academics in China have been grappling with theoretical definitions of women and gender and vigorously debating the appropriateness and usefulness of applying imported theories of gender and feminism to the Chinese context since the early 1980s (Tan, 1991; Lin, Liu and Jin, 1998; Min, 1998). Furthermore, the practical activities that women's organisations, groups and networks engage in and their direct contact with the immediate problems confronting women have led to the development of alternative views and interpretations of gender relations and of feminisms as activism. The process of addressing women's immediate needs potentially leads to new understandings of prevailing gender equality ideals and practice as women identify and challenge the relations of power and gender that circumscribe their lives (Naples, 1998).

In analysing women as political subjects Molyneux (1985) has distinguished between practical and strategic gender interests. Practical gender interests arising from concrete conditions of women's positioning within the gender division of labour are usually a response to an immediate perceived need. These differ from strategic gender interests by not generally entailing a strategic goal such as women's emancipation or gender equality and not challenging the prevailing forms of gender subordination (Molyneux, 1985; Moser, 1993). In order to assess the types and aims of activities engaged in by the Club it is useful to categorise in terms of these two forms of gender interests. However, in order to avoid replicating the hegemonic interpretations of feminist activism that have excluded activism that was not based on an articulated gender analysis, a broader definition of feminist activism that includes actions that challenge women's disadvantaged position in society, whether or not these are articulated as feminist (Gluck, 1998), is applied.

Exploratory and qualitative research interviews (Kvale, 1983, 1989) with organisers, members and staff of the Migrant Women's Club form the main data of this chapter. Interviews were carried out in Chinese with five main organisers and staff of the club and with eight members. These interviews were supplemented by documentary sources and observations at organised club activities and a series of visits to the club. Interviews were carried out mainly over the course of three visits to Beijing in 1996–97. Additional visits to the club and an interview with one of the two club initiators took place in 1998.

Background and structure – an organisation within an organisation

The Migrant Women's Club was set up by staff at the magazine *Rural Women Knowing All* (*Nongjianü baishitong*) when they started receiving letters from rural women about problems they were encountering in the cities they migrated to.[3] Administratively the magazine, published monthly since January 1993, is a subdivision of the newspaper *Chinese Women's News* (*Zhongguo funübao*), which has in turn been published by the All-China Women's Federation (ACWF) since 1984. Among some 10000 newspapers and magazines published in China, including about fifty published by the ACWF, there was none specifically intended for a rural female readership although the great majority of women in China are from rural areas (Xie, 1995b, p. 222). According to co-initiator of the club and consultant to the magazine Professor Wu Qing the reason was that

> Nobody would take on the task of creating a magazine for country bumpkins, as well as the double handicap of dealing with something concerning both *rural* and *women*. No one dared. People are afraid of losing money . . . Xie Lihua had the guts to do it. She has had opportunities to go to rural areas, so she knew the needs and demands and the market.
>
> (Wu Qing, interview, 23 July 1997)

The setting up of the club within the structure of the ACWF is a strategic choice on the part of the two main initiators, editor Xie Lihua and Professor Wu Qing, based on their activist experience from two of the first popular women's organisations in Beijing. Their choice reflects that the western civil society opposition between state and society is not directly replicated in the Chinese context in which one main action strategy applied by the new organisations is based on personal networks that cut across institutions regardless of their structural links to the party/state. The ACWF for its part doubtlessly views a new organisation set up within its own structure as less threatening than those outside its domain. Furthermore, whereas accommodation and funding are major problems for independent organisations that are mainly dependent on support from foreign donors, the club holds the relatively privileged position of being supported by both foreign donors and the ACWF.

In terms of recruitment of members the Migrant Women's Club is an innovative type of membership organisation in the Chinese women's organisation context. All women in China are in principle automatically associated to their local-level branch of the Women's Federation and membership of professional women's organisations usually automatically includes all women within a certain profession. Contrary to routine membership, the Migrant Women's Club recruited its first members by issuing 2000 letters in March 1996 to hospitals and factories employing rural women and to eight service enterprises that facilitate contact between rural migrants and urban employers in Beijing. By December that year 196 members had registered.[4] Members' ages reflect the tendency for women in China to migrate predominately when they are young and unmarried (Davin, 1999). The average age of members was 21.5 years, the eldest being 36 and the youngest 16. Most had been in Beijing for more than three years at the time when they became members. In the capital most members were engaged in various forms of unskilled labour as domestic maids, factory workers, waitresses and shop assistants. Only a few were engaged in skilled labour such as typing and accounting (Li, 1996, p. 17).

The Migrant Women's Club is a popular initiative set up by women. However, it is also the initiative of highly educated urban professionals for a dissimilar group of rural women with the aim of addressing their problems. As has been noted by studies of organisations, organisations staffed and elected by the people they are meant to serve and represent, and organisations staffed by people who are different (socially, professionally, ethnically) from their members tend to have different relationships with their constituencies in terms of member participation in defining needs and determining the activities of the organisation, with organisations staffed by members generally representing a more participatory approach (Farrington et al., 1993, p. 3). Although the organisers and main decision makers of the club are not themselves rural women, the organisers say that they attempt to represent the interests of members by basing their work on the needs and interests of its members as well as on their active participation in determining the activities of the organisation, in contrast to viewing members as 'passive receivers' (Li, 1996, p. 14).

Given a situation in which rural migrants are generally ostracised by the urban population, the choice of engaging a migrant rural woman as one of two office staff can be viewed as a significant step reflecting a recognition on the part of the organisers that they do not share the members' experience of being rural migrants and that they are in fact attempting to include and base their work on their needs. At this early stage of the organisation's history this does not necessarily mean that the organisers are in practice able to realise fully their objective of basing their work on members' expressed needs, partly because the club does not yet have a (formal) structure to ensure the participation of members in setting the agenda of the club. However, a meeting in March 1997 to plan future club activities showed that although the few members present were not the main actors they were actively involved and listened to. Further research is needed to understand in more detail the club decision-making process, including the extent to which organisers and staff are willing to withdraw control and members are inclined and able to take on responsibility. At present, in the context of the possibilities for and difficulties of organising from below in China, the club is a first step that may at a later stage lead to women migrants organising on their own initiative.

Addressing immediate needs and challenging women's subordination

The two fundamental issues addressed by the Migrant Women's Club are, first, the social and economic gap between urban and rural China and, second, gender inequality. As described by the club, rural to urban migrants come to personify the gap between the life-styles of an agricultural rural and an industrialised urban society. Rural women in the city are discriminated against in terms of working conditions, they find their knowledge and skills inadequate to cope with urban life and they have problems related to their rural household registration. Club members are shocked that they are not only taken advantage of by employers, but that the urban population also seems to be generally hostile towards them (Li, 1996, pp. 9–10). In a letter to the magazine one woman wrote that she felt extremely humiliated when she first met her potential employer who looked at her, not as a fellow human being, but 'at best as if she were buying a high quality commodity' (Xie, 1995a, p. 6).

Much of the discrimination experienced by rural migrants is not gender-specific. However, according to the club initiators, rural women migrants are particularly exposed and vulnerable in the urban context. Their decision to work for rural women is based on their view that if China in general, despite much attained progress under Communist Party rule, has a long way to go in achieving gender equality in a cultural context where women are in many ways viewed as second class citizens, then rural women are those who are most disadvantaged (Xie Lihua, interview, 28 July 1997; Wu Qing, interview, 23 July 1997).

Letters and articles published in *Rural Women Knowing All* provide examples of the problems confronting rural migrants, while a number of surveys and studies provide a more overall picture of the extent of the problems. These include long working hours, poor working and living conditions, lack of labour contracts and social security measures, physical and verbal abuse, sexual harassment and rape (Davin, 1999; Tan, 1995; Solinger, 1998).

As a contrast to these problems the aim of the club is to provide a space where members can feel at home. 'A warm place to go where there is no discrimination, no cold indifference and no inequality' and a place where 'everyone can speak as much as they like without inhibition' and where women can mutually support each other and find friends, are phrases from the open letter written to solicit members ('Dagong mei zhi jia' bangongshi, 1996). My visits to the club gave me the impression of a relaxed atmosphere. Members who telephone or visit the office during the week to chat or seek advice show that they find the club safe and supportive. The two members of staff Yu Jinglian, a retired editor, and Zhang Xin, herself a rural migrant, are readily available with help and advice. In one case an unmarried member turned to the club for help when she became pregnant[5] and in another case staff checked up on the workplace of a member who was not receiving the training agreed on in her work contract.

Having brought together women in the club to share their experiences, the next aim is to support them to create change to improve their lives, initially to help members to recognise precisely where their problems and weaknesses lie, and then to support them in confronting these both when they are structurally imposed on them in the form of gender roles and urban/rural hierarchies and when they stem from lack of education and skills. The aim is also to support migrant women to recognise their own strengths in a situation where they are constantly being told that they lack 'quality'. The club aims both to provide education to members and also to support them to recognise that even though they may lack formal education they have other strengths. Since December 1996 the club has offered primary school classes in maths, Chinese and English as the majority of members have attended only six years of school or less. The teachers are club members and staff, and pupils emphasise that they appreciate being taught by teachers who do not make them feel inferior (Chinese class students, conversation, April 1997). In 1998 a new book for Chinese classes was being compiled by Zhang Xin, the aim being to collect a series of texts relevant to the lives of the rural women themselves. In mid 1997 classes in typing and computer skills were started and there were plans to start classes in sewing.

A manual on legal rights was also being compiled. Based on a series of case studies, the idea was to translate laws and regulations relevant to the lives of rural migrants into a language comprehensible to them and to provide them with information on relevant authori-ties and institutions to contact when in need of support. Often, rural women are not aware that they have legal rights in the labour market and that these are being violated. And even if they are aware they do not necessarily know where to seek assistance. Although the club, in co-operation with *Rural Women Knowing All*, has been involved in solving specific problems encountered by members, it does not have the capacity to resolve conflicts by providing social services and legal aid on a larger scale. When members seek support to solve problems related to their employment or other matters, in principle the role of the club is mainly to provide information, moral support and guidance and to facilitate contact with the ACWF and employment authorities, which can deal specifically with the problems (Yu Jinglian, interview, 21 July 1997).

The approach applied by the Migrant Women's Club in supporting rural women migrants is based on equality between men and women being legally guaranteed in the constitution, the marriage law and the law on the protection of the rights and interests of women. The club views insufficient labour market legislation as one of the reasons that rural migrant women are discriminated against and emphasises the importance of improving the law. However, the aim is primarily to rectify the imbalance between the legislated and proclaimed equality and the actual discrimination in daily life by ensuring that women know their rights and by creating awareness in society in general of rural migrant women's situation and their rights. The club's objective is both to provide members with knowledge of their legal rights and to unite rural women and their urban employers in breaching the urban–rural gap. In aiming to improve the relationship between migrant and host populations the club is engaged in a delicate balancing act between supporting rural migrant women and simultaneously convincing employers that in the long run this is not contrary to their interests.

While lectures on legal rights are given by professional lawyers, at other meetings speakers are rural women who talk from their personal experience. At one meeting held in May 1996, Zhang Huanrong, a 28-year-old successful poultry breeder, talked about her experience of setting up an enterprise. Following Zhang Huanrong's speech, Xie Lihua reminded the some fifty members attending the Sunday meeting that due to the household registration system they would probably have to leave Beijing at some point. Xie Lihua emphasised the importance of every single member deciding on and preparing herself for her future. She stressed that Zhang Huanrong's story could provide support and strength for others. Because you are a woman your only choice is not to find a husband to support you – was Xie Lihua's message to club members. On the contrary, if you believe in yourself you can find the strength to overcome difficulties and arrange your own future instead of depending on others to make decisions for you. The theme that women have a right to making decisions about their own lives rather than being obliged to adhere to dominant gender roles that emphasise the importance of women's sacrifice of personal needs for the benefit of their husband or family is central to Xie Lihua's thinking and the agenda of the club. The purpose of the meeting was to create a gender awareness among members that would sustain them when they were confronted with their own and other people's conceptions of normative gender roles, and to translate awareness into a practice enabling women to overcome the difficulties they encounter by recognising their own strength.

Members of the club, like the majority of migrants in China, fall into the category of what is termed the 'floating' population. This means that their residence in the city is temporary and they are permanently registered in their rural place of origin. Most migrants will at some point leave the city, from choice or because they cannot gain permanent residence in the city. All citizens in China are registered at birth as either urban or rural residents. Apart from temporary urban residence permits it is extremely difficult to change from a rural to an urban status.

Originally this registration system was set up in order to limit rural–urban migration. According to Xie Lihua, the club does not encourage members to return to rural areas but plays a role in supporting them to be prepared to cope if and when they do choose or are compelled to return (Xie Lihua, interview, 28 July 1997). Some members have been sent to the city to earn money to support their family and plan only to stay in the city as long as their family requires them to do so, but other members are set on avoiding return (member interviews, 20 July 1997 and 23 July 1997).

In mid 1997 Xie Lihua discovered that a group of 20 rural migrant women in Xiamen (a south China coastal city) had been granted urban residence permits in recognition of the contribution rural migrants were making to the development of the city. The Migrant Women's Club invited these women to visit Beijing for a meeting that had the dual objective of morally supporting club members' wish to remain in the city and to stage a media event to promote a change of attitudes towards granting urban residence to rural women migrants, especially when they marry an urban resident (Xie Lihua, interview, 10 August 1998). In order to prevent rural to urban migration the household registration system registers children according to the mother's registration with the consequence that children of a rural mother living in the city cannot, even when their father holds an urban household permit, receive urban schooling (Davin, 1999, p. 6). Xie Lihua's view is that

> It is important to solve the household registration issue for migrants. In its present form the system is harmful to women. Some places now permit the child to follow the registration of the father or the mother. This benefits the education of the children and corresponds to changes in society. Even though the problem had only been resolved for 20 women I consider this as progress. Media publicity of the case of these 20 women will cause government officials to start thinking about the issue.
>
> (Xie Lihua, interview, 10 August 1998)

The club is enabling only a relatively small number of members to receive basic education and legal education and to develop group support and mutual, as well as to some degree official, recognition of their wishes and needs as in the meeting between the Xiamen women and club members. However, the message that women can question unequal gender relations, put forward demands on the basis of their own definition of their interests and create change is being spread to a much larger number of women via the magazine. Furthermore, the urban population, administrators and policy makers are being influenced through the media to change attitudes to rural migrants.

The link between the magazine and the club is not only structural but is functionally incorporated into club activities. In one of the early cases, before the establishment of the club, magazine staff helped Chen Cundi, who later became a Migrant Women's Club member, to obtain a divorce from the husband she had been sold to. This case illustrates a practice of addressing a specific immediate problem, providing information and practical support and then going beyond the immediate practical gender interests of the migrant woman in question to challenge women's subordination in general.

Chen Cundi was abducted by a woman who offered her a job in another province. When she arrived there she discovered that she had been sold into marriage. Although she managed to escape from her husband, five years passed before Chen Cundi reached Beijing, where she came into contact with magazine staff. A journalist and a lawyer travelled with her to her own and her husband's province where they assisted her in contacting the relevant Women's Federation and legal authorities in order to obtain a divorce. Because her husband had paid her mother a large sum of money Chen Cundi believed that she did not have the right to leave him or obtain a divorce. Following the divorce Chen Cundi said that she would have stayed with her husband had it not been for the fact that he was beating her:

> He had a very bad temper. He often abused and hit me. So I did not stay for more than a couple of months. He would lock the door when he left for work. I tried to run away and he beat me. My brother tried to help me but then he beat my brother. Finally, my brother helped me to run away across the fields. I wanted to end the marriage but I did not dare. Without my consent my household registration had been moved to my husband's province and I had been married. The authorities in Shaanxi would not help me as I was now registered in Hebei. And as long as I was married I could not move my registration. My husband said I could get a divorce if I repaid him all the money he had spent to buy me. I felt just like an egg hitting against a stone. My mother wanted me to return to my husband. She is a very typical Chinese rural woman.
>
> (Chen Cundi, interview, 20 July 1997)

Chen Cundi was susceptible to the deceit that led her to be sold in a situation where her family was desperately poor following the death of her 50-year-old father due to the family's lack of funds for medical care. She considered committing suicide, but finally managed to flee. Contact with magazine staff and joining the Migrant Women's Club meant an enormous change for her. In early 1997 she was part of a group of three club members who gave talks in Beijing to recruit new members. Previously, she said, she would never have dared to stand up in front of many people. In fact, she hardly dared approach the club to join because she felt inferior as she was 'only a maid'. It is unlikely that she would even in her wildest dreams have imagined that she could actually end the marriage she had been sold into, not least because divorce initiated by the woman does not accord with still-prevalent cultural assumptions of gender relations. When she left her husband and returned to her home village Chen Cundi was looked down on by fellow villagers because she was not complying with her role as a married women by accepting her destiny (Chen Cundi, interview, 20 July 1997).

The idea that Chen Cundi could divorce her husband without paying him back was 'imposed' on her by magazine staff intervention. In going beyond the expressed practical gender needs of rural women, as in this case, the magazine and the club represent strategic gender interests because rights, privileges and gender relations that subordinate women, and are often taken for granted in Chinese society, are challenged. By representing the strategic interests of rural migrant women the club is, as discussed by Nussbaum (1995) in the context of women's projects in India, imposing the values of an urban, intellectual women's movement upon women who have come to perceive their own second-class status as 'right' and 'natural'. They are assuming that these women, although they are not able to articulate these needs, do need and value autonomy.

Furthermore, the club extends its feminist activism beyond the small number of a few hundred urban members. When the club and the magazine help individual women to solve specific problems the case is covered in the magazine in order to create (gender) awareness about a general problem and to illustrate that alternative patterns of action are possible. Xie Lihua defines the link between the activities of the club and media coverage in *Rural Women Knowing All* and *Chinese Women's News* as essential to the objective of creating awareness in rural China in the sense that 'only the media can convey an understanding of the outside world, and only if there exists an alternative can the wish and impetus to change backward features arise' (Xie, 1995b, p. 226).

Via its link to *Rural Women Knowing All*, which in 1997 had reached a distribution of 230000, the Migrant Women's Club is able to spread its message in support of creating gender equality and social justice not only to the relatively small group of members but to a larger group of rural women in both rural and urban China. The club also engages the urban media in an effort to change the stereotypically negative image of the cheating, criminal migrant. Television, radio and other media regularly publicise activities of the club such as the first anniversary. Commenting on the importance of presenting social issues from an alternative perspective Xie Lihua says:

> We cannot know to what degree we have been successful in changing attitudes, but I do have examples of journalists who have changed the perspective of their writing about the migrant population once they came to know the club and its activities. Some people say I am just publicising my own work. I do not agree. I am publicising a belief and a way of working that represents a trend of development in society, so I really find that media publicising is very important. We bring forward social problems that deserve reflection.
>
> (Xie Lihua, interview, 10 August 1998)

By creating events such as the first anniversary and making use of the interest of the media in such events, the club is able to reach a broad audience. The main aim is to create a change of attitude among the urban populace towards rural migrants by presenting an alternative image of rural migrants. In contrast to the image that exaggerates their numbers and stresses their most visible and negative aspects an alternative, positive image of migrants engaged in constructive activities is presented.

The main aim of the celebration was to convey this positive image. The celebration included singing, talks and members' individual lifestories, all of which were aimed at the media. The celebration was held in a large hall. At one end a long table for the main speakers was set up with rows of chairs for members and other participants facing this panel. Between the panel and the rows of participants was a space filled by TV reporters and their equipment. The result was that the massive number of media representatives separated participants from the panel, so that the some 200 club members and their supporters became not only participants in the celebration but also spectators to a media event. This was apparent in the function the sharing of life stories took on at the event. Within the context of the club itself, at Sunday meetings, when stories are shared among members, the recognition that their problems are not individual serves as the basis for action for change. In the context of the celebration these same stories served the purpose of illustrating the great difficulties of migrant women. Storytelling then serves to create an image of this group of rural migrants as honest, hard-working contributors to the construction of the modern city.

Conclusion

The setting up of an organisation with the specific objective of looking after the interests of rural migrant women is an expression of the creation of a new culture of and about women and gender relations that has developed as a reaction to the contradictory effects of economic reforms (see also Croll, 1995). The objective of the Migrant Women's Club is to create social change that goes beyond its members. Despite the limited outreach of a small organisation it is important as one component within a new phase of the Chinese women's movement which emerged in the 1980s–90s. While individuals doubtlessly have benefited from membership of the club, it is questionable whether members are aware that their membership and participation in media events such as the celebration of the first anniversary is utilised as part of the club's strategy to influence and change urban attitudes to rural migrants. Nevertheless, the anniversary was also a political manifestation symbolising the continuing expansion and vitality of a plurality of feminist activisms in China and their imaginative interaction with the media to create social change.

Notes

1   I am grateful to Diana Martin, Maria Jaschok, Lin Chun, Min Dongchao, Harriet Evans and Geir Helgesen for suggestions that led to the present version of this chapter. Research visits to Beijing were supported by the Nordic Institute of Asian Studies (May 1996), the British Academy (March–April 1997 and 1998) and the European Science Foundation (July–August 1997 and 1998). All visits were hosted by the Institute of Sociology, the Chinese Academy of Social Sciences.

2   The All-China Women's Federation (ACWF) was set up with the main objective of transmitting party policy to a constituency of all women in China and also with the aim of transmitting opinions from grassroots women to the party (Davin, 1976). Historically, the organization, due to its tight links to the party, has had a tendency to subordinate the concerns of women to those of the party (Howell, 1996). Similarly, the All-China Federation of Trade Unions

and Youth League were mandated to transmit party policy to, and represent, workers and youth.

3   Other activities organized by the magazine include literacy training, the establishment of a rural women's development fund, a reproductive health programme, and an investigation on suicide among rural women.

4   To become a member registration with relevant migration authorities and a temporary residence permit in Beijing are required.

5   Due to the population control policy pregnancies are only allowed for married women according to a quota system (see Milwertz, 1997).

References

Croll, E. (1995) *Changing identities of Chinese women: rhetoric, experience and self-perception in twentieth-century China*. Hong Kong: Hong Kong University Press; London and New Jersey: Zed Books.

'Dagong mei zhi jia' bangongshi (Migrant Women's Club Office) (1996) 'Zhi lai Jing dagong jiememen de yi feng gongkaixin. (Open letter to sisters who have come to the capital to work)'. *Nongjianü baishitong zazhishe*, March.

Davin, D. (1976) *Woman work*. Oxford University Press: Oxford.

Davin, D. (1999) *Internal migration in contemporary China*. London: Macmillan.

Farrington, J., Bebbington, A., Wellard, K. and Lewis, D. J. (1993) *Reluctant Partners? Non-governmental organizations, the state and sustainable agricultural development*. London: Routledge.

Gluck, S. B. (1998) 'Whose feminism, whose history? Reflections on excavating the history of (the) US women's movement(s)'. In N. C. Naples (ed.), *Community activism and feminist politics. Organizing across race, class, and gender*. London: Routledge.

Howell, J. (1996) 'The struggle for survival: prospects for the Women's Federation in post-Mao China'. *World Development* 1, 129–43.

Jaschok, Maria (1998) 'Chinese educational reforms and feminist praxis: on ideals, process and paradigim', in Michael Agelasto and Bob Adamson (eds). *Higher education in post-Mao China*. Hong Kong: Hong Kong University Press, 321–43.

Kvale, S. (1983) 'The qualitative research interview'. *Journal of Phenomenological Psychology*, 2, 171–96.

Kvale, S. (1989) 'To validate is to question'. In *Issues of validity in qualitative research*, ed. S. Kvale (ed.), 73–92, Lund: Studentlitteratur.

Li Tao (1996) Tigao suzhi moqiu fazhan. 'Dagong mei zhi jia' de renwu yu qiantu (Improve quality, strive for development – the tasks and future of the Migrant Women's Club). Unpublished paper.

Lin Chun, Liu Bohong and Jin Yihong (1998) 'China'. In A. Jagger and I. Young (eds), *A companion to feminist philosophy*, Oxford: Blackwell.

Mallee, H. and Pieke, F. N. (eds) (1999) *Internal and International Migration Chinese Perspectives*. Richmond, Surrey: Curzon Press.

Milwertz, C. (1997) *Accepting population control – the perspective of urban Chinese women on the one-child family policy*. Richmond, Surrey: Curzon Press.

Min Dongchao (1998) 'Tranlation as crossing borders: a case study of the translations of the word "feminism" into Chinese'. Unpublished paper.

Molyneux, M. (1985) 'Mobilization without emancipation? Women's interests, the state, and revolution in Nicaragua'. *Feminist Studies*, 2 (Summer), 227–54.

Moser, C. O. N. (1993) *Gender planning and development*. London: Routledge.

Naples, N. (1998) 'Women's community activism'. In N. C. Naples (ed.), *Community activism and feminist politics. Organizing across race, class, and gender*. London: Routledge.

Nussbaum, M. (1995) Women and cultural universals. Paper presented at the International Symposium on Chinese Women and Feminist Thought. Beijing, June 21–24.

Solinger, D. J. (1998) 'Job categories and employment channels among the 'Floating population'. In Greg O'Leary (ed.), 3–47. *Adjusting to capitalism. Chinese workers and the state*. London: M. E. Sharpe.

Tan Shen (1997) 'Nongcun laodongli liudong de xingbie chayi. (Sexual difference in the flow of rural labour)'. *Shehuixue yanjiu*, 1, 42–7.

Tan Shen (1995) 'Biange zhong funü de liang ge hang zhong da wenti'. Translated as 'Two major issues emerging in the reform of today's China', paper presented at the International Symposium On Chinese Women and Feminist Thought, Beijing, 21–24 June.

Tan Shen (1991) Dui jinnian funü yanjiu xianxiang de shehuixue kaocha (A sociologicl study of the phenomena of women's studies during recent years). In Li Xiaojiang and Tan Shen (eds), *Funü yanjiu zai Zhongguo*. (Women's studies in China), 23–42. Henan: Henan renmin chubanshe.

White, G., Howell, J. and Shang Xiaoyuan (1996) *In search of civil society*. Oxford: Clarendon Press.

Xie Lihua (1995a) 'Guniang, nimen weishenme jin cheng. (Girl, why do you come to the city)'. *Nongjianü Baishitong* (Rural Women Knowing All), 1, 4–7.

Xie Lihua (1995b) 'Women de guwen – Wu Qing (Our advisor – Wu Qing). *Nongjianü Baishitong* (Rural Women Knowing All), 8, 4–6.

Xie Lihua (1995c) '*Nongjianü baishitong zazhi* de ban kan sixiang he faxing celüe' (The management ideology and distribution strategy of the magazine *Rural Women Knowing All*). In *Dangdai nongcun funü fazhan yu duice*. (The development and strategy of contemporary rural women), eds. Rural Women Knowing All and Tianjin shifan daxue funü yanjiu zhongxin, Beijing: Zhongguo Funü chubanshe.

Zhang, Junzuo (1994) 'Development in Chinese reality: rural women's organizations in China'. *The Journal of Communist Studies and Transition Politics*, December, 4, 71–92.

Zhang Naihua with Wu Xu (1995) 'Discovering the positive within the negative: the women's movement in a changing China'. In Amrita Basu (ed.), *The challenge of local feminisms: women's movements in global perspective*. Boulder, San Francisco, Oxford: Westview Press, 25–57.

14
Frustrated Housewives or Unemployed Workers?: the Case of Domestic Returners[1]

Helen Russell

Women's employment has become increasingly visible in British cities and towns. Currently, 48 per cent of all employees in Britain are female, and within the next few years women are predicted to form the majority of employees (Metcalf, 1997). The increase in female employment has been particularly noticeable among mothers, for example between 1983 and 1992 employment rates among women with children grew by 20 per cent compared to an increase of 9 per cent among women without children (Brannen et al., 1994). British women are now having fewer children and are returning to work much sooner after childbirth (McRae, 1993; Macran et al., 1996). The fact that much of this employment is in the service sector, where workers deal directly with the public, further raises the profile of women's employment. However, while women's employment is becoming more visible, the same cannot be said of their unemployment.

Public debate and academic research on unemployment in Britain has tended to focus on male unemployment or on typically male industries. Furthermore, much of the policy directed towards the unemployed, including both income maintenance schemes and training policy (Callender and Metcalf, 1997), has favoured male workers. Eligibility for unemployment benefits and therefore being officially designated as 'unemployed' is based on typically male employment patterns, privileging full-time, continuous and higher-paid work. For example, in 1995 it was estimated that two million women workers in Britain fell outside the social insurance net because their pay fell below the earnings threshold; the majority of these women were part-time workers (ONS, 1996, p. 346). Furthermore, the linking of insurance-based unemployment benefit to recent contribution payments penalises those who have a gap between their period of employment and their period of unemployment, such as women returning to work after child rearing. Searching for part-time employment can result in failure to meet the actively seeking work criteria that apply to both means-tested and insurance-based unemployment benefits (Brown, 1990; Poynter, 1996). These rules have resulted in the underrepresentation of women on the unemployment register.

The focus on male unemployment reflects a general perception that women's unemployment is much less serious than men's, either because women have fewer financial responsibilities than men or because employment is believed to be less central in women's lives. Women, especially those with young children or those working part time (Hakim, 1996) are thought to place greater importance on their family role than their work roles; therefore, it is argued, unemployment poses 'no serious threat' to their identity (Ashton, 1986, p. 123). Others have argued that regardless of whether women are committed to employment or not, the domestic role can offer them an alternative form of satisfaction and fulfilment and therefore unemployment will not have the same psychological impact on women as it does on men.

> even if women prefer to have a job, unemployment hits them less hard than men psychologically speaking because an alternative is available to them in the return to the traditional role of housewife that provides some time structure, some sense of purpose, status and activity even though it offers little scope for wider social experiences.
> (Jahoda, 1982, p. 53)

One group of women who are particularly invisible in discussions of unemployment and who are largely excluded from official counts of unemployment and government training schemes are those attempting to re-enter the labour market having spent a period of time as full-time housewives. This group of women have been termed 'domestic returners' (Cragg and Dawson, 1984, p. 8).

Because of their discontinuous employment record many returners will not qualify for insurance benefits. Furthermore, if they are living with an employed partner they will usually be ineligible for means-tested unemployment benefits. This ineligibility for benefits also has implications for access to training. While women returners and those receiving lone parents allowance are eligible to participate in government schemes for the unemployed, priority usually goes to the registered long-term unemployed. The Equal Opportunities Commission has pointed out that the output-related funding for training also discourages the enrolment of women returners (EOC, 1993). Trainees other than lone parents do not qualify for childcare expenses and part-time training opportunities are uncommon; both these factors further restrict participation by returners (Callender and Metcalf, 1997).

The questions raised about the seriousness of female unemployment in terms of finances, identity and psychological well-being are particularly salient for domestic returners who have not lost jobs (or regular pay-packets), who are likely to have considerable family commitments and who have spent time outside the labour market 'voluntarily'. Some would argue that by taking a break in employment and restricting the type of work they will accept because of family responsibilities, these women have demonstrated a lack of commitment to employment (Hakim, 1991, 1996). Moreover, if the domestic role compensates for employment as Jahoda has suggested, then domestic returners should be particularly immune to any psychological impact of unemployment because they have been fully immersed in this role. Neither have these women experienced an 'abrupt exclusion from a social institution that previously dominated their daily lives', which is also identified as an important factor linking unemployment and psychological distress (Jahoda, 1988, p. 17). This chapter addresses the question of whether or not women seeking to re-enter employment after a period spent in the home should be considered unemployed. The answer to this question has implications for the visibility of women's unemployment in our cities and for the treatment of female unemployment in public policy. We first outline what existing research tells us about domestic returners.

Research on female unemployment and returners

Recent research on women's life and work histories has greatly enhanced our knowledge of the return to work following child rearing (Macran et al., 1996; Joshi and Hinde, 1993). These studies have shown a marked reduction in the period of time spent out of work at the birth of the first and last child. While Macran et al. (1996) recognise the possibility that employment opportunities at the time of re-entering the job market may lead to 'period effects', they do not explicitly address the effect of unemployment on the re-entry period. The implicit assumption is that the length of the employment gap is largely voluntary. Joshi and Hinde (1993) include the national unemployment rate as the variable in some of their analysis but do not consider the individual's experience of unemployment. McRae's (1993) study of women returners explicitly addresses the issue of whether the length of time before returning to work is extended involuntarily by an inability to find work. Among those whose intention to return to work had not been fulfilled, 26 per cent said they had been unable to find a job and a further 12 per cent said they could not find a job with suitable hours or location (p. 133).

Research addressing the job search experience of domestic returners is rare. Chaney's study of the topic throws some doubt on the assumption that employment is often financially optional for this group – 85 per cent of the women said that they had returned to work for financial reasons (Chaney, 1981). Cragg and Dawson's (1984) qualitative research on unemployed women also included domestic returners. Their findings undermine the argument that the domestic role offers women protection against the psychological distress that often accompanies unemployment. They concluded that the majority of unemployed women in their study, especially married women, wanted paid employment 'at least as much to escape the confines of domestic life as to enjoy the inherent satisfactions of employment' (p. 71). The study suggests that negative aspects of the domestic role such as boredom and social isolation may push women into the labour market and heighten their psychological distress. A further implication of this argument is that there may be a *selection effect* among domestic returners, whereby housewives who are most dissatisfied or who are in greatest financial need select themselves into the labour market and hence into unemployment.

In the remainder of this chapter we will evaluate the extent to which domestic returners can be identified as unemployed. Using survey data we will explore the two main areas of contention. First, we investigate the claim that these women lack real commitment to employment and therefore that their joblessness is to some extent voluntary. Second, we will test the assumption that domestic returners are sheltered from the deprivations that usually accompany unemployment. The level of employment deprivation, psychological distress and financial hardship experienced by domestic returners will be compared to the situation of others inside and outside the labour market.

Data

The data used for this investigation come from the Social Change and Economic Life Initiative (SCELI). The initial survey was carried out in 1986 in six urban labour markets: Aberdeen, Coventry, Kirkcaldy,

Northampton, Rochdale and Swindon. A representative sample of approximately 1000 individuals aged between 20 and 60 was interviewed in each area (for dertails see Gallie, 1994, pp. 338–9). A follow-up survey of approximately 200 respondents in each area was carried out in 1987. The SCELI data-set was chosen for this study because it contains detailed work histories, which are needed to distinguish different groups of unemployed women based on their previous labour market experience. Furthermore the survey oversampled the unemployed and therefore provides a bigger sample of unemployed women than other sources.

In order to capture those re-entering the job market a broad definition of unemployment is adopted. We include those in one or both of the following groups:

1 those who have been looking for employment in the last four weeks; and
2 those in receipt of benefit for reasons of unemployment.

Cragg and Dawson (1984) distinguish domestic returners from other unemployed women on the basis of their reasons for leaving their last job. Those who left for domestic reasons were defined as domestic returners while those who left for some other reason were classified as job losers. However, as the authors themselves note, these categories are not entirely distinct and women may leave a job for one reason but stay out of the labour market for another. Therefore, this study identifies returners by using respondents' work histories, categorising individuals on the basis of their activity prior to unemployment. Women who moved from employment to unemployment are defined as job losers and women who entered unemployment from full-time housework are defined as domestic returners. Those who were in full-time education immediately prior to their unemployment spell are excluded from the current study. This means that women who left jobs for domestic reasons but who immediately started to look for another more suitable job are classified as job losers because they have not experienced a spell of economic inactivity.

In total, 80 of the unemployed female respondents (20 per cent) were identified as domestic returners and 325 (80 per cent) were defined as job losers. Table 14.1 summarises the characteristics of these two groups and compares them to employed women. The proportion of women married or cohabiting was fairly similar in both unemployed categories, but there were clear differences in caring responsibilities. A much higher

Table 14.1 Descriptive statistics on three groups of women

	Job losers (%)	Domestic returners (%)	Employed (%)
Married/Cohabiting	47.7	55.0	77.4
With children	61.2	91.2	62.3
With children under 5 years	25.5	53.8	11.2
With three or more children	8.9	26.3	9.5
Receiving unemployment benefit[a]	71.7	50.0	—
Mean age	34.1 (11.8)[b]	31.7 (8.1)	38.5 (10.8)[b]
Mean time since last job (months)	27.3 (41.7)[b]	84.7 (75.6)	—
Base N	*325*	*80*	*1961*

[a] Includes those receiving insurance-based or means-tested unemployment benefits.
[b] The figures in brackets are standard deviations.

proportion of domestic returners had children in the household. Domestic returners were also more likely to have preschool-age children and larger families. These greater family commitments are likely to be partly responsible for the wide discrepancy in the length of time which had elapsed since the women's last jobs. Domestic returners had spent an average of seven years without employment compared to a mean of 2.3 years for job losers, but there was a high degree of variation within both groups.

Domestic returners' lower eligibility for benefit was also evident: only half were claiming benefit compared to 72 per cent of female job losers. The equivalent figure for unemployed men in the survey was over 90 per cent. The proportion of domestic returners receiving benefits was somewhat higher than expected because a significant minority were lone parents (40 per cent) and therefore more frequently qualified for means-tested benefit.

The family characteristics of job losers were very similar to employed women on a number of dimensions: an equal proportion had children and a similar proportion had large families. However, two distinct differences emerged: employed women were more likely to be married or cohabiting and were less likely to have young children. These differences suggest that single parenthood and responsibility for preschool children are associated with higher unemployment risks for women.

If having access to a more involving domestic role protects against the psychological impact of unemployment or detracts from women's employment commitment then these summary figures suggest that domestic returners' experience of unemployment were quite different from that of job losers. In the following sections we put these propositions to the test.

Employment commitment

The most fundamental argument for excluding domestic returners from the ranks of the unemployed is that they are uncommitted to employment and therefore that their joblessness is voluntary. This claim is backed by evidence of discontinuous careers and restrictions on working hours and location. However, it fails to take into account the constraints under which women's labour market decisions are made (Finch, 1989; Ginn et al., 1996). The lack of affordable childcare in Britain means many couples may have little option but for one partner to give up paid work or reduce hours to care for children (McRae, 1993; Gornick et al., 1997). Sex differentials in pay and prevailing gender norms mean that it is usually the female partner who adapts her employment behaviour (Brannen and Moss, 1992).

Those who deduce women's employment commitment from their labour market behaviour also implicitly adopt what might be termed a 'trade-off' model of commitment. It is assumed that commitment to paid work and to family are mutually exclusive. The measure of employment commitment adopted in the SCELI survey does not presuppose such a trade-off, nor is commitment extrapolated from behaviour. Employed respondents were asked, 'If you had enough money to live as comfortably as you would like for the rest of your life, would you continue to work, not necessarily in your present job, or would you stop working?' The unemployed were asked whether in the same financial circumstances they would 'want to work somewhere or would you want to remain without a job?' This measure tells us whether employment has a meaning in peoples' lives other than as a source of money. Those who work solely for financial reasons are defined as uncommitted to employment.

The results from this question show that domestic returners, far from being uncommitted to employment, display greater commitment than most other groups in the labour market (Table 14.2). Their commitment surpasses that of female job losers and of employed women and men, and is matched only by the commitment of unemployed men. The returners cannot therefore be excluded from the category of unemployed on the basis of their lack of employment commitment, when their commitment is assessed using a non-behavioural measure.

Table 14.2   Employment commitment among different groups in the labour market

	Domestic returners (%)	Female job losers (%)	Employed women (%)	Unemployed men (%)	Employed men (%)
Committed	74.0	69.0	60.3	74.9	66.8
Not committed	26.0	31.0	39.7	25.1	33.2
Base N	*77*	*313*	*1957*	*466*	*2079*

Employment deprivation, psychological distress and financial hardship

We next test the argument that domestic returners cannot be considered unemployed because they do not experience the same deprivations as other unemployed individuals in either psychological or financial terms. At the same time we can test the counter-hypothesis raised by the qualitative evidence outlined above, which suggests that domestic returners may be in an equally poor position because dissatisfaction and financial hardship have played a role in pushing them into the job market. Here we use three measures of deprivation. The first, which is termed 'employment deprivation' assesses respondents' dissatisfaction with joblessness. The second measure evaluates respondents' level of psychological distress. Finally, we examine respondents' financial deprivation using both objective and subjective measures of poverty.

Employment deprivation

Survey respondents who were unemployed or outside the labour market were asked to state their level of agreement/disagreement with a range of statements about what it is like not to have a paid job (see Table 14.3). Five response categories were available, ranging from agree strongly to disagree strongly. The questions used refer only to non-financial aspects of being without a job. These questions are examined individually and are also combined to form an overall scale of dissatisfaction, ranging from one to five (most dissatisfied). The scale has an internal reliability of 0.86 (Cronbach's Alpha). The responses of domestic returners are compared to those of other unemployed women, unemployed men and economically inactive women. If domestic returners' joblessness is to some extent voluntary we would expect them to express similar responses to economically inactive women. If the domestic role can substitute for some of the functions of employment we would expect

Table 14.3 Employment deprivation among the unemployed and economically inactive

	% Agreeing somewhat or strongly				
	Unemployed women			Unemployed men	Housewives
	Domestic returners	Job losers	All[1]		
Find being at home very satisfying	29.1	28.5	28.6	20.0	63.2
I get bored being at home	77.2	71.8	72.9	73.0	37.9
Not having a job doesn't worry me	22.8	19.0	19.8	13.1	60.8
Not having a job makes me feel rather useless	60.8	54.7	55.9	65.5	21.7
Often get depressed about not having job	43.0	52.8	50.9	65.9	18.3
Miss daily routine of a job	62.0	62.2	62.2	70.3	24.6
More difficult to make friends when don't have job	81.0	83.9	83.4	76.2	58.9
Other people look down on me because I don't have a job	24.1	24.5	24.4	43.6	15.3
Mean dissatisfaction score	*3.4*	*3.5*	*3.5*	*3.8*	*2.4*
Total N	(79)	(322)	(401)	(477)	(892)

domestic returners to display lower levels of dissatisfaction than female job losers and unemployed men.

In practice, the responses of domestic returners were very similar to those expressed by women who had lost their jobs. An equal proportion of the two groups were bored, dissatisfied, worried, miss the routine of employment, and felt stigmatised and socially excluded. Despite having extensive caring responsibilities, domestic returners were just as likely to report feeling useless as job losers. The only significant difference between the two groups of women was that domestic returners were less likely to report getting depressed about their joblessness. These results undermine any claim that women re-entering the job market are less serious in their desire to leave unemployment and weaken the argument that the domestic role offers these women an alternative source of satisfaction.

Domestic returners' claim to an unemployed status is further strengthened by the comparison with housewives. There were large and significant differences between domestic returners and full-time housewives on all of the attitudes measured, and domestic returners had substantially higher mean dissatisfaction scores. These differences were of a much greater magnitude than those found between domestic returners and unemployed men. Therefore, in terms of employment deprivation these women had more in common with unemployed men than housewives. Clearly, the desire for paid work creates a crucial difference between these two groups of women.

These findings provide some support for our selection hypothesis that dissatisfaction with the domestic environment pushes domestic returners into the labour market and distinguishes them from women who remain full-time housewives. In order to test this proposal more rigorously we need to use longitudinal information on women's satisfaction prior to entering the job market. Using data from the follow-up Household Survey we can identify women who were full-time housewives in 1986 but who were employed or unemployed in 1987. These women were significantly more dissatisfied with joblessness in 1986 (2.7) than women who remained full-time homemakers (2.2) ($p < 0.005$). This provides more conclusive evidence that women who are most unhappy with the domestic environment are more likely to rejoin the labour market. In the following section we will examine whether this dissatisfaction with joblessness translates into higher levels of psychological distress.

Psychological distress

The measure of psychological distress used in the analysis is a shortened version of the General Health Questionnaire (GHQ) (Goldberg, 1978). The GHQ is a well validated and reliable measure of psychiatric morbidity which has frequently been used to measure psychological distress among the unemployed (for example Leana and Feldman, 1991; Warr, 1987). The reduced version consists of the four items that are most highly correlated with overall scores on the full version. The four items ask whether the respondent has recently

1 been feeling reasonably happy all things considered?
2 been able to enjoy normal day-to-day activities?
3 been feeling unhappy and depressed?
4 been losing confidence in themself?

Responses to each item were graded on a four-point scale and these have been summed to form a scale ranging from 0 to 12, with higher scores indicating greater psychological distress (see Table 14.4). Cronbach's alpha for the scale is 0.79. This short version cannot be used to detect psychiatric morbidity but can be used as a general indicator of psychological well-being.

Table 14.4 Mean GHQ scores by employment, status and sex

	Mean GHQ score	Base N
Domestic returners	4.8	323
Female job losers	4.8	80
All unemployed women[a]	4.8	403
Unemployed men	4.6	473
Employed women	3.3	1948
Employed men	3.1	2081
Full-time housewives	3.7	886

Note: Higher GHQ scores indicate greater levels of psychological distress.
[a] First time job seekers are excluded.

There is no evidence to suggest that the well-established link between unemployment and psychological distress is any weaker among domestic returners. Female job losers and returnees recorded the same level of psychological distress. Unemployed women recorded marginally higher levels of distress (4.8) than men (4.6), however, as there is a general tendency for women to display worse psychological well-being than men (Goldberg, 1978). The more crucial test is whether the difference between the employed and unemployed is the same for women and men. The difference between the two scores is the same for men and women. Full-time housewives have lower distress scores than unemployed women, but have significantly worse mental health than employed women, which gives support to the counter-hypothesis that aspects of the domestic role may be detrimental to psychological well-being.

Again, it is possible to test the theory that the most distressed among the economically inactive population *select* themselves into the labour market by comparing the original GHQ scores of women who remained full-time homemakers and those who moved into the labour force. As predicted, women who re-entered the job market between the two surveys had a higher average GHQ score at the first interview than women who remained engaged in full-time housework (3.9 compared with 3.4). However, the difference was not statistically insignificant.

Neither levels of employment deprivation nor psychological distress suggest that returners' involvement in the domestic role means that they find unemployment easier to cope with than job losers do; indeed, there is some support for the view that some negative aspects of this role push them into the labour market. However, our focus on women's dissatisfaction with the non-financial aspects of full-time homemaking should not obscure the significant pull factors such as the intrinsic and extrinsic rewards of employment. The financial motivation to find employment will be examined next.

Financial hardship

Although domestic returners were shown to exhibit a high degree of non-financial employment commitment there remains doubts about the extent to which they experience the financial deprivation which usually accompanies unemployment. It is assumed that many of these women will be financially supported by a male breadwinner and therefore that their employment is more optional than men's. Furthermore, it might be argued that domestic returners (and the households to which they belong) have not experienced any immediate income loss unlike those who have lost jobs.

The financial position of domestic returners will be examined in two ways. First using a poverty line measure and, second, using respondents' own assessment of their economic situation. The argument concerning the financial significance of female unemployment is framed within the household, therefore a poverty line based on household income is adopted. Such measures are problematic because they assume an equal distribution of income within the household and obscure women's economic dependency. Nevertheless, the argument will be tested within its own terms.

Total household net income was adjusted for household size using the standard OECD equivalence scale. This sets the equivalence factor at 1 for the first adult, 0.7 for additional adults and 0.5 for each child. The poverty line is set at 50 per cent of median income; households falling below this threshold are classified as poor. The income data was sometimes incomplete, therefore the sample numbers are somewhat smaller for this analysis.

Contrary to the arguments outlined above, women domestic returners displayed no weaker financial need for employment than other female job seekers. If anything, their economic situation was slightly worse than that of female job losers (see Table 14.5); however, the difference was not statistically significant.[2] The prediction that domestic returners will be better off was not supported, partly because the assumption of a male breadwinner is often false. As we saw in Table 14.1, 45 per cent of domestic returners were not currently married or

Table 14.5 Household poverty among unemployed women and men

	Unemployed women Domestic returners (%)	Job losers (%)	Unemployed men (%)
Above poverty line[a]	51.4	57.4	44.3
Below poverty line	48.6	42.6	55.7
Base N	(74)	(272)	(397)

[a]The poverty line is placed at 50% of median equivalised household income.

cohabiting. Indeed, 40 per cent of the domestic returners were single parents and therefore were sole breadwinners for their dependants. Even among married/cohabiting returnees almost a quarter (23 per cent) had partners who were not in work. Even among the married/cohabiting group, a higher proportion of returners (35 per cent) than job losers (17 per cent) were living below the poverty line.

The analysis was repeated using a measure of respondents' perceived difficulty making ends meet (see Table 14.6). Answers were placed on a five-item scale ranging from very easy to very difficult. The measure revealed a higher incidence of financial hardship among all groups compared to the poverty-line figures. Domestic returners were again found to experience greater financial difficulty than female job losers: over 70 per cent have experienced difficulty making ends meet. The level of hardship among returners was very close to that of unemployed men. These results suggest that financial need may be another factor which prompts economically inactive women to join the labour market. Furthermore, these findings undermine the assumption of financial support from a male breadwinner. In spite of their financial need many of these returners do not receive government transfers for unemployment (see Table 14.1). The absence of State support is likely to contribute to the hardship experienced by these women.

Conclusion

While women workers are becoming increasingly visible in British cities, their role within the family has meant that their unemployment is sometimes disguised as voluntary breaks from the labour market. This ambiguity surrounding the employment status of women trying to re-enter the workforce has meant their problems often go unrecognised, and many of this group find themselves excluded from benefit

Table 14.6　Difficulty making ends meet among unemployed women and men

	Unemployed women Domestic returners (%)	Job losers (%)	Unemployed men (%)
No	29.6	38.8	27.8
Yes	70.4	61.2	72.2
Base N	*74*	*272*	*471*

provision and other forms of support for the unemployed. The recent government Welfare to Work strategy has focused attention on the situation of certain groups of domestic returners, namely those aged under 25 and lone parents. However, provision for childcare within the New Deal is limited. Those participating in the Employment Option (expected to account for 45 per cent of places) are ineligible for childcare expenses, and among other participants support is restricted to lone parents or couples where both partners are unemployed, whose children are under 11 and in specific types of childcare. The opportunity to participate in programmes on a part-time basis is also restricted. Lone parents aged over 24 are entitled to participate in the New Deal for Lone Parents; however, there is no specialist training or money for childcare (Donnelly et al., 1998). Older returners who are not lone parents are excluded from these new developments, and as discussed above are often indirectly excluded for schemes directed towards the long-term unemployed.

This chapter addressed the question of whether domestic returners should properly be considered unemployed and therefore whether the low priority attached to this group in policy terms is justified. The analysis has shown that domestic returners have a genuine desire for employment that is being thwarted. This conclusion is evident from the women's high level of employment commitment and their dissatisfaction with joblessness. Domestic returners' attitudes to joblessness are much closer to those of female job losers and unemployed men than those of full-time housewives. The results show that the caring responsibilities of this group of women cannot be taken to 'reveal a preference' for home making *vis-à-vis* employment, and discredit the view that returners' joblessness is voluntary.

The analysis also provided considerable evidence to counteract the second objection to defining domestic returners as unemployed, that is, that they do not experience the same deprivations as other unemployed individuals. It was found that returners recorded equally high levels of psychological distress as male and female job losers and greater financial difficulty than other female job seekers. Indeed, the evidence supported the view that for some women there are deficiencies in the domestic environment which push women back into the labour market. Retreating into the traditional home maker role is often offered as a solution for unemployed women (Hakim, 1996, p. 209), however, this is clearly not an option for domestic returners who have entered the job market as an escape from domesticity and its deprivations.

These findings suggest that the needs of domestic returners should be given equal priority to other groups of unemployed individuals. Particular attention should be given to the training and informational needs of these women in order to enable them to avail themselves of the employment opportunities in their localities. The results also suggest a more general need to broaden concepts of unemployment in order to take account of women's more discontinuous patterns of participation and their sometimes considerable unpaid work commitments. Only then will this 'private' problem become a more public issue.

Notes

1 This research was undertaken as part of a D.Phil. thesis and I wish to thank my supervisor Duncan Gallie, for his support throughout the project. Financial support from the ESRC and Nuffield College, Oxford is gratefully acknowledged.
2 The placement of a poverty line is somewhat arbitrary, therefore a number of other poverty lines were tested. At 60 per cent of median income a significantly higher proportion of domestic returners' households are in poverty compared to those of female job losers.

References

Ashton, D. N. (1986) *Unemployment Under Capitalism: The Sociology of British and American Labour Markets*. Brighton: Wheatsheaf.
Brannen, J., Mészàros, G., Moss, P. and Poland, G. (1994) *Employment and Family Life: A Review of Research in the UK*. London: Employment Department Report No. 41.
Brannen, J. and Moss, P. (1992) 'British Households after Maternity Leave'. In S. Lewis, D. Izraeli and Hootsmans (eds), *Dual-Earner Families: International Perspectives*. London: Sage.
Brown, J. (1990) *Victims or Villains? Social Security Benefits in Unemployment*. York: Joseph Rowntree Memorial Trust.
Callender, C. and Metcalf, H. (1997) *Women and Training*. London: Department for Education and Employment.
Chaney, J. (1981) *Social Networks & Job Information: the Situation of Women who Return to Work* E.O.C./S.S.R.C. Joint Panel on Equal Opportunities.

Cragg, A. and Dawson, T. (1984) *Unemployed Women: A study of Attitudes and Experiences*. London: Department of Employment, Research Paper No. 47.

Donnelly, C., Nimmo, M. and Convery, P. (1998) *The New Deal Handbook*. London: Unemployment Unit and Youthaid.

EOC (Equal Opportunities Commission) (1993) *Formal Investigation into the Publicly-funded Vocational Training System in England and Wales*. Manchester: EOC.

Finch, J. (1989) *Family Obligations and Social Change*, Cambridge: Polity Press.

Gallie, D. (1994) 'Methodological Appendix'. In D. Gallie, C. Marsh and C. Vogler (eds), *Social Change and the Experience of Unemployment*, Oxford: Oxford University Press.

Ginn, J. et al. (1996) 'Feminist Fallacies: A Reply to Hakim on Women's Employment'. *British Journal of Sociology*, 47(1), 167–73.

Goldberg, D. (1978) *Manual of the General Health Questionnaire*. Windsor: NFER Publishing Company.

Gornick, J. C., Meyers, M. K. and Ross, K. E. (1997) Supporting the Employment of Mothers: Policy Variation Across Fourteen Wefare States. *Journal of European Social Policy*, 7(1), 45–70.

Hakim, C. (1991) 'Grateful slaves and self-made women: fact and fantasy in women's work orientations'. *European Sociological Review*, 7(2).

Hakim. C. (1996) *Key Issues in Women's Work: Female Heterogeneity and the Polarisation of Women's Employment*. London: Athlone Press.

Jahoda, M. (1982) *Employment and Unemployment: A Social-Psychological Analysis*. Cambridge: Cambridge University Press.

Jahoda, M. (1988) 'Economic Recession and Mental Health: Some Conceptual Issues'. *Journal of Social Issues*, 44(4), 13–23.

Joshi, H. and Hinde, P. R. A. (1993) 'Employment after Childbearing in Post-War Britain: Cohort-Study Evidence on Contrasts Within and across Generations'. *European Sociological Review*, 9(3), 203–27.

Leana, C. R. and Feldman, D. C. (1991) 'Gender Differences in responses to Unemployment'. *Journal of Vocational Behavior*, 38, 65–77.

Macran, S., Joshi, H. and Dex, S. (1996) Employment After Childbearing: A Survival Analysis. *Work, Employment and Society*, 10(2), 273–96.

McRae, S. (1993) 'Returning to Work After Childbirth: Opportunities and Inequalities'. *European Sociological Review*, 9(2), 125–38.

Martin, J. and Roberts, C. (1984) *Women and Employment: A Lifetime Perspective*. London: Department of Employment/OPCS.

Metcalf, H. (1997) *Half Our Future: Women, Skill Development and Training*. London: Policy Studies Institute.

ONS (Office for National Statistics) (1996) *Labour Market Trends*, 104(8).

ONS (Office for National Statistics) (1998) *Labour Market Trends*, 106(4).

Poynter, R. (1996) *Jobseeker's Allowance Handbook*. London: Child Poverty Action Group.

Warr, P. (1987) *Work, Unemployment and Mental Health*. Oxford: Oxford University Press.

15
The Future of Women

Elizabeth Wilson

Over the past decade cities and urban space have become an important focus for theoretical work in the social sciences, part of the 'culturalisation' of sociology and of an increasing interdisciplinarity in which the subject of cities fits particularly well since it can encompass geographical, architectural, artistic and cultural consumption and gender studies. The 'city' may also have inadvertently become an organising concept for a wide range of theorists in the 1980s as Marxism was ceasing to play that role. One of the important contributions of Marxism had been to challenge the conventional divisions between so-called academic disciplines, and the subject of the city and urban life facilitates a similar (although also very different) blurring of boundaries. For several reasons sociology became culturalised, geography became glamourised, art became politicised.

This blurring was part of the debate on postmodernism, since postmodernism itself was an overarching concept – although it was paradoxically based on the idea that there could no longer be overarching or 'totalising' theoretical systems, such as Marxism, which purported to explain everything. Part of the critique therefore of postmodernism is that it simply constructs yet another totalising theory. Yet while I remain sceptical as to its merits, and have never signed up to its political implications, (see Eagleton, 1996) I do find 'postmodern' a useful adjective in gesturing to an ambience, a mood, sometimes a style. The idea of the postmodern city, in particular, or what writers claimed the postmodern city was, seemed to epitomise a new, fragmented postmodern world in which meanings were opaque and ambiguous, and experience contradictory.

In the writings of Marxists on the city in the 1970s the specificity of the city sometimes tended to collapse into the generality of the capitalism formation. Another problem with Marxist analysis was that it could become deterministic, ending in a position in which nothing could change until everything had changed. Yet there is equally an implicit determinism, or perhaps pessimism, in postmodern writings, even if many postmodern writers have seen possibilities for improvements in urban life through small-scale change and through the regeneration of localities, reviving the idea of the urban village.

One of the most important aspects of the debate, or debates, on urban space has been that it brought sociology, geography and planning into contact with the realm of architecture, art and aesthetics at a time when art and culture were being used by municipal authorities throughout the Western world as a motor for the regeneration of inner cities. Another boundary that has collapsed, or been blurred, is that between academic writing and a more personal and literary kind of writing,[1] and this may be seen in some of the writing about cities, where distinctions between theory and experience, between fact and fiction, between sociology and autobiography have been breached. A much earlier example would be Walter Benjamin's *Berlin Chronicle* (1979), which described his childhood in terms of the different districts of Berlin as he became familiar with them; two more recent examples are the work of Iain Sinclair, primarily a novelist, and especially his 1997 book about London, *Lights Out for the Territory* (Sinclair, 1997) and Richard Sennett's *The Conscience of the Eye* (Sennett, 1993). Even Jane Jacobs' influential polemic from 40 years ago, *The Death and Life of Great American Cities*, (Jacobs, 1961) was based on her own experience of living in Greenwich Village as it was then. Now the semiautobiographical discourse on cities has burgeoned, a discourse that brings together the general and the particular, and a revival, perhaps, of some of the protocols of the Chicago School of the 1920s with its ethnographic concern with the detail of urban lives.

Deutsche (1996) and others have argued that the discussion of urban space has been dominated by male writers and masculine concerns, but she and her fellow feminists have sought to remedy this and to introduce gender issues into the debate. Indeed, the retreat from Marxist analysis brought issues of ethnicity and gender to the fore, and although the tendency to treat these as a substitute for class has led to a discourse every bit as one-sided as the old class analyses were said to be, and although ethnic groups, women and gays are themselves internally divided by class difference, the fuller recognition that cities are gendered and racialised is welcome.

In practice the issues that dominate the work of women who are researching into or writing about women and urban life are similar to the issues that would have concerned Marxists or Marxist feminists 20 years ago: the unequal chances of women in cities (as elsewhere, of course) in terms of public services, health, childcare and employment. We know that in general women are poorer than men; that families headed by a woman are more likely to remain in the inner city as others flee to what they perceive (rightly or wrongly) as the more comfortable and safer world of the suburb, the village or the small town or satellite town. We know that women often feel very unsafe in cities, and we know that their housing, and the educational opportunities of their children are likely to be restricted. This has less to do with urban life *per se* as with inequalities in wealth, but one result is that women working in these areas continue to prioritise welfare and planning issues that appear not to have changed significantly since the 1970s. Women are still trying to resolve the issues related to what is sometimes known as the feminisation of poverty.

It seems to me therefore (although this may be a too subjective or anecdotal observation) that researchers tend to focus on these urgent issues and to be less concerned with the aesthetic and subjective dimensions of urban life insofar as these relate to women. If this is the case, it does raise the possibility of another gender division, in which women writers, researchers, activists and academics are – one may argue necessarily – primarily concerned with that side of city life that represents danger, disempowerment and deprivation, whereas their male counterparts feel freer to explore the urban as a site of pleasure, excitement and empowerment.

One may argue that such a division, if it exists, reflects an inescapable reality. Nevertheless, it has been an important component of feminism to claim the right to pleasure and empowerment for women as well as protection. In the 1970s and early 1980s sexuality was much discussed as one source of pleasure and empowerment that had to be claimed by women, and in 1982 there was a women's conference in New York entitled Pleasure and Danger, which addressed the difficulties of women struggling to explore hitherto forbidden and transgressive areas of eroticism. The conference was controversial and was criticised by other groups of feminists for not prioritising issues of rape and pornography, but the argument then was that feminists should be free to look for pleasure as well as combating the causes of danger. The same must be true of gendered urban studies. Eroticism and the city interconnect, in any case, in many ways; it is urbanisation that has made prostitution, erotic spectacles and transgressive encounters possible, and even made possible the emergence of a distinct gay culture. Men were largely the beneficiaries of these, but some feminists have argued for their right to emulate men in seeking sex in public, in toilets, in bathhouses.

Urban life, like women's lives, is inherently contradictory, and not only for women – although perhaps particularly for them – but for all those living in cities. It even raises the contentious issue whether there can be excitement without an element of risk. After all, the attack on the suburban way of life before and after the Second World War had partly to do with a perception of the suburb as endlessly and boringly safe – as, in fact, a feminised environment from which something essential to life had been lost.

Here, however, we are moving away from a consideration of practical policy and towards an assessment of the representation – in art, literature, film – of the city, the urban landscape and the many strange aspects of urban life. The representation of both rural and urban life has been endlessly romanticised, again largely, although not exclusively, by male artists and writers. There are, of course, examples of women who have described urban life in positive terms: Simone de Beauvoir (1989, 1990) in her autobiographies, Charlotte Bronte (1994) in *Villette*, and Virginia Woolf,[2] for example in *Mrs Dalloway* (1974), spring to mind; but it is interesting and significant that so many of the men who have romanticised the city have romanticised it precisely because of its dangers: for example, Fredric Jameson in a famous polemic on postmodernism describes the hellish landscape of the postmodern city in curiously glamourised terms (Jameson, 1984). Dickens, while purporting to describe the gloom and horror of Victorian London, produced rather an effect of the sublime; Francis Carco (Carco, 1929), to take just one more random example, built a successful literary career on the romanticisation of the semicriminal, semibohemian underworld of Monmartre with its violence, pimping and tragic prostitutes, a romanticism upon which Edith Piaf capitalised with her plaintive songs of lost love and victimised women (Vincendeau, 1987); while in films this kind of inverted romanticism has been equally powerful: above all in *Film Noir* where the danger of the urban is often linked to the 'evil woman' and/or female sexuality (Kaplon, 1978; Dyer, 1993).

In the 1990s feminist theorists have made major contributions to theories of postmodernity, yet these debates have often seemed rather separate from another set of debates which place women at their centre: debates concerning the changing roles of men and women, the decadence, as it is often alleged (although that word is seldom used) of contemporary consumer society, the fate of children and the family, and the transformed nature of work. On the one hand we are told that girls now outperform boys at all levels of the educational system; that boys, as they grow up, are more likely to become deviant, criminal, unemployed and suicidal; that 'deindustrialisation' had destroyed the work structure for men while creating new jobs for women in the tertiary sector; that feminism has been so threatening for men that it has decimated their sperm count and created a need for Viagra; and that a stable and orderly society can only be restored by the return of the 'breadwinner/homemaker' model of the nuclear family. At the same time we are told that women have more opportunities than ever before, that feminism is no longer needed since women are doing so well, that single mothers must be encouraged into the workforce, that women – younger women at least – are becoming as drunken, promiscuous, 'laddish' and obscene as their male peers, and that even if the glass ceiling hasn't yet been shattered, this too is only a matter of time. The usually unspoken implication is that it is women's advancement that has caused all this masculine anguish – an assertion that Coward (1999) has finally brought out of the closet. If it is really the case that men in general simply cannot cope with the emancipation of women, this is surely a damning indictment of them rather than of women, but this conclusion, too, is seldom directly confronted. The whole sometimes euphoric, more often panicky discourse is, moreover, occurring at a time when women's movements are fragmented or quiescent and feminism largely confined to the academy. This means that what is happening on the ground – women's lives spent juggling home and career, the fact that surveys suggest that they still shoulder almost the whole burden of domestic work even when fully employed, the yawning gulf between the oversexualised images of women and heterosexual relations splashed all over the media and the often drab and insecure reality of daily life – bears little relation to the discourse on the status of women, since relatively few practical solutions are advanced. Thus we see, on the one hand, the initiative by the British Labour government to get single mothers back to work and off benefit, and, on the other, journalistic articles celebrating women's return to the home. These journalists tend to suggest that there is a new generation of high-powered women (admittedly they have to have rich husbands if they can afford to retire from paid employment) who have willingly left their harried lives as hotshot barristers or media women in favour of the 'richness' of meeting the kids from school, making friends with other mothers at the school gate and going on impromptu picnics. All the mothers who have no choice but to stay at home or work part time might have a wry smile for this grand rediscovery of the joys of domesticity by a privileged minority.

How to make sense of this cacophony of assertion and opinion? I have always believed that it is impossible to understand women's situation in terms of a simple progression forwards or backwards. In many ways things have got both better and worse for women during the past 25 years. It has got both better and worse for some of the *same* women (now you have a career but your husband's gone off with the au pair); but also there are growing differences between the life chances of different groups of women. How foolish are those who say class doesn't matter any more when we see how the division widens between women at the top of the pile and those at the bottom. Of course, if we look at any group of women professionals or managers, their career prospects are still to some extent thwarted by the men in their environment, by prejudice and sexism, the glass ceiling; at the other end of the scale, unemployed women are often attached to unemployed men; their difficulties may well be even greater than those of their partners, and they may be more likely to suffer in a number of ways, partly due to sexist behaviour, a sexist welfare system and so on; but the gulf between those two different sets of women is huge.

What are we to make of this, and of the quiescence of feminism – or perhaps I should say the absence of a feminist movement – in spite of the fact that there are still many women working on a whole range of issues of concern to women, and that there are still so many aspects of women's lives that urgently need to be changed. I want to mention briefly two responses to this situation, both published in 1997. The first is the report, *Tomorrow's Women* (Wilkinson and Howard, 1997) published in March of that year by the 'left of centre think tank', Demos. In many ways its conclusions were sensible and uncontroversial; its authors, Helen Wilkinson and Melanie Howard, point out that women's equality at work is hindered in Britain because employers are reluctant to make adequate provision for maternity leave and generally to recognise women's family responsibilities. Scandinavia has coped much better, and in countries such as France and Belgium women are more likely to be employed full time and enjoy better nursery and nursery school provision. In Britain, by contrast, 'work has not been adequately adapted to the needs of the family and parenting'.

Feminists have been pointing to these inequalities and campaigning for change almost throughout the twentieth century, and the feminists of the 1970s certainly placed them at the centre of their campaigns. Where the Demos report differs from the writings of the 1970s generation is in emphasising the differences between different groups of women. Second-wave feminists were soon accused of racism for their promotion of a universal sisterhood, which was seen (I believe not entirely accurately) as a denial or refusal to recognise the different oppressions of ethnic minority women or women in the developing world, and as an imperialist claim that white, Western middle-class women could speak for all women. But not only do Helen Wilkinson and Melanie Howard present as a new discovery the way in which class, ethnicity, earning power and varying value systems act to fragment women, they also argue that this makes the revitalisation of a single, unified women's movement unlikely; there will be feminisms, not feminism, because women's life experiences are so diverse today that the idea of a single, unifying women's movement no longer makes sense.

> Only fifteen per cent of women now define themselves primarily by gender, fewer than define themselves by their intelligence. Although women are becoming more assertive, they are unlikely to coalesce into a single movement, and politicians, advertisers and businesses will find it increasingly hard to appeal to a 'typical' woman.

The unity of all women was always, of course, a fiction. None the less it is politically naive *automatically* to conclude that because women's lives and aspirations vary so greatly a feminist movement is an inappropriate goal. Political movements and parties are always coalitions (as the benighted state of the Tory party, now that it has ceased to be one, demonstrates) that actively construct the constituencies they aim to represent.

An additional problem with the Demos report is that it assumes too glibly that its data, based on market research, can be unproblematiclly translated into politics. Market research is not the best basis for political prediction, since the goal of marketing is to create and amplify consumer differences – the opposite of the goal of a political movement.

The Demos report (1997) tries to have it both ways. It makes much of the advance of so-called 'feminine values' – environmentalism, the therapeutic agenda and 'spirituality' (a few stereotypes there, I think). At the same time it emphasises the increasingly 'masculine' behaviour of some women. Women's lives are of course contradictory, and the report tries to illustrate this by describing the five types of 1990s woman: Networking Naomi, New Age Angela, Mannish Mel, Back to Basics Barbara and Frustrated Fran. Personally I found it difficult to identify with any of these caricatures, but perhaps that's because I could be described as Dinosaur Daphne, the only socialist feminist left in Britain.

Yet across the lives of these five types, the old problems are clearly visible. The report, for all its desire to stress the positive in terms of 'women's lives' and the negative in terms of the future for feminism as a movement, cannot conceal that for many women the problems identified not only by women's liberation in the 1970s, but also by the suffrage movement at the turn of the century, remain with us, unresolved.

Helen Wilkinson and Melanie Howard acknowledge the widening gulf between rich and poor women – there are more successful professional and businesswomen in the enterprise culture; but there are also more women sinking into the benefit culture of welfare dependency. The report's solution for this is to rename the two groups euphemistically the 'time rich' (that is, the unemployed) and the 'time poor' (that is, well-paid women with professional partners who don't share the burden of housework and childcare fairly), and suggests that there is 'a common interest in encouraging working women to buy more services from currently unemployed women'. But the return of the domestic servant, although possibly inevitable, is hardly the optimum solution to the decline in unionised, adequately paid manufacturing or white-collar work, and nannies and cleaners don't really resolve the problems of professional women forced to put in excessive hours at work. In fact, the Demos solution – the return of the domestic servant – seems an astonishingly retrograde solution when stated thus starkly. Is the availability of more nannies and cleaners really an adequate goal for feminism?

Tomorrow's Women is essentially a reflection rather than an analysis of contemporary attitudes, which are well caught (better, possibly, than the authors realise) in the report. Demos is close to New Labour and seems to share with them a concern with the media, presentation and the concerns of the new managerial class. There is similar Blairite rhetoric about the future, being 'modern' and a wish to be in the mainstream of contemporary mass culture, with references to the Spice Girls, the soap opera, East Enders and and the women's road movie, *Thelma and Louise*, but the end result is rather the same as the New Labour government – a wish to make all the right noises and support the right 'radical' causes, such as environmentalism, but an equally strong wish not to offend the powerful and not to appear to be 'rabidly' feminist. Above all, like New Labour, it has no alternative economic strategy that might mitigate the effects of monetarist 'flexibility' on both women and men in the work place. As things stand, there seems no reason to feel optimistic that employers will listen to Helen Wilkinson, Melanie

Howard and Demos and 'reduce working time, providing support to make sure that childbearing and work are genuinely . . . compatible'.

Yet while it is easy to criticise this 'modern' voice of (semi-)feminism; and the voice of the more thought-out feminism of the 1970s does not seem right for the millennium either. This voice was also represented in 1997 with the publication of *Who's Afraid of Feminism: Seeing Through the Backlash*, edited by Ann Oakley and Juliet Mitchell (Oakley and Mitchell, 1997), two of the most influential British feminists of an earlier time. The articles in this volume are scholarly and serious. Most address specific issues of relevance to women that have arisen in recent years; nevertheless, to organise a whole book round the assertion that there has been a backlash against feminism, which these editors do, seriously oversimplifies the ways in which women's lives have changed during the last two decades, and does scant justice to the extraordinarily contradictory experience it has been. Equally contradictory are the ways in which women's oppression and women's lives have been discussed over this period and the concept of 'backlash' distorts, and indeed misrepresents, this immensely varied discourse.

Neither of these interventions in contemporary debate adequately accounts for the strangeness of the world we inhabit. Helen Wilkinson and Melanie Howard appear to be dazzled by media representations and consumer-survey hype; some of the articles in *Who's Afraid of Feminism* look back with nostalgia at the optimism of the early 1970s, and especially to its sexual optimism and the importance accorded to the sexual revolution (Walters, 1997).

Both these contemporary texts raise two questions: what was the women's liberation movement of the 1970s really about, what was it like, what did it achieve?; and, how should we interpret the confusions of the 1990s?

I lack space to answer either of these questions now – nor do I feel competent to answer them. I shall conclude by mentioning the death of Princess Diana – a very recent event at the time of the Oxford conference at which this paper was originally given – and briefly discuss the public response to the death of the Princess and the explanations for the widespread mourning that circulated at the time.

While I was not myself among those who felt deep grief, or even enormous interest (Wilson, 1998) I understood that Diana's life would have resonance for many women. The television psychologist Oliver James, who was much in evidence at the time, was probably right to suggest that 80 per cent of the visitors to the various sites were women and that this was because our society has offered women so much more than it can deliver. Even the women's movement of the 1970s itself was perhaps part of that, with its promise of at least the right to glorious and continuous sexual and personal fulfilment.

I did not and do not believe that this signifies the feminisation of British culture as some (most women) commentators suggested at the time, when the British stiff upper lip trembled and the nation broke down and cried. For one thing, that idea depends on a stereotypic view of gender in which men have the stiff upper lips and women alone are capable of expressing their feelings. In a culture whose religion is football, I see little evidence of the feminisation of culture. In films? In relation to driving behaviour? In shared childcare? In workplaces where aggression and horn locking are no longer the norm? I don't think so.

But whatever the meaning of that event – already half forgotten and seeming now altogether less momentous and meaningful than it did at the time – Princess Diana did personify the contradictory and difficult nature of many contemporary women's lives. Her position was unique and exceptional, yet her difficulties were similar to those of many women: an unhappy marriage, an insensitive and unfaithful husband, hateful in-laws, a snatch at happiness with another, on the face of it rather unpromising, lover. Her looks and clothes glamorised her predicament, yet her bulimia reminded her audience that beauty is a poisoned chalice for the modern woman. Finally, her efforts to find a new role for herself must also have resonated with many women. She was in fact a confused, contradictory individual, iconic of the incoherence of our society's attitude towards its women.

Yet if we look at women's lives, in all their diversity, we can take heart and hope for a happier outcome than Diana's. For after all, Diana was not like us, but was caught in a bizarre imperial time warp, and instead of noting the similarities between her position and that of so many women, it might be more constructive to measure the distance and the difference between her and us. It is true that bread-and-butter, economic issues still lie at the heart of women's most pressing problems, that women at all levels still tend to earn less than men, that paid employment and domestic life have yet to be reconciled, and that women continue to suffer as a result of their financial dependence on men. Yet attitudes do change and have changed. Even Princess Diana couldn't have been and done what she was and did if they hadn't. And although conservative writers from Francis Fukuyama to Melanie Phillips of the *Sunday Times* thunder their polemics on the subject of women's place in the home and the need for a return to the patriarchal family, this is not a full-blown backlash. Apart from anything else, a patriarchal backlash doesn't suit the logic of 'late' capitalism. Deregulation and flexible working favour the continued employment of women, albeit often on very disadvantageous terms and conditions (typically low-paid, part-time, casualised work). This is not exclusively a problem for women, however, and at least in theory could form the basis for oppositional movements in which men's and women's interests coincide, thus strengthening both. The voice of women's groups and organisations are particularly urgently needed to voice an alternative set of economic and social propositions to those that currently dominate government. This is because it is women who are at the sharp end of the two major colliding aspects of contemporary life: the contradiction between flexible markets and all the paraphernalia of monetarism the one hand, and the fragmentation of social life on the other. Despite, therefore, the pessimism of the Demos duo, who can envisage only fragmented feminisms to mirror a fragmented society, there could be a different scenario: one in which women's improved education, training, employment and consequent greater visibility give them a lever with which to intervene in politics of all kinds, as the mother of Stephen Lawrence and Mo Mowlam have done. They indeed provide more sustaining role models for the future than Princess Diana could ever do, and give us considerable hope for women's increasing influence in the world.

Notes

1 Although some would argue that there has been a simultaneous polarisation between books written for the general public and academic discourse, with fewer 'crossover' books.
2 Although Woolf particularly has been severely criticised by some feminist theorists on the grounds that her pleasure in the city, in, for example, *Mrs Dalloway*, is that of a woman privileged by her class and ethnicity.

References

Benjamin, W. (1979) 'Berlin Chronicle'. In W. Benjamin, *One Way Street*, London: Verso.
Bronte, C. (1994) *Villette*. London: Penguin.
Carco, F. (1929) *From Montmartre to the Latin Quarter: The Last Bohemia*. Trans. Madeleine Boyd, London: Grant Richards and Humphrey Toulmin.
Coward, R. (1999) *Sacred Cows: Is Feminism Relevant to the New Millennium?* London: Harper Collins.
de Beauvoir, S. (1989) *The Prime of Life*. London; Penguin,

de Beauvoir, S. (1990) *Memoirs of a Dutiful Daughter*. London: Penguin.

Deutsche, R. (1996) 'Men in Space' and 'Boys Town'. In Deutsche, Rosalyn, *Evictions: Art and Spatial Politics*, Cambridge, MA: MIT Press.

Dyer, R. (1993) 'Homosexuality and film noir'. In R. Dyer, *The Matter of Images: Essays on Representation*, London: Routledge.

Eagleton, T. (1996) *The Illusions of Postmodernism*. Oxford: Blackwell.

Jacobs, J. (1961) *The Death and Life of American Cities*. Harmondsworth: Penguin.

Jameson, F. (1984) 'The Cultural Logic of Late Capitalism'. *New Left Review*, No. 146, July/August, 53–92.

Kaplan, E. A. (ed.) (1978) *Women and Film Noir*. London: British Film Institute.

Oakley, A. and Mitchell, J. (eds) (1997) *Who's Afraid of Feminism: Seeing Through the Backlash*. London: Hamish Hamilton.

Sennett, R. (1993) *The Conscience of the Eye*. London: Faber.

Sinclair, I. (1997) *Lights Out for the Territory*. London: Granta.

Vincendeau, G. (1987) 'The *mise en scène* of Suffering: French *chanteuses réalistes*', *New Formations*, No. 3 (Winter), 107–28.

Walters, M. (1997) 'American Gothic: Feminism, Melodrama and the Backlash'. In A. Oakley and J. Mitchell (eds), *Who's Afraid of Feminism*: Seeing Through the Backlash, London: Hamish Hamilton.

Wilkinson, H. and Howard M. (1997) *Tomorrow's Women*. London: Demos.

Wilson, E. (1998) 'The Unbearable Lightness of Diana'. In M. Merck (ed.), *After Diana*, London: Verso.

Woolf, V. (1974) *Mrs Dalloway*. Harmondsworth: Penguin.

Index

217